ALSO BY BARRY LEVINE

*All the President's Women* (with Monique El-Faizy)

# THE SPIDER

# THE SPIDER

### INSIDE THE CRIMINAL WEB OF
### JEFFREY EPSTEIN AND GHISLAINE MAXWELL

# BARRY LEVINE

CROWN

NEW YORK

Hardback ISBN 978-0-593-23718-2
Ebook ISBN 978-0-593-23719-9

Printed in the United States of America on acid-free paper

crownpublishing.com

2 4 6 8 9 7 5 3 1

First Edition

*Book design by Susan Turner*

*For Sharri and August (and Cooper),*
*for their support during the difficult months of work*
*on this book in quarantine*

# CONTENTS

# INTRODUCTION

## THE SPIDER'S LAIR

SIXTEEN HUNDRED TWENTY-SEVEN MILES OF OCEAN SEPARATE CONEY Island's gaudy boardwalk at the southern tip of Brooklyn—where Jeffrey Epstein grew up—from the white sand beaches of the U.S. Virgin Islands, where he later made his home.

There, amid the few dozen islands and cays off the southeast tip of St. Thomas, sits a seventy-acre cay called Little St. James. Epstein acquired the island in 1998 for $7.95 million and purchased the adjacent one, Great St. James, for $17.5 million almost two decades later. Estimates now peg the islands' combined value at about $86 million.[1]

The onetime schoolteacher turned financier called his private getaway Little St. Jeff's. During his visits—two or three times a month, usually—he lived in a cream-colored villa with a bright turquoise roof. The estate also featured a movie theater, library, and detached Japanese bathhouse. Meditative music was piped in around the property, its two pools, and the cabanas.

Five other structures dotted the island, including staff quarters; at one point, around 2008, the staff had ballooned to some seventy people. There was an outdoor massage room, as well as a mysterious building that resembled a temple. Farther from the villa sat a helicopter pad and, beyond it, a secluded cove Epstein called "the grotto." Two massive U.S. flags flew on either end of the island, where security guards patrolled the water's edge.

When Epstein was on his island, the polo-shirt-clad employees were to stay out of sight. There were reportedly other rules as well. The temperature in his bedroom was kept at a chilly 54 degrees.[2] Towels had to be replenished constantly. Mats had to be readied for his frequent yoga practices. Vegetarian food—the teetotaling Epstein's favorite—was always on hand.

The house contained several oddities. Epstein kept his collection of "pirate treasure" not in jewelry boxes but in "old rum bottles and crockery" discovered on the island by workers, according to one report.[3] Other items were less benign. A contractor who worked in the house told a journalist that Epstein had installed a "ten-showerhead shower—for group showers," adding that he observed framed pictures of "young, barely clothed or semi-nude girls."[4]

Many characteristics about the island stuck out in the minds of visitors, but what left the biggest impression on locals were Epstein's guests.

On Little St. James, Epstein entertained a variety of boldfaced names. Most famous was Bill Clinton, who was a passenger on Epstein's jet at least twenty-six times. Two witnesses placed Clinton on the island in 2002, although his spokesperson has denied he ever visited.

Other visitors included captains of industry, celebrities, and royalty. Prince Andrew visited, and so did his ex-wife, Sarah Ferguson, as well as Epstein's patron, businessman Les Wexner, and the lawyer Alan Dershowitz. In March 2006, Epstein hosted the Cambridge professor and theoretical physicist Stephen Hawking and twenty other renowned scientists for a conference called "confronting gravity" in St. Thomas. Science was a passion for Epstein, an interest that manifested in sometimes bizarre ideas, as well as in financial gifts and ties to institutions that would later disavow them.

Nearly everyone who fell into Epstein's web later came to regret it.

. . .

WHILE PLENTY OF VIP GUESTS visited Little St. James in the years Epstein resided there, another type of visitor stands out in the minds of many locals.

Epstein would shuttle his visitors to the island by helicopter or boat from St. Thomas, about a mile away. According to a lawsuit filed by the attorney general of the Virgin Islands against Epstein's estate in early 2020, local "air traffic controllers and other airport personnel" reported seeing Epstein accompanied by girls who appeared as young as eleven and twelve years old, and as recently as 2018.[5] According to the suit, Epstein flew his victims into Cyril E. King Airport in St. Thomas on either one of his two Gulfstream jets or his Boeing 727-200, which later became known in the media as the Lolita Express.

The court papers detail a "pattern and practice of human trafficking, sexual abuse, and forced labor of young women" on the island. While Epstein liked to brag about his "Zen-like retreat," for others it was a place of horror. One fifteen-year-old victim was so desperate to escape the island that she tried to swim to freedom.[6] Prince Andrew was once seen groping an underage girl on a balcony on the island that was "right out in the open."[7]

One victim who was raped by Epstein on his island said, "I spent two weeks vomiting almost to death in a hospital after that first encounter."[8] Still another victim told CBS News that Epstein "trapped me in his bedroom on the island where he had a gun strapped to his bedpost. I couldn't leave."[9]

A former air traffic controller told *Vanity Fair* that on multiple occasions he saw "Epstein exit his helicopter, stand on the tarmac in full view of my tower, and board his private jet with children—female children."[10] Another employee at the airstrip observed that Epstein's companions "were always wearing college sweatshirts" that seemed intended as "camouflage."[11]

When I traveled to St. Thomas in January 2020, a cabdriver told me locals referred to Epstein's island as Dicks Island, while others, she said, called it Obeah, meaning "a bad omen." A place of evil.[12]

In the Virgin Islands, Epstein spun his web from a "business" office he maintained on St. Thomas. Known officially as Southern Trust Company, Inc., the office was tucked away in the American Yacht Harbor complex in the Red Hook quarter on the far eastern side of St. Thomas.

On the morning I visited, the office's glass doors were closed and covered with heavy hurricane shutters painted blue. To the right of the entrance were neglected potted palms and tropical plants. In the marina below, I could see yachts, catamarans, and sailboats. (Epstein reportedly co-owned the 127-slip marina with real estate tycoon Andrew Farkas, a past business partner of Jared Kushner.) Across a road was a small shopping center with a place called Duffy's Love Shack in front.

Epstein, who sexually abused at least one young victim in the office, passed off Southern Trust as a company researching genetic sequencing databases for cancer treatment and DNA sequencing.[13] What the 3,200-square-foot office also housed, according to Virgin Islands attorney general Denise George, were databases to track the movements and availability of young women and underage girls.

The dark side of Jeffrey Epstein was always hidden in plain sight.

BY NOW, THE BASIC CONTOURS of Jeffrey Epstein's horrendous crimes—his decades-long obsession with and abuse of young women and underage girls, often initiated under the guise of seeking out masseuses—are well known.

Beginning in November 2018, the *Miami Herald*, led by reporter Julie K. Brown, published a multipart investigation on Jeffrey Epstein. The paper called it "Perversion of Justice," and, in the paper's words, "it awakened the world to a decades-long injustice suffered by dozens and perhaps hundreds of young girls, many of whom had never spoken about their abuse at the hands of Jeffrey Epstein."

The number of rapes in Epstein's story is both sickening and hard to comprehend. In legal documents, police reports, and published reports, more than three dozen individual victims have accused Epstein of rape—some multiple times.[14] But an untold number of additional victims have never come forward.

The reports in the *Miami Herald* brought about a renewed interest in Epstein on the part of law enforcement, culminating in his dramatic arrest at Teterboro Airport in New Jersey in July 2019.

Barely a month later he would be found hanging from a noose in a Lower Manhattan jail cell.

IN THE MONTHS LEADING UP to and following Epstein's death, hundreds of articles would be written about his life, crimes, and passing. Conspiracy theories emerged—promoted with the Internet refrain "Epstein didn't kill himself"—about the unexplained circumstances of his jailhouse demise, while journalists probed his network of connections among the wealthy and powerful, and the mysterious circumstances of his vast wealth, reportedly $577 million at the time of his death.

Much has been made of Epstein's network of high-placed friends and acquaintances. Among them he counted politicians and lawmakers, even heads of state. There were eminent lawyers, like Dershowitz, and billionaire businessmen, including Wexner and Microsoft founder Bill Gates. Some, like director Woody Allen and producer Harvey Weinstein, would see their own later years consumed by allegations of sexual abuse.

There were some of the world's smartest men, like Hawking and former Harvard president Larry Summers, along with celebrities and their hangers-on. There were also bankers, a Saudi arms dealer, and the head of an international modeling agency.

Still, for all that has been written about Jeffrey Epstein, an astonishing amount is still unexplained. He was elusive in life—a criminal who did not play by the rules of polite society—and he has remained just as elusive in death.

What other secrets did Epstein possess when he died?

Where did he get his money? How did a kid from Brooklyn who never graduated from college worm his way into the highest ranks of political, business, and scientific circles? Why did so many powerful men stay loyal to him even after he pleaded guilty to sex crimes in Florida in 2008? How did he manage to elude real justice for so long? And how did his entourage of assistants and companions, including Ghislaine Maxwell, sustain their employer's habits, and why?

How did Epstein spin his web, and why did so many people fall into it?

I HAVE BEEN FOLLOWING THE Jeffrey Epstein saga since the fiasco of Epstein's first indictment in Florida, and I became even more intrigued as I talked to sources and conducted interviews while reporting my previous book, *All the President's Women: Donald Trump and the Making of a Predator,* which was published in 2019.

While author James Patterson's 2016 work *Filthy Rich* gave an accurate basic outline of Epstein's life up to then, and Brown's subsequent *Miami Herald* series skillfully brought forward so much in the Florida case that remained below the surface, I was struck by how the complexities of Epstein's life—especially his relationship with Ghislaine Maxwell—have not been fully traced in a book of investigative reporting or any other medium.

What especially gnawed at me was how he moved so easily between the various worlds of the multidimensional life he had created for himself—literally going from a conference that included some of the world's most prominent billionaires to, days later, victimizing another young person. This pattern—oscillating between venues of power and respectability and hidden lairs seemingly designed to perpetrate heinous crimes—was one that repeated over and over again in the last three decades of Epstein's life. What was buried in Epstein's psyche that led him to both places—and allowed him to inhabit both for so long virtually without consequence?

This book is my attempt to answer that question, and many others, and to sketch the most complete portrait yet of one of the most extraordinary and despicable criminals of our recent history. I hope the reader will find satisfactory answers in the chapters ahead.

The reader will see how the circumstances of Epstein's youth set the course of his adult life, including how a fixation on a high school crush resulted in some of Epstein's earliest predatory behavior. These new disclosures are among the many previously unreported details of Epstein's life unearthed in the research for this book.

Just as a spider has eight legs, Epstein had numerous dimensions to his life. To adequately pursue them, I knew I would need help. Two veteran journalists, Sharon Churcher and Philip Messing, worked tirelessly for many months to help me fill out this portrait of Epstein and his world. Almost a decade before the *Miami Herald* began its investigation, Churcher was already producing groundbreaking reporting on the Epstein case, exposing allegations of sexual wrongdoing on the part of Prince Andrew when she published the first interview with longtime Epstein victim Virginia Roberts Giuffre in 2011. Churcher opened up her reporting notebooks for the present project, providing never-before-published details from her conversation with Giuffre and other sources.

To learn the full account of Epstein's final days in jail before his death, I turned to Messing, who developed unrivaled contacts in law enforcement as a hard-charging and longtime police reporter for the *New York Post*. Messing came with another horseshoe in his glove—he overlapped with Epstein at school back in Coney Island. Thanks to Messing's efforts, the reader will get the fullest accounting yet of Epstein's time in the Manhattan Correctional Center before his death, including previously unreported details about what happened while Epstein was on suicide watch and disturbing claims involving the New York City medical examiner's findings in Epstein's death.

A FEW WEEKS AFTER RETURNING from the Virgin Islands, and thanks to the intervention of Phil Messing, I was welcomed into Epstein's former boyhood home in Sea Gate, the gated community in Coney Island where Epstein grew up.

The house is an unremarkable Cape Cod–style three-story three-family dwelling with a front porch. In the Epstein family's former unit, two bedrooms and one bath are connected by a narrow hallway that opens onto a small kitchen and living room. In the rear, I walked into the bedroom Jeffrey once shared with his brother, Mark. The window overlooks the small walled-in backyard, revealing a tiny patch of gray sky. I thought about what Jeffrey Epstein might have seen in his imagination when he looked out this same window.

Adam Davis, who now lives in Epstein's boyhood home, told me: "Trying to understand him is like trying to understand Hannibal Lecter."[15] Davis is a religious man; he has a framed painting of the Virgin Mary flanked by angels on his living room wall. In Epstein's former boyhood bedroom, a painting of Jesus hangs on one wall, a crucifix on another. Seeing them made me think of the photo of Epstein and Ghislaine Maxwell meeting Pope John Paul II that was discovered decades later in Epstein's home in Palm Beach, Florida.

Joyce Carol Oates once wrote: "The pedophile's curse has something almost supernatural about it, like the bite of a vampire infecting an entire life."[16]

Or maybe like the bite of a spider.

The spider waits at the center of its web, waiting for the vibrations of its prey before it attacks.

This book is intended to capture all of those vibrations in Jeffrey Epstein's life in the hope that a spider like him will never bite again.

## PART ONE

# THE BOY FROM BROOKLYN

I am not a madman.
—JEFFREY EPSTEIN[1]

# 1

## WONDER WHEEL

THE FENCED-IN ENCLAVE OF SEA GATE SITS AT THE WESTERNMOST end of Brooklyn's Coney Island peninsula, surrounded on three sides by the waters of Gravesend Bay and the Atlantic Ocean. Built more than a hundred years ago as a summer retreat for some of Manhattan's most illustrious families—the Morgans, the Dodges, the Auchinclosses, the Vanderbilts—Sea Gate and its palatial homes constituted some of the first glimpses afforded to the new immigrants from Italy and Eastern Europe who rushed to the decks of overcrowded steamers as they entered New York Harbor.[1]

In 1933, the original clubhouse of Sea Gate's Atlantic Yacht Club burned down. Without a place to be catered to and seen, and as the allure of the city dimmed amid the Great Depression, patrician families gradually abandoned the area. Sea Gate would now attract some of the city's new arrivals—first-generation working-class families eager to escape the overcrowded neighborhoods of Brooklyn, then America's fourth-largest city—for their own home on the wishful shores of the ocean. In particular, Sea Gate became a middle-class haven for Jewish intellectuals, artists, and families. Lavish homes were torn down, replaced by single- and two-family homes. Isaac

Bashevis Singer, the famed Yiddish novelist, lived in Sea Gate, as did Beverly Sills, the world-renowned soprano who ultimately ran the New York City Opera, and Irwin Winkler, the Academy Award–winning producer and director.[2]

Even after the ultra-wealthy departed, trappings of its former prestige persisted. Access in and out of the half-square-mile Sea Gate community consisted of just two crossings, at Surf and Neptune avenues. Even today, cars may enter only after a guard raises a reinforced barrier, and pedestrians must negotiate an elaborate turnstile that leads them to a security desk. Though it is a part of Brooklyn and New York City, the community maintains its own police department—a force of thirty peace officers protects the community's eight thousand or so residents.

West Thirty-Seventh Street is the three-thousand-foot-long north-south DMZ separating Sea Gate from the rest of Brooklyn and New York City. Three-quarters of the way up West Thirty-Seventh Street, behind a twelve-foot-high chain-link fence topped off by barbed-wire concertina and a sign warning NO TRESPASSING AND NO DUMPING, is Maple Avenue.

WHEN JEFFREY EDWARD EPSTEIN WAS born on January 20, 1953, his parents, Seymour Epstein and the former Pauline Stolofsky, had been married barely more than a year.

Jeffrey's paternal grandfather, Julius, came to the United States from czarist Russia around 1900. When he was naturalized as a citizen in 1906, he was working as a contractor, according to his immigration paperwork. In 1916, Julius married Bessie Tesher. The pair had two sons.

Jeffrey Epstein's maternal grandparents, Max and Lena Stolofsky, arrived at Ellis Island in 1912. Max was a tailor and worked at a clothing factory in Manhattan; he would also work as a chauffeur at a furniture company, and later he was self-employed. Max and Lena had four daughters, including Pauline. Max was originally from

Lithuania, Lena from Berlin. They fled the pre–First World War pogroms of czarist Russia and Eastern Europe and sailed into New York Harbor aboard one of the countless rickety steamers en route to Ellis Island. Most of Epstein's extended maternal family had stayed behind in Europe and perished in the Holocaust.

A first-generation sense of patriotism in what many saw as the inevitable fight against Hitler suffused the Epstein side of the family. Seymour Epstein completed only three years of high school, enlisting in the U.S. Army on August 8, 1941, at Camp Yaphank, in Suffolk County, four months before Pearl Harbor. Seymour's younger brother, Arnold, became something of a hometown hero after he left to fight in the Second World War in 1944 as a navigator inside a B-24 bomber. He would fly fifty-one missions over Italy and Romania with the Air Force 450th Bomb Group's 720th Squadron.

After the war, Seymour Epstein worked for the New York City Department of Parks as a groundskeeper and gardener. Pauline, Jeffrey's mother, was a housewife who also had to work to afford the family a middle-class lifestyle. The pair were described by neighbors as simple and gentle people.

Shortly before they were married in January 1952, Seymour moved into an apartment with Pauline and her parents at 2992 West Thirty-First Street in Coney Island. The apartment, which has since been destroyed to make way for public housing, was home to many working-class Jewish families at the time, including the family of Joseph Heller. Heller would live in the building with his widowed mother and two siblings shortly before he left for the Second World War in 1942. Like Jeffrey's uncle Arnold, Heller would fly B-25 bombers over Europe for much of the war, experiences that would shape Heller's novel *Catch-22*.

Even after Pauline's parents died in the early 1950s, the couple would continue living in the apartment, even paying bills in Max Stolofsky's name until well after he died in 1954. The building would also be their home at the time of the births of both their sons, Jeffrey and Mark.

After nearly a decade of living on West Thirty-First Street, Pauline and Seymour were finally able to move into their own place in 1962, deciding to keep their family in Coney Island, though opting for a more middle-class neighborhood. Taking the middle flat in a triplex apartment building, in 1962 the Epsteins would finally make a home for themselves, just a few blocks from where Pauline's parents had lived.

Seymour and Pauline moved into the house at 3742 Maple Avenue in 1962. The three-story house was divided into three apartments with two separate entrances. The Epsteins lived in unit 2, and conditions inside were cramped. The rooms were nowhere near the size of the prewar apartments that many New Yorkers were known to boast about. A small hallway connected the parents' bedroom, the kitchen, and the living room; exposed water pipes, painted over and over, interrupted the layout in the kitchen and bathroom. Eggshell-colored wallpaper draped the drywall. The home was furnished eclectically; there was no need—or ability—to acquire matching sets.[3] Most of the writers and musicians had moved on to more prestigious neighborhoods by this time, and the secluded slice of Brooklyn shore became home to working-class families—civil servants and laborers—who worked long hours to provide the American postwar dream for their children. Kids played in the street, and everyone knew everyone else. Residents rarely locked their doors.

Seymour and Pauline Epstein weren't known as a particularly religious couple, but their house was just five blocks from Sea Gate's largest synagogue, and Jeffrey was bar mitzvahed at the age of thirteen. When Jeffrey and his brother, Mark, eighteen months his junior, sat on the steps in front of the house, over time they would have observed the community becoming more orthodox as more observant families moved in.[4]

Young Jeffrey adored his mother, whom neighbors remembered as a slightly overweight woman who was seen in the neighborhood wearing *shmattes,* the Yiddish word for rags.[5] By contrast, Jeffrey's relationship with his father was somewhat distant; his father was old-school and believed that good grades and Jewish savvy were the pathways to success in America.

The Epstein boys shared a small bedroom whose three windows looked out on a cement wall in their backyard that had been chipped by the thick and salty ocean air; they could peek into the backyards of similar multifamily homes but could see little else. They lived close enough to the ocean that they could hear the waves and smell the salt in the air, but for the most part, the ocean was out of sight, as were the wonders and frenzy of Manhattan, though they were just one hour and fifteen minutes away by public transportation.

In 1954 in nearby Coney Island, Nathan's Famous sold forty thousand hot dogs in a single day. But even Coney Island and Sea Gate could not escape New York City's slow march to decline in the 1960s. A mile and a half down Surf Avenue from Epstein's apartment, the famed Luna Park in Coney Island was on the downswing when Jeffrey Epstein was a child. The wooden Cyclone roller coaster still ran, but the amusement park had lost some of its luster as a beacon of family summer entertainment. Nonetheless, kids from nearby Sea Gate still hung out in Coney Island.

One attraction that remained was Lillie Santangelo's World in Wax Museum, which opened in 1926. Lillie, whom the locals called "Grandma Moses on LSD," ran an old sideshow house of horrors that reproduced an array of curiosities and crimes with mechanical dummies.[6] For a dollar admission, a visitor could ogle a freak show complete with moth-eaten mechanical chimpanzees playing poker, an exhibit of a "two-headed baby," or a wax likeness of bank robber Willie Sutton.

JEFFREY AND MARK EPSTEIN BOTH attended PS 188, a ten-minute walk from home, on Neptune Avenue. The public school was a mosaic of New York diversity—primarily Italians, Jews, and Irish kids, with a burgeoning number of Puerto Ricans and Blacks. Seymour and Pauline were adamant that their boys do well in school, and they played games at home like Concentration to sharpen their boys' mental focus and memory skills.

Jeffrey's nickname at PS 188 was Bear (when he was even younger, it was simply Eppy), classmates recalled. A classic nerd who liked math and science, Epstein was light-years ahead of most of his peers academically. He liked music and played the piano. Even though his parents possessed limited financial resources, Epstein's parents sent him, in the summer of 1962, to Michigan's Interlochen National Music Camp, where, according to records, he studied the bassoon, orchestra, and radio.[7]

Epstein would have been the kind of student that a teacher dreams of—bookish, artistic—but he was bored. Some former classmates recall an aloofness to his demeanor. Epstein was classified as being gifted and talented—so advanced that he had skipped the third grade. He later enrolled in the seventh grade at Mark Twain Junior High School, a troubled institution with a significant number of students who faced personal challenges due to extreme poverty and families with drug and alcohol problems; Mark Twain would evolve into the city's first magnet school, highly competitive and reserved for kids who were intellectually gifted or possessed unique talents.

Epstein entered the intermediate school just as the demographics of his slice of Brooklyn began to shift dramatically. Real estate developer Fred Trump, future president Donald Trump's father, turned vast stretches of land once crowded with beach bungalows into what became known as Trump Village, a series of seven highrises. Alongside New York City's ambitious but ill-fated "urban renewal" plan that provided housing to lower-class tenants, Coney Island changed from a predominantly Jewish and Italian neighborhood. Higher crime rates and considerable white flight to the suburbs only served to further isolate Sea Gate.

New York City and its institutions were in financial free fall, and Lafayette High School, which Jeffrey Epstein was zoned to attend, was considered rough. In later years, Epstein confided in friends about his disgust at the circumstances of his upbringing. He was angry about the lower-middle-class tag placed on his forehead. The cloistered community of Sea Gate made him feel trapped in a life of poverty, according to Steven Hoffenberg, a later business associate in whom Epstein confided about his life. "He grew up as a nobody. And he couldn't take that."

IN THE SEVENTH GRADE, EPSTEIN was assigned to an SP, or Special Progress, class, which would allow him to skip yet another grade, the eighth, and progress directly into the ninth. By this point, Epstein was lumbering, taller than many of his classmates even though he was younger. He appeared to have a five o'clock shadow even though he was only twelve, a time when most boys were still a long way from beginning to shave.[8]

In September 1966, Epstein entered the tenth grade at Lafayette High School. The school was large enough to accommodate four thousand pupils from Coney Island and Bensonhurst crammed together into a single building on Benson Avenue. Lafayette was not, at the time Epstein arrived, a high-performing school. It had few college-bound students, and parents were mostly untroubled that it wasn't quite the melting pot intended when the Board of Education districted schools to the local population. Epstein's classmates fell into three groups: Sea Gaters like himself, white and generally middle- or upper-middle-class; lower- or middle-class white students from Coney Island; and poor Black and Puerto Rican kids from Coney Island, whose parents were largely reliant upon public assistance.

Lafayette was also known as a school that produced baseball stars. Sandy Koufax, the legendary southpaw ace for the Los Angeles Dodgers, was a Lafayette graduate, as was Mets pitcher John Franco a generation later. Epstein, who had retained baby fat and freckles into his teenage years, showed little interest in sports and was a target for bullies.[9] But even if Epstein did not count as popular, classmates recall that he moved about as if he glowed with a halo, with seeds of the seemingly carefree charisma and sometimes arrogance that would mark his personality as an adult.

"There are three types of kids when you're going to high school," Bruce Reznick, a former classmate, recalled. "There are kids who are dumb, and it doesn't matter how much work they do, because they'll always be dumb. There are kids like most of us, who have got to work hard to achieve. And then some kids don't have to work hard to excel. Epstein was one of those."[10]

Melody Stern, who would later become a courtroom stenographer, also knew Epstein. "You wanted to not like him, but he was so smart and so funny," she said. Stern recalled an incident in the fall of ninth grade when Epstein offered up a boastful prediction about his future in front of her and three other classmates. She cannot forget the syntax of his startlingly prescient words. "He had his hands at his sides," Stern recalled, "and he said, 'I'm going to be rich when I grow up.' He didn't say, 'When I grow up I'm going to be rich.' He said, 'I'm going to be rich when I grow up.'"[11]

One of the girls listening to Epstein brag was named Kathleen Suter. Some former Epstein classmates remember Epstein as having few romantic interests in junior high school, but, according to others, he was smitten with "Kathy." Blond, with shoulder-length hair, long legs, and a pretty smile, Suter looked as if she had walked off a tennis court at a tony private club in Greenwich, Connecticut, rather than come from a New York City housing project, said one former classmate. Robert Rosenbaum, a neighbor, remembered, "She had a whispering beauty to her, an aura that was just angelic." When Suter was in her early teens, according to Melody Stern, Suter won a teenage modeling contest sponsored by Abraham & Straus, a now defunct department store that was located in downtown Brooklyn.

If Epstein was in love with Suter, Suter thought of Epstein only as a friend, according to one classmate. Nonetheless, their relationship would persist for decades.

. . .

THE BULLYING AND TEENAGE ANGST did little to hamper Jeffrey Epstein's academic excellence. He also joined Lafayette's math club, tutored students who were older than him, and banked an impressive list of afterschool extra-credit groups that fast-tracked to a good school after graduation.[12] But there was still a threat that he wouldn't get his diploma.

One of Jeffrey Epstein's closest friends from childhood was Warren Eisenstein, who died in February 2014.[13] In a legal document prepared by Epstein's defense lawyers in 2007, Eisenstein would recall that he and Epstein were told they couldn't graduate because they had failed physical education. What ensued was an early example of Epstein's powers of persuasion. "After ten minutes of negotiating with our teacher, Jeff convinced him that we would do anything he asked us to do until graduation," Eisenstein stated. "Jeff managed to volunteer us to not only lead gym class every day, but we both had to double every exercise that the rest of the class did . . . including track. Our gym teacher gave us a C and we graduated."[14]

Epstein walked out of high school with a diploma at the age of sixteen.

ACCORDING TO HIS FRIEND Steven Hoffenberg, Epstein was once fixated on attending Harvard University—it would be "his way to show the world that he's one of them."[15]

However, Epstein chose to continue his education locally. He applied and was accepted to Cooper Union, a university in Lower Manhattan known for producing some of the best engineers and architects in America. The institution, founded in 1859, was perhaps best known for offering full scholarships to all its accepted undergraduates. It was also one of the most selective schools in the country, accepting fewer than 13 percent of all applicants.

Situated on Astor Place, where the neighborhoods of Greenwich Village and the East Village met, the school and its area epitomized the downtown Manhattan counterculture of artists, drugs, and protests. The school—and everything about the neighborhood around it—might as well have been on a different planet from sheltered Sea Gate.

Epstein, living at home, lasted only two years at Cooper Union. It wasn't a matter of grades; there was no family crisis at home; nor did Epstein change his interests and shy away from math and the sciences. Quite the contrary, he was considered a brilliant student who didn't have to work very hard for a stellar grade point average. It wasn't a matter of money, either. Cooper Union was tuition free, and both he and friend Warren Eisenstein drove taxis during the summer breaks for extra money.[16] (Years later, a classmate would snicker about the similarities between Epstein and the character Travis Bickle, famously played by Robert De Niro in Martin Scorsese's classic 1976 film *Taxi Driver*.) He also worked as a roofer for some extra cash.[17] But Epstein seemed bored with conventional prestige. He seemed intent on following an unconventional path.

When he dropped out of Cooper Union, Epstein didn't go far, enrolling in New York University's esteemed Courant Institute of Mathematical Sciences, just a few blocks west. Epstein stayed almost three years at New York University but again dropped out without completing a degree.

It was 1974: time to conquer the city—and the world—at his own pace.

# 2

## TO SIR, WITH LOVE

YEAR AFTER YEAR, THE DALTON SCHOOL ON MANHATTAN'S UPPER East Side is ranked as one of the nation's top preparatory academies.[1] Originally known as Children's University School, the school dates to 1919, and its founding was an expression of an educational reform movement that questioned the traditional role of classrooms as settings of rigid structure emphasizing drills and memorization. Instead, reformers of the new progressive model sought "total enrichment of mind, body, and spirit" in their students through individualized learning plans.[2]

In time the Dalton School shed its reputation as a revolutionary "laboratory" of education and simply became one of the city's most prestigious schools. It is also one of the most selective, admitting only those students who, according to the school's mission statement, "are of sound character and educational promise."[3] The admissions process was on par with that of colleges in the Ivy League—and for good reason. If one was admitted to Dalton, as one former student put it, "you were all but destined to have your pick of college and graduate school." Getting into the Dalton School became something of a high-society gladiator competition—a blood sport with no quarter given. Having a child as a student in the school was as much a Manhattan status symbol as a summer home in the Hamptons.

Tuition at the Dalton School in 1974 was $3,200 a year (it's roughly $54,000 today), and parents expected the best for that sum. The Dalton School boasted that 75 percent of its teaching staff had advanced degrees. The remaining members of the faculty had all completed their bachelor's degree.

All except Jeffrey Epstein, that is.


IN THE SUMMER OF 1974, the Dalton School hired the once shy and nerdy kid from Sea Gate, now just twenty-one, as a calculus and physics teacher. In normal times, the chances of a man like Epstein being interviewed, let alone hired, for a teaching job at the Dalton School would have been nil. But these were not normal times. The last embers of political revolution and upheaval still burned in the city, and Dalton found itself embroiled in something of a culture war, with left-leaning, artsy parents on one side and a strict new head-master on the other.[4]

The Dalton School hired Donald Barr—a former intelligence officer in the Office of Strategic Services during the Second World War and an English professor at Columbia University—precisely to instill a sense of order and discipline into the learning institution. Barr's edicts prohibited unconventional clothing at Dalton; denim jeans were out, as were miniskirts. To avoid expulsion in the Barr regime, marijuana-using students were required to see a therapist.[5]

But if Barr could be seen as overbearing, he also seemed to pos-sess a fondness for eccentrics, individuals who couldn't be catego-rized by any cookie-cutter definitions. He was reportedly fascinated by how Epstein calculated answers, worked out complex stories in response to mundane questions. There were rumors that Barr may have been a recruiter for the American intelligence fraternity—chatter later picked up by Epstein's friend Steve Hoffenberg. Could Barr have seen Epstein in this light?

Whether or not Barr had any association with the intelligence world, he and Epstein both struck acquaintances as complicated and at times downright strange. In 1973, a year before Epstein came to Dalton, Barr had published a novel titled *Space Relations: A Slightly Gothic Interplanetary Tale* whose plot centered on "intergalactic sexual slavery."

Some students found little to like in the headmaster. "Donald Barr was a real puritanical asshole," Karin Williams, who graduated from Dalton in 1978, remembered. Williams said that after Barr left Dalton, she heard a story that when Dalton staff "renovated the office, they discovered a whole stash of pornography behind the old panels."[6]

Barr's decision to hire Epstein left many perplexed. E. Belvin Williams, a former Dalton trustee and associate dean of Columbia University's Business School, told the *Miami Herald,* "I think it was unusual that a school focused on quality education would hire a person with no experience and no college degrees, especially when the Dalton teachers we knew were excellent."[7] (Barr reportedly left the Dalton School almost immediately after hiring Epstein.)

Perhaps Epstein couldn't believe his luck. Although some published reports list his starting salary as only $12,000 a year, he was making $20,000 (close to $105,000 a year in 2020, adjusted for inflation).[8] The twenty-one-year-old who filled out the application at the Dalton School in the summer of 1974 was slick and sure of himself.

The taxi-driving dropout's job would now be teaching the privileged offspring of powerful Wall Street financiers and the city's cultural elite.[9] Two of Robert Redford's children were students at Dalton, as well as Jennifer Grey, daughter of the Academy Award–winning actor Joel Grey.

As Epstein entered one of Manhattan's fortresses of learning, the once chubby kid was now a slim and confident adult.

DALTON KIDS WERE NOTHING LIKE Brooklyn kids. Epstein's new pupils were from a different planet completely, self-assured and unafraid. Excitement for students at Dalton didn't mean heading out to the boardwalk at Coney Island during school breaks. They traveled out west for whitewater rafting, and they went skiing in Switzerland; some even could enjoy long weekends in Paris. Many of the kids came from divorced homes where one parent was across town or on the other side of the earth; they were cared for by nannies and housekeepers.

The cultural shock was mutual. Students—and faculty—at Dalton had never seen anyone like Epstein before. He wore tight-fitting clothing with his shirt—usually of mid-1970s polyester—open wide. "It was a very preppy kind of school," Pam Brenner-Newton, a Dalton alumna who graduated in 1977, recalled. "He would wear lots of gold chains with shirts kind of open down inappropriately and big fur coats. . . . He didn't look the part, and he didn't want to look the part."[10]

Epstein also didn't speak like the quintessential Dalton teacher. A male student named Ken[*] who attended Dalton at the time recalled being struck by Epstein's "Brooklyn" demeanor amid the upper-crust trappings of the school. "I come from a similar lower-middle-class Jewish background as [Epstein]. He was very Brooklyn, almost in a blue-collar way, the way he spoke and dressed flamboyantly by the standards of the day. He didn't code-switch. . . . He always spoke that way."[11]

The setup at Dalton was designed to enhance interaction and close contact between students and teachers. The school encouraged each student to make his or her own educational choices, and the menu of study boasted a rich assortment of classes.[12] Each subject area had a "lab" where students were encourged to meet with teachers outside normal classroom hours.

In interviews, students do not seem to recall "Mr. Epstein" as being an inspiring or talented teacher. At best he earned mixed reviews. Joshua Persky, a class of 1977 graduate of Dalton, had

[*] A pseudonym. Ken has requested that his identity be concealed.

Epstein for physics and rated Epstein an "okay" teacher to the *Miami Herald*. On Facebook, another Dalton alumnus, Peter Thomas Roth, described Epstein as an "amazing" physics teacher.

More than his pedagogical abilities, what stands out in the memories of Dalton students is Epstein's Studio 54–like appearance. "When I think of him, I think of him walking down the hall with this big floor-length fur coat," one former student remembered. "You know, hair very large—kind of like John Travolta—with an open shirt and a lot of chains, which was not the norm for a teacher at Dalton during that time."[13] Students thought his dress odd. "I was just sort of like bamboozled, as a kid, just looking at this guy saying, 'Why is he wearing that?'" Karin Williams recollected. "Maybe in your private life, but not at your workplace."[14]

Being a teacher conveyed an amazing amount of power—and control—for one so young to have over people only a few years his junior. And it is here at Dalton that Epstein's involvement with young girls likely began.

In September 1975, ABC debuted a television comedy called *Welcome Back, Kotter,* about a hip young teacher who returns to his old high school in Brooklyn to teach a class of incorrigible kids, a group of students nicknamed the Sweathogs. In the show, the students routinely interacted with the teacher as if he were a friend, even being guests at his home. The show was a smash hit and was the launching pad for the career of John Travolta. But when Jeffrey Epstein began appearing at the homes of students to attend parties thrown by some of the Dalton kids—especially when their parents weren't home—the phenomenon was seen as an anomaly. According to one former student, he only visited the homes of the girls who were considered attractive.[15]

Another student remembered: "It was not normal for teachers to come to student weekend parties. People would have parties, their parents would go away for the weekend, there's a party at so-and-so's house. You would be there—with somewhere between three and six high school students. Everybody would be like, 'Wow, that's weird that Epstein's here.'"[16]

Alcohol and drugs were common at these soirees. The student named Ken remembered one encounter with Epstein at a party in a large apartment on the Upper East Side where students were drinking and smoking marijuana without adult supervision. "[Epstein] showed up, which was very strange. People took notice of it. It was a topic of discussion, like 'What the fuck was up with that.' I don't think he was partaking in anything. The very fact he was there was disconcerting. I was not a heavy drug or alcohol user, so I had my faculties about me, and I remember thinking, 'Oh, this is weird.'"

Ken recalled that he and Epstein happened to leave the party at the same time and began walking in the same direction. "Then he said, 'Excuse me' and rang a buzzer of a small walk-up [apartment building]. . . . The person answered, and he said, 'Hi, can I come up?' . . . Then he looked at me and said, 'Okay, 'bye I got to go.' It was like a classic out-of-the-blue booty call kind of thing."[17]

Reflecting on his own interactions with Epstein, Scott Spizer recalled, "There was overall this sense of something inappropriate going on here. He's way too friendly, way too close. He's a bleeping teacher."

YEARS LATER, IT IS EVIDENT to some former Dalton students that Epstein showed special attention to certain female students, especially girls who were more physically diminutive. "He had this grin; it was kind of a leer," remembered one female former student. "What I felt was, you know, keep moving, slimeball. I probably gave him a look to that [effect], because the leer left his face instantly. . . . I now realize that given his reputation for solicitation of minors, he was testing the water [with me]."[18]

Karin Williams recalled a similar incident. "I have two friends who were in the same classroom, one who he approached, and she shut him down," the former Dalton student remembered. "She said that in class he would be very physically close. You know, when you're helping with the homework and those assignments, you know, kind of touching and stuff like that. Not directly groping per se but that she could see that he was being inappropriately near when they were working."[19]

Not everyone saw ulterior motives in Epstein's actions, however. In an interview with *The New York Times,* one former Dalton student named Leslie Kitziger, whose parents were going through a divorce at the time, said, "I was a fourteen-year-old and he helped me through a time when there wasn't anybody else to talk to."[20] She told the *Times* that Epstein had conducted himself appropriately around her.

Years later, in one of the many depositions that Epstein would give to lawyers, he skirted the issue of whether he had inappropriate relationships with any of his students. When asked if he had "sexual contact with the girls that you were teaching at Dalton," Epstein answered, "No." When asked if he had sex with any of his students after he left Dalton, Epstein declined to answer. "I'm [going] to answer that question like every other question I've answered today, which is, I intend to respond to all relevant questions regarding this lawsuit; however, at present, my attorneys have counseled me I cannot provide answers to any questions that may be relevant to this lawsuit. I must accept this advice or risk losing my Sixth Amendment right to effective representation. Accordingly, I assert my federal constitutional rights as guaranteed by the Fifth, Sixth, and Fourteenth Amendments to the U.S. Constitution."[21]

In interviews for this book, several former Dalton students said they suspected that Epstein had pursued one of his students, a woman who is now deceased. During their time at Dalton, the relationship between Epstein and this former student struck these observers as particularly close, "outside the norm." Other students detected no signs of impropriety in the relationship, while a family member of the woman's said, "I have nothing bad to say about Jeffrey."[22]

• • •

JEFFREY EPSTEIN PARTED WAYS WITH the Dalton School after the 1975–76 school year. The official Dalton line was that he was let go because of his haphazard and uninspiring approach to educating young minds. According to Peter Branch, the school's interim headmaster, "It was determined that he had not adequately grown as a new teacher to the standard of the school."[23] That narrative, however, appears to be something of a whitewash.

In the spring of 1976, during a parent-teacher conference at the Dalton School, Epstein met Bear Sterns CEO Alan "Ace" Greenberg, who was the father of one of his students, Lynne Greenberg.[24] Epstein reportedly dazzled Greenberg—and also confided in the older financier that he didn't want to be a teacher anymore.

Greenberg defined the expression "rags to riches." He started his financial career as a clerk in the Bear Sterns mailroom, eventually catapulting himself to CEO. Greenberg, who was the son of an Oklahoma City clothing store owner, found a young mirror image of himself in Epstein and he adored those who showed PSD—"poor, smart, and desperate to be rich"—qualities.[25]

Greenberg reportedly summoned the young man to his office, barked out a few questions, and hired him on the spot, despite Epstein's admission that he didn't know the difference between a stock and a bond.

Epstein learned an invaluable lesson at Dalton: It wasn't what you knew, but who you knew. He would never be poor again.

# 3

## MONEY NEVER SLEEPS

BEAR STEARNS WAS ONCE ONE OF THE MOST RESPECTED EQUITY TRADING houses on Wall Street. Founded in 1923 by Joseph Ainslie Bear and Robert B. Stearns, the company name rolled off the tongue sounding like an immovable force of banking and investing. The firm had a reputation on Wall Street as being immune to failure. Not only did Bear Stearns survive the crash of 1929, it did so without laying off a single employee.

In the 1970s, Bear Stearns would have been a prestigious trading house for a young and hungry broker eager to launch his career. Getting in the front door wasn't easy; attracting the attention of the firm's persnickety recruiters was just the start. There was a thorough background check; references were meticulously examined. Bear Stearns executives liked to boast that their people were rock solid and brilliant. It also boasted that it was a different type of investment house—one that was scrappy and hungry, and where middle-class dreams of upper-class dividends were within reach.[1]

Once in the door, a new trader or analyst learned everything the Bear Stearns way. The Bear Stearns "school" was a "learn how to get rich academy," and the wealth-hungry recruits savored every minute of it.

In the summer of 1976, Jeffrey Epstein, having ditched the Dalton School, was such a recruit. But Epstein had a significant differentiator—his powerful mentor. CEO Ace Greenberg and Epstein shared a special bond. "Jeffrey loved Ace Greenberg like a father. And Ace Greenberg loved Jeffrey like a son," Steven Hoffenberg recalled. "Ace was everything Jeffrey had dreamed about." For his part, Greenberg appreciated Epstein's "super-intelligence in math" and felt the young man had "a fire in his belly." Epstein was poised to "become a master of options trading."[2]

Greenberg was proud of his hire, even showing Epstein off to friends and business associates. In an interview for this book, Lynne Koeppel, Greenberg's daughter, remembers Epstein coming to their family home a few times as a guest at dinner parties. The kid from Brooklyn stood out to her. "He had a great personality. He was everything my father liked. Poor, smart, and with a deep desire to become rich. Everyone thought that he was brilliant."[3]

Epstein told *The Wall Street Journal* in 2003 that he was specifically fast-tracked at Bear by Greenberg, whom he called "amazing." Greenberg, Epstein said, wanted his protégé to learn every area of the business, beginning with the American Stock Exchange and later moving up to the trading desk to "learn all the different areas of the firm including the margin department."[4]

For all his talent at math, finance was something completely new to Epstein, but, according to Hoffenberg, the new vocation was a perfect match. "He found the home that he had been searching for up to that [time]," Hoffenberg said.[5]

There was no other junior associate there like him.

Epstein stood out at Bear, but this time it wasn't because of his fur coats or open shirts. By the time he reached Wall Street, Epstein wore a Moe Ginsburg suit purchased from the legendary low-cost, no-frills "pipe-rack" operation in Lower Manhattan where many men starting their first real job sought respectable three-piece suits.[6] Epstein was unique at Bear because of his uncanny ability to comprehend the pricing of options, the financial derivatives given to buyers for the rights to sell or buy based on the value of underlying assets.

He applied a scientific approach to his trades, and his success was immediate and lucrative. To Epstein, finance was like physics. There were "a fixed number of rules" and, in finance as in physics, one could experiment. "If you didn't violate those rules and if your experiment worked, you hit the target." And the target might mean you get "to fly first class to Paris," as Epstein put it.[7]

Jeffrey Epstein used to tell his clients at Bear Stearns that he was a tax expert who was skilled in sophisticated investment strategies.[8] In reality, he was an options trader. At the time, options trading was an arcane and dimly understood field, just beginning to take off. To trade options, one had to value them, and to do that one needed to be able to master such abstruse mathematical confections as the Black-Scholes option pricing model.

For Epstein, breaking down such models was pure sport, and within just a few years he had his stable of elite clients. In 2002, *New York* magazine quoted Bear Stearns CEO James Cayne about Epstein. "He was not your conventional broker saying 'Buy IBM' or 'Sell Xerox,'" Cayne remarked. "Given his mathematical background, we put him in our special products division, where he would advise our wealthier clients on the tax implications of their portfolios."

Among the A-list clients that Epstein soon handled was Edgar Bronfman, Sr., the Canadian American businessman whose family owned Seagram distillers. Bronfman, a pro-Israel activist who was very involved in Jewish causes, was a huge client for Bear Stearns, and for the up-and-coming twentysomething eager to boost his salary and his standing at the prestigious investment house.

Teaching at Dalton might have unleashed a hidden beast inside Epstein, but working at Bear Stearns, where he was regarded as a prodigal son who could do no wrong, turned him into something of a Gordon Gekko. His starting salary at Bear, according to some reports, was $200,000—ten times what he made at Dalton.

Greed wasn't good, it was great. And it paid dividends—not just money, but power.

BY THE TIME HE BLEW out the candles on his twenty-fifth birthday cake, Jeffrey Epstein was already a million miles from the modest blocks of Sea Gate. He now lived in a nice apartment on East Sixty-Sixth Street on the Upper East Side. Epstein was now ensconced in an atmosphere of wealth and the privileges that came with it.

New York City was a great place to be flush with cash in the late 1970s. In the years between when it teetered on the brink of bankruptcy in the mid-1970s and the onset of the AIDS epidemic in the mid-1980s, the city was an epicenter of decadence. For a junior associate like Epstein, a young man with bonus money in his wallet and a chip on his shoulder, there were restaurants like Elaine's and clubs like Studio 54; there were also places like Plato's Retreat, the legendary swingers' club on Thirty-Fourth Street, for unabashed debauchery.

Money was power, and it paid for any and all vices. Epstein, though, would later say he was a loner, not the kind of person to hang out in discos or nightclubs, and that he never touched alcohol or drugs.[9] Just as he stood out from his peers in other respects, Epstein's vices, too, would mark him as different.

JUST AS JEFFREY EPSTEIN SEEMED to be at the top of the world, a strange incident occurred with the former classmate on whom he had once set his boyhood romantic sights, Kathy Suter.

Though Epstein was finding success and newfound wealth in his new life in finance, he also allegedly showed signs of a fixation with a part of his past: his high school flame. Epstein had maintained something of an on-again, off-again relationship with Suter since finishing public school. There were phone calls between the two, an occasional burger. At some point things fizzled, but it seemed Epstein simply couldn't forget his childhood sweetheart.

According to Bernard Laffer, who also maintained a relationship with Suter, she had grown disenchanted with Epstein after his transformation into a financier. "[Kathy] had told me she had been dating Jeff, [but] she said she didn't like who he had become," Laffer recalled in interviews for this book with journalist Philip Messing.[10] "She said he was very arrogant and difficult to deal with and she just couldn't handle it. He had started making Wall Street money and she felt this had turned him into someone different."

One evening in 1979, Laffer and Suter went on a date to the movies. When the couple emerged from the Kingsway Theater near Coney Island several hours later, they were startled to see Epstein getting out of a chauffeur-driven town car in front of the theater. It is unclear to Laffer whether Epstein encountered them by chance or had purposely followed them, but Laffer suspected the latter. "I think he had been following her. How the fuck would he know that she was there?" Laffer recalled.

When Epstein saw Suter with another man, according to Laffer, he became volatile, unhinged.

As Suter approached Epstein, the conversation became heated, according to Laffer's account. In an effort to intervene, Laffer said he walked over to where the two were arguing. "I said to him—I think I called him Bear—I said, 'Bear, I hope you're paying your limo driver a lot of money because when I start beating your ass, he's going to have to pull me off you.'"

In response to Laffer's remarks, Epstein retreated, but he turned to Suter with a parting message. "He backed up and yelled to Kathy something like, 'I'm not finished with you!'" Laffer recalled. "And he got into his limo and the driver drove away."[11]

After the alleged incident of stalking, Epstein would maintain contact with Suter for the next thirty years.

THOUGH EPSTEIN WAS MADE A limited partner at Bear Stearns, his tenure at the Wall Street giant proved short-lived and ended in 1981.

Numerous accounts have emerged as to what upended Epstein's Bear Stearns career. According to one, human resources discovered that Epstein had lied on his résumé and had never completed his bachelor's degree. When word reached Ace Greenberg, he found himself in a difficult position—Epstein was reportedly dating his secretary. Greenberg wanted to treat his prodigy like everyone else, but Epstein knew how to talk to his boss, and he explained why he lied about his educational background. For Greenberg, Epstein was a success. There was little incentive to allow this white lie to torpedo a promising career.[12]

But there were other signs of trouble. During a separate investigation into Epstein's work practices he was accused of an insider trading "Reg D" violation after lending $20,000 to Warren Eisenstein, his close friend from Sea Gate, so that he could buy a particular stock. Investigators found that no stock purchase had taken place. According to Eisenstein's widow, Linda, the loan that the couple received was to purchase an apartment. "We were trying to buy a condominium," Linda Eisenstein recalled, "and [Warren] went to Jeffrey about it, to see if he would help him out. It was twenty thousand dollars, which is nothing, and that was what I understood happened. It wasn't like he [Epstein] blamed Warren, and there were no hard feelings because their relationship, to my knowledge, never changed."[13]

Other irregularities surfaced as well. Serious issues emerged with Epstein's expense accounts; he was also embroiled in a Securities and Exchange Commission (SEC) investigation of insider trading relating to work he was doing for Edgar Bronfman, Sr., his most lucrative client.

Under this cloud of allegations, Epstein handed in his resignation on March 12, 1981, shortly after he received the summons from the SEC to talk about Bronfman and Epstein's attempt to take over a mineral company.[14] Bear Stearns boss James Cayne told the authors of *Filthy Rich* that Epstein left of his own volition.[15] According to other reports, Epstein was forced out. His career in conventional finance—regardless of the spin—was over.

According to one former business partner, a huge fight ensued among the brass at Bear over what to do with Epstein. Some wanted to keep him. But Epstein had lost his licenses—known as the Series 7 and Series 63—that entitled the holder to sell and solicit orders for securities products; they were prerequisites for a long and illustrious career on the trading floor. Epstein could still be an adviser on investment banking, packaging terms, but he could no longer trade in his name.

Ace Greenberg's affection and clout weren't enough. Faced with little choice, Epstein cleaned out his desk at Bear Stearns, collected a $100,000 bonus—a fortune in 1981—and headed uptown to his apartment on East Sixty-Sixth Street.

It was time to grab a piece of the world for himself—with no rules or regulations to rein him in.

# 4

# THE "COSMO" GUY

JEFFREY EPSTEIN WALKED OUT OF THE BEAR STEARNS OFFICE ON Madison Avenue carrying a cardboard box of his belongings, the Shit Can Case, as it's called in finance. The contents consisted of some papers, a few office props he had collected, and two of his most prized possessions from his time at one of the world's most prestigious financial houses: an award from Helen Gurley Brown's *Cosmopolitan* magazine bestowing upon him the title of Cosmo Bachelor of the Month for July 1980, and an 8 x10 glossy photograph of Morgan Fairchild, the blond siren of soap opera and television fame.

So far in his adult life, Epstein had turned a one-in-a-million opportunity to teach at the Dalton School into a one-in-a-million opportunity to climb the ranks at one of America's top financial firms. He negotiated the land mines of the financial markets—along with an SEC investigation—and emerged with barely a scratch.

But Epstein was now on his own. So far, his life had seemed to teach him that he could leverage anyone and anything to his benefit. It was a wide-open world for someone who had the determination never to fall below the poverty line.

In 1981, he filed corporate papers launching a financial consulting firm called Intercontinental Assets Group.

The sky was the limit.

IN THE DAY AND AGE before start-ups, establishing an investment firm from inside the dusty confines of a small Upper East Side apartment on East Sixty-Sixth Street was considered quite novel.[1] The Intercontinental Assets Group had the ring of a powerhouse firm. In fact, there was no proprietary software to bestow an edge; there was no receptionist, no other employees at all. Epstein stacked company files on the sofa and in his kitchenette.

What Epstein did have was ambition. He aimed to take advantage of the lessons learned at Dalton and Bear Stearns. He would focus only on the truly flush. To the hyper-rich clients, he imagined giving financial advice on investments, trusts, estates, asset allocation, and how to organize and manage a family fortune. His business model was simple: Extreme wealth creates a host of unique and often intractable problems. Epstein would solve those problems for his clients.

The trouble was that he didn't have any clients. Without the safety net of a Bear Stearns salary or annual bonus, Epstein's New York City life fell victim to the penny-pinching reality of a self-employed financial consultant. However, just as he had done with Donald Barr and Ace Greenberg, Epstein looked to take advantage of any influential individuals who might fall into his web.

At some point, Epstein shifted his company's focus to recovering stolen money from fraudulent brokers and lawyers. This was a murkier world than the conventional world of stocks and finance, but it was lucrative. He landed a prestigious clientele, including Andrew Levander and Robert Gold, who had lost most of their net wealth when a company called Drysdale Government Securities crashed.[2]

The super-rich weren't the only clients Epstein was courting.

Around this time Epstein began to tell friends that he sometimes consulted for governments—and government agencies—to help them recover embezzled funds. At the same time, Epstein reportedly also searched for clients who had embezzled funds themselves—and needed to relocate them, perhaps in offshore accounts.[3] Epstein had turned himself into something of a financial bounty hunter double agent.

In the case of the Drysdale Government Securities debacle, Epstein's "hunting" prowess made him a hero to Spanish actress Ana Obregón.[4] Obregón, a model and actress, would later pose for *Playboy*. Her father had lost millions of dollars with Drysdale Government Securities, and Ana requested Epstein's help to get it back. He did, though the details of the intricate operation remain hazy. Reportedly, Epstein earned millions by locating the Obregón millions in a maze of hidden accounts.[5]

If Epstein's relationship with Obregón was purely business, one relationship that wasn't was Epstein's affair with Eva Andersson. Andersson was the kind of Nordic beauty that men fantasized about. The Gothenburg-born Andersson was also smart, possessing a razor-sharp mind that was academically focused. Gerard W. Ford, who with his wife, Eileen, ran the Ford Modeling Agency, one of the world's most prominent agencies, discovered Eva on the streets of the Upper East Side. "Jerry," as he was known, approached the Swede and offered her a job on the spot; supposedly, he brought her to the agency, marched her inside, and shouted to his wife, "Look what I found in the street!"[6]

Andersson's modeling career was short-lived by choice. After going back to her native Sweden, she entered the beauty pageant world, earning the title of Miss Sweden and being selected as fourth runner-up in the 1980 Miss Universe pageant in Seoul, South Korea. She then returned to the United States to commence medical school in the early 1980s.

She met Jeffrey Epstein in Manhattan. The relationship was romantic and serious. Epstein was infatuated with Eva, according to friends. He encouraged her to complete medical school and even helped her with tuition. The relationship was one of the handful of long-lasting relationships that Epstein ever shared with a woman.

People who knew Epstein in the early 1980s were certain that the pair would wed, but, as Steven Hoffenberg would later reflect, "Marriage is normal. Jeffrey was abnormal."[7] Another friend, Stuart Pivar, who founded the New York Academy of Art with Andy Warhol in 1982 and was a longtime confidant of Epstein's, cited another factor: "I know that he hated kids. And that's the reason that he was reluctant to marry her."[8]

The relationship between Epstein and Andersson would last nine years, from 1981 to 1990.

Epstein's associations with Andersson and Obregón came at a pivotal moment in his life. These two glamorous women brought him legitimacy and access—access to a world of high finance and celebrity that would be light-years ahead of what he could ever have imagined from a desk at Bear Stearns. In the case of Andersson, it brought Epstein into a more conventional adult social world of dating and relationships.

But those weren't the relationships he desired.

# 5

## DIRTY DEEDS, DIRTY MONEY

BY 1984, JEFFREY EPSTEIN SEEMED TO BE CAUGHT IN A DOWNWARD spiral. Business was slow, slower than he had hoped when he left Bear Stearns, and to make matters worse, one of his clients was suing him. A pinball machine manufacturer named Michael Stroll had sued Epstein in federal court for the $450,000 he lost in an oil deal. As in many legal entanglements to come, Epstein, who won the lawsuit, proved that if you were steadfast, clever, and arrogant, you could stay above the law.

Epstein's sense of being coated by a suit of Teflon armor was reinforced in the summer of 1984.

During a vacation on Hilton Head Island, South Carolina, Epstein met a thirteen-year-old girl, identified only as Jane Doe 4 in court papers filed in 2019. The girl was the daughter of a woman from whom Epstein had rented a beach house. Jane Doe 4 routinely worked as a babysitter for vacationing couples and thought nothing of it when Epstein hired her. But Epstein had no children, of course, and when the girl arrived at the house, he offered Jane Doe 4 alcohol and drugs. Epstein raped her for the first time later that night.[1]

The rapes would continue over the next few years on subsequent trips to Hilton Head, according to court documents. Epstein took secret nude photographs of Jane Doe 4—possibly while the girl was asleep or under the influence of narcotics or alcohol. When Jane Doe 4 learned of the images and demanded that they be returned to her, Epstein became violent and refused to surrender them.

The abuses continued over the next several years, according to a lawsuit Doe joined with other Epstein victims in 2019. Epstein flew the girl across state lines, to New York on three or four occasions, according to the court filing, to offer the young woman as "fresh meat" to a circle of male friends.[2] The lawsuit contains disturbing descriptions of how Doe was raped and beaten by this group of Epstein's friends, who are not identified. The suit describes how one of the men slapped Doe in the face after she was forced to perform oral sex on him; the same man penetrated her both vaginally and anally.

By his thirty-first birthday, Jeffrey Epstein seemed to have turned a fateful corner into a life of outright deviancy. But he had seemingly also learned that there were two kinds of people in the world: those who could make a fuss about his actions, like Michael Stroll, and those who could be compelled into silence, like Jane Doe 4.

PERHAPS LEVERAGE WAS THE TRUE love of Epstein's life.

The high-profile individuals to whom Ana Obregón connected Epstein were not just the glamorous; some of them were dangerous.

Douglas Leese and Adnan Khashoggi were members of a small and insular community of arms brokers who approached flexible-minded members of governments, primarily from the Third World, and offered one-stop shopping for the arms and munitions needed to keep their regimes in power.[3] These characters who populated Leese and Khashoggi's world were a motley crew of former spies, retired generals, and opportunists with no moral compass. Nothing in this community was black-and-white. It was murky and gray, and fueled by cash.

The mid-1980s were a lucrative time to be an arms merchant.

The American-supported Central American regimes were under communist assault; Colombia and other Latin American countries were embroiled in the last of their communist rebellions; sub-Saharan Africa was rife with internecine bloodshed; and there were always paramilitary and guerrilla groups in southeast Asia in need of AK-47s, rocket-propelled grenades, and ample supplies of Czech-made explosives. And of course there was the Middle East. There was the Arab-Israeli conflict, a civil war in Lebanon, conflicts in and around North Africa, and the Iran-Iraq War, which had both sides in desperate need of material. For sellers who had access to cluster bombs, supersonic fighter bombers, and advanced radar systems, there were many buyers.

Leese was one of the most successful arms merchants working in the Third World, as well as the highly lucrative kingdoms and dictatorships of the Arab world. The British citizen was certainly greatly respected, as were most men who maintained offices near Mayfair and Whitehall in London where the telex machine churned confidential messages twenty-four hours a day. Leese had close relationships with Third World despots as well as with senior executives from the arms consortiums.

Leese's company's activities spanned banking, insurance, arms dealing, and other off-the-traditional-radar enterprises that entailed huge profits, danger, and risk.[4] Men like Leese always looked for brilliant, personable, mathematically inclined men who knew enough about how the world worked to be discreet. Jeffrey Epstein was one such man.

Epstein did well for Leese, devising offshore tax havens and creative accounting that enhanced the already astronomical profits that came from selling weapons. Leese also introduced Epstein to one of his associates: Adnan Khashoggi.

Khashoggi, a Saudi arms dealer, was a man of marvel and mystery. He was born in Mecca, and his father was said to have been the personal physician of Saudi king Abdullah bin Abdulaziz Al Saud. Khashoggi was one of the world's wealthiest arms brokers. He moved around the world surrounded by heavily armed bodyguards—men trained in the art of killing at Fort Bragg in the United States and at Hereford in the United Kingdom. The Saudi soon became another trusted client of Epstein's.

Epstein relished watching Leese and Khashoggi operate. The Byzantine way of doing business was all about personal leverage—who you knew. What you knew was less important than being known and vouched for. Being able to get something precious via a phone call was the currency among this breed of well-connected men—and women—who operated in their own insulated universe. Little by little Epstein toed his way into this crowd. Epstein, who had at times struggled to find his company's financial footing, was fascinated by this covert and dangerous world of yachts and conspicuous consumption. Leese, for example, owned a three-hundred-acre estate, which also served as his heavily fortified home office, outside of Bath, Great Britain. Epstein was frequently helicoptered onto his estate.[5]

Being a middleman meant that you could take advantage of the greed or perversion of both the buyers and the sellers to get a contract signed and paid for. The terms of hundred-million-dollar weapons deals were discussed in private clubs over glasses of brandy. The details of these arrangements were always secretive; discretion was guaranteed in a handshake, and bribes were the currency of day-to-day business.

Epstein began living the fantasy, and the universe of his imagination grew by leaps and bounds the more successful he became. He started telling people that he was a spy. It was, of course, bullshit.

But Epstein was nonetheless mastering the trade of deceit.

JEFFREY EPSTEIN MADE IT A point to learn from those with whom he worked. It was an intriguing trait for someone so brash and self-confident. The mentor-protégé relationship was extremely important for Epstein, and Douglas Leese was one such individual whom

Epstein looked up to and admired. When Leese presented Epstein with a source of new business, Epstein leaped at the opportunity.

Leese was the one who introduced Epstein to Hoffenberg, also a Brooklyn native, in 1987. Hoffenberg ran Towers Financial Corporation, a firm that purchased bad debt at pennies on the dollar and then turned the collections into considerable profit. Epstein impressed Hoffenberg right away. "He appeared to be brilliant, extraordinarily gifted and talented in convincing people to buy from him," Hoffenberg would later say.[6] Hoffenberg wanted to grow his company, and Epstein said he could get access to new investors.[7]

Epstein and Hoffenberg immediately hit it off. They shared the common background of Brooklyn to help cement their relationship, and they often reminisced about their experiences growing up in the borough. "Jeffrey and I had an extraordinarily different kind of relationship," Hoffenberg recalled. "I thought he was a friend, a dear friend. He had an extraordinary ability to bond. . . . Epstein's supernatural ability was to discern what the other person was looking for."[8]

Hoffenberg would later claim that he took Epstein on as a favor to Douglas Leese and that Epstein had been stealing from Leese—and later from Hoffenberg. Nonetheless, soon after his initial meeting with Hoffenberg, Epstein was flying around the United States—and beyond—on Hoffenberg's private jet. Hoffenberg, who, like Epstein, never finished college, had the trappings of the lifestyle that Jeffrey so voraciously craved: chauffeur-driven limousines, fast boats, and 72-foot yachts.[9]

If Epstein learned the value of a lie at Dalton, with Hoffenberg he learned its molecular structure. Epstein worked out of Hoffenberg's office in the Villard Houses, an imposing historical landmark of Renaissance Revival architecture behind St. Patrick's Cathedral on Madison Avenue. It was the type of office building or residence where titans of industry held court, not two-bit investors thinking of ways to undercut the system.[10]

Epstein is believed to have earned $25,000 a month as a consultant for Hoffenberg at Towers Financial—a mighty package for someone who lacked a degree and the necessary trading licenses. Reportedly, he grew the company's revenue-raising division from $20 million annually to just shy of $1 billion.[11]

But Epstein joined the team at Towers during a critical juncture in the company's history. In 1987, Towers Financial acquired the parent companies of two Illinois-based insurance firms, Associated Life Insurance and United Fire. The plan was to use the assets of these two companies to boost Towers Financial's chances of a corporate takeover of Pan American Airways, at the time one of the largest airlines in the world.

The bid to take over Pan Am failed. On the night of December 21, 1988, a terrorist bomb ripped through the cargo hold of Pan Am 103, a Boeing 747 flying over Lockerbie, Scotland, and 270 people were killed. Pan Am never recovered from the terrorist attack and its resulting reputation for being a carrier with lax security; the company filed for bankruptcy shortly after the incident. Towers Financial also attempted to take over Emery Air Freight. That effort failed, too. But the thwarted takeover attempts had depleted the insurance firms of their assets, and eventually, thousands of investors were bilked out of more than $450 million.[12]

To recover their losses and start again, Towers Financial perpetrated a fraud, selling promissory notes hinting at returns close to 20 percent. It was an enormous Ponzi scheme, though Hoffenberg would later describe it as a standard business practice. "A Ponzi scheme means you take in new money and you use the new money to pay old money," Hoffenberg recalled. "Every company in America does it."[13]

Both Hoffenberg and Epstein siphoned money for themselves in the process. According to Hoffenberg, Epstein was the person in charge of all the transactions. Yet when U.S. attorneys in Illinois and New York concluded their investigation and charged Hoffenberg with a phone book full of financial wrongdoings, Epstein escaped indictment. Hoffenberg served eighteen years in a federal penitentiary.

• • •

IN 1990, NO LONGER STRUGGLING financially, Jeffrey Epstein pur-
chased a two-story mansion at 358 El Brillo Way in Palm Beach,
Florida. The address was in one of the ritziest areas of already ritzy
Palm Beach, stretching from the Intracoastal to the Atlantic Ocean;
Everglades Golf Course was a couple of streets away.

New York developer Donald Trump had a place down the road.[14]

# 6

## PATRON

THERE WAS ALWAYS A BROOKLYN CONNECTION. IT WAS DIFFICULT TO find an American who wasn't six (or fewer) separations from New York's famed Borough of Kings. In 1908, Bella Cabakoff, then only a few months old and the first in her family to be born in the New World, far from the poverty and pogroms of czarist Russia, made the long trek from Williamsburg, Brooklyn, to Columbus, Ohio—her parents, who came to this country penniless and without speaking a word of English, were in search of new opportunities far from the squalor of the disease-infested tenements of New York's Lower East Side. Bella would go on to marry Harry Wexner in Dayton, and in 1937 she gave birth to a son, Leslie.

America was good to the Wexner family. They ran a clothing store, a small downtown retail operation. They named the establishment Leslie's after their son. According to Wexner in a 2003 interview, his parents "worked eighty-hour weeks to scratch out a living, but they never made ten thousand dollars a year."[1] But Wexner's parents knew how to save a penny, and they knew how to stretch its value. A middle-class existence soon followed. The parents invested heavily in the education of their kids so that they could be successful.

Wexner's parents paid a king's ransom for him to attend a posh high school in the exclusive Bexley section of town. He graduated from Ohio State University with a degree in business administration.[2] He even served in the Air National Guard.

Wexner, like many kids of his generation, worked in his parents' store when he was a child. He wielded a broom, folded the merchandise, and manned the cash register; it was an invaluable education, one of cost versus expenditure, that he could never have learned wearing his Buckeyes sweatshirt. Wexner knew business because it was ingrained inside his DNA from day one. Wexner was smart. It was the 1960s; cultural and sexual norms were changing around the country and the world. With his degree and some seed money—$5,000 from a spinster aunt and $5,000 from a bank loan—he envisioned turning the small clothing franchise into a multinational powerhouse.[3] The company he created was called The Limited. It began with a small store in Columbus.[4]

The Limited was an amazing success—a testament to Wexner's business acumen and his uncanny ability to predict market trends and execute business plans to meet and brand those demands. Wexner took the company public in 1969.

In 1982, Wexner discovered a new type of store—designed somewhat like a Victorian brothel—selling sexy lingerie in a way it had never been sold before. The business, Victoria's Secret, had been started by a man named Roy Raymond, and when he faced bankruptcy, Wexner bought him out for what has been reported at over one million dollars. Victoria's Secret was incorporated into the Limited family of companies—an empire that would ultimately include Bath & Body Works, the White Barn Candle Company, and La Senza. Roy Raymond threw himself off San Francisco's Golden Gate Bridge in 1993, a decade after Wexner had turned his fledgling business notion into an international empire.[5]

The acquisition of Victoria's Secret helped to make Leslie Wexner the richest man in Ohio and one of the richest men in the United States. His yacht, the 315-foot *Limitless,* was the largest in the

United States at the time of construction.[6] He was courted by politicians and political causes for donations; he was a lifelong Republican. Wexner was benevolent, supporting charities in the United States and beyond. A supporter of a myriad of Israeli and Jewish causes, he established an entity called the Wexner Foundation that offered programs to young Jewish students.[7]

WEXNER WAS IN HIS FIFTIES—and a bachelor—when Robert Meister, an executive at the global insurance giant Aon, introduced him to Jeffrey Epstein.[8] Meister had met Epstein in the first-class cabin on a flight from Palm Beach to LaGuardia Airport in New York. The two men immediately hit it off. Their relationship blossomed, and eventually Meister felt inclined to introduce Epstein to a contact of his: Les Wexner.

For Epstein, Wexner was the Big Fish, a man with unending wealth whose cash reserve exceeded those of the small Third World nations to whom Leese and Khashoggi sold weapons. Wexner's empire was booming beyond anyone's wildest imagination. It was as if the money would never end. And he needed help managing it.

Epstein, of course, was everything that Wexner found charming. He was brash, that New York brand of quick-witted, street smart, and funny that was missing in Midwest Jews. Epstein, like Wexner's mom, Bella, was from Brooklyn—Brooklynites always considered themselves belonging to the borough more than to the city. Epstein had a sterling résumé—Dalton, Bear Stearns—and, like Wexner, he was an entrepreneur. "Wexner doesn't know much about money. He doesn't know a stock from a bond. He knows fashion, he knows how to dress people," explained Thomas Volscho, a sociology professor at the City University of New York, College of Staten Island, who has been researching the financial history of Jeffrey Epstein.[9]

Why did Les Wexner and his new friend hit it off so well? Sandy Lewis, a Bear Stearns banker who had once managed some of Wexner's money, told *Vanity Fair* that Wexner was "a shy man who got taken" by Epstein, a "con artist." Wexner "had been seduced," in Lewis's telling. Wexner was not "seduced [by Epstein] in a physical sense," Lewis explained to *Vanity Fair*. "I mean emotionally seduced out of his loneliness."[10]

Whatever connected Leslie Wexner and Jeffrey Epstein, the relationship seemed to be anchored in a foundation of money and trust. Epstein set up his 10,600-square-foot "guesthouse" on Wexner's 336-acre New Albany, Ohio, property; by 1991, he had talked his way into getting power of attorney over Wexner's money.

Leslie Wexner soon turned into one of Jeffrey Epstein's only clients. With Wexner, Epstein had immediate respectability, access to the men who stood in line to be near Wexner, and even access to the Victoria's Secret brand and the young women who competed for a spot in the catalog.

Wexner also allowed Epstein to use his private plane at will. Around the time he met Epstein in the late 1980s, Wexner purchased a mansion at 9 East Seventy-First Street on the Upper East Side off Central Park and Fifth Avenue for $13.2 million. Less than a decade later the property was transferred to a company controlled by Epstein for $20 million, according to *The Wall Street Journal*.[11]

# PART TWO

# HIGH SOCIETY

My clients are not in any way near the middle,
they're at the tippy tip of the top of the pyramid.
—JEFFREY EPSTEIN in an interview with
*Science* magazine, August 2017[1]

# 7

# DADDY'S LITTLE GIRL

ROBERT MAXWELL WAS LARGER THAN LIFE IN EVERY WAY. BORN JÁN Ludvík Hyman Binyamin Hoch in 1923, he grew up in a shtetl called Slatinské Doly in the Czechoslovakian mountains, today part of Ukraine. He was one of seven children and in later years would tell anyone willing to listen that he didn't own a pair of shoes until he was seven.[1] Neither poverty nor anti-Semitism would keep him down. As a teenager, he towered a defiant six feet tall, and he swaggered with a barrel chest and fists that were always ready to pounce.

Ján was fifteen when German forces marched into Prague on September 30, 1938; a year later, Hitler's Hungarian allies seized the area around Slatinské Doly from Czechoslovakia. Jan joined an underground organization that ferried young men and women to France. There he joined up with the 1st Czech Division, a corps of refugees from the Czech Army that merged with the French Army.[2] When France fell, Ján was one of the four thousand Czechs who made it to England. He transferred into the British Army and took part in the D-Day landings at Normandy and was later awarded a Military Cross for leading an assault against a German machine-gun post in Holland.

While Maxwell fought the Germans on the Western Front, his entire family was exterminated in the Nazi death camps. "At the end of the war I discovered the fate of my parents, and my sisters and brothers, and my relatives, and my neighbors," Maxwell would later say. "I don't know what went through their mind as they realized they've been tricked into a gas chamber, but one thing they hoped is that they wouldn't be forgotten."[3]

After the war, Ján Hoch remained in occupied Berlin as an administrative officer for the British Army. Now bearing the rank of captain, he completed his transformation from Old World Jew into English gentleman by changing his name once again. From this point on, he would be known as Ian Robert Maxwell.

THE NEWLY MINTED ROBERT MAXWELL was confident, boisterous, and blessed with the gift of gab. He served in the Foreign Office's press section in Berlin—a natural posting for him since he boasted fluency in seven languages, including Yiddish and German. Maxwell used his contacts in the divided German capital to launch his first company, a publisher of scientific journals and textbooks he acquired from its German and British owners, renaming it Pergamon Press.[4] Those communication skills caught the eye of MI6, Britain's overseas intelligence service. MI6 provided Maxwell with seed money for Pergamon in the hope that his access to scientists could help recruit the Soviet Union's top minds for the West.[5] Pergamon Press would eventually become a multimillion-dollar publicly traded company.

At the height of the Cold War, Maxwell embarked on several successful enterprises inside the Soviet Union and the Warsaw Pact nations. It was a time when Britain's intelligence services were penetrated by moles working on behalf of the Soviet espionage service, men like Kim Philby and the Cambridge Five, but Maxwell's relationship with the Soviets failed to raise anything more than a few eyebrows, which meant that the intelligence services knew what he

was doing and either approved or turned a blind eye to the relation-
ships he had behind the Iron Curtain because they benefited Britain.
He traveled frequently to Moscow and met with the top leaders
within the ruling Communist elite. "Maxwell was a special person,"
Leonid Shebarshin, former head of the First Chief Directorate of the
KGB, commented.

Rumors also circulated that while Maxwell was in Berlin he was
secretly working for the Irgun, the anti-British guerrilla group fighting for Israeli independence. Israel's pre-independence armies had
cultivated emissaries stationed around the world, including in the
United States.[6] Maxwell used his position in the British Army to supply funds, arms, and transit papers to Irgun agents aiming to smuggle
people and guns into Palestine. His nom de guerre was Ha'Tzshechi
Ha'Katan, or "the Little Czech." His handler was a man named
Yitzhak Shamir, a brilliant field operative who would go on to a long
career in Israel's intelligence service, the Mossad, and ultimately be
elected Israeli prime minister.[7] There were always suggestions that
Robert Maxwell also worked for Israeli intelligence. While he might
not have been a fully fledged agent, he certainly considered himself
an asset.

His fortune brought him to politics as a member of Parliament
for the Labour Party, but his creative accounting caught up with him.
In 1970, the British Department of Trade and Industry concluded
that "notwithstanding Mr. Maxwell's acknowledged abilities and
energy, he is not in our opinion a person who can be relied on to
exercise proper stewardship of a publicly quoted company."[8]

That wasn't, however, the end of Maxwell's career. His political
ambitions thwarted, Maxwell would seek to recapture fortune and
glory in other ways. He was a master of self-promotion, paying for
publicity and granting only interviews that were guaranteed to shower
him with praise. He taught his sons to be ruthless in business and to
carry on the family tradition. He wanted his daughters—especially
his youngest, Ghislaine—never to know the life of poverty that he
had experienced growing up.

• • •

ROBERT MAXWELL MET ELISABETH MEYNARD in Paris before he shipped off to England in 1940 to fight the Nazis. The two married after the war and had nine children together in a fifty-three-room mansion called Headington Hill Hall, near Oxford. The Maxwell children were all raised with nannies and private schools, and no luxury was denied to them.

Ghislaine Maxwell was born in France on December 25, 1961. Although Robert Maxwell trusted his business affairs to his sons Ian and Kevin, Ghislaine, the youngest sibling, was his favorite. Journalist Sharon Churcher first encountered her at Headington Hill Hall on June 10, 1968, when Ghislaine was six years old. Their home, she recalls, "served the dual purpose of being the headquarters of 'Captain Bob' Maxwell's Pergamon publishing empire and giving him the appearance of being a 'proper Englishman.'" The occasion for Churcher's invitation was a ball celebrating Maxwell's birthday after he bailed out Oxford's struggling student magazine, *Isis*. Churcher, among a group of aspiring journalists who were present, recalled that Ghislaine and her three older sisters were dressed like Victorian maidens in identical long gowns trimmed with lace and velvet. The outfits, Churcher learned, were ordered for the festivities from Gina Fratini, a designer whose celebrity clients included Elizabeth Taylor.[9]

Maxwell implied that he was teaching his children the egalitarian lessons that only a man of humble beginnings could understand. He and Elisabeth "teach them that having money isn't everything," he claimed in an interview for British television. "The privilege of money also imposes duties and limitations."[10]

In reality, there were few limitations. Maxwell was chauffeured around in a Rolls-Royce; more often than not, he was helicoptered to meetings in London and across the English Channel. No one ever argued with Maxwell, in part because he would never let anyone win; as a result, there was never any dissent. Maxwell's employees were sycophants, and their loyalty and silence were bought with large salaries.

Robert Maxwell was fixated on control. He and he alone steered the publicity, the branding, and the financing of his publishing business. He was even obsessed with controlling how the outside world saw him. Maxwell was horrified by gray hair and made a point of not being photographed—or seen, for that matter—without his jet-black hair slicked back like a movie star from the forties.[11] His signature look—bushy eyebrows and a carefully selected bow tie—was instantly recognizable.

Robert Maxwell saw himself as a Czech-born Joseph P. Kennedy: the patriarch of a dynasty that he hoped would wield financial and political power on a global scale. Maxwell, much like Kennedy, had grandiose expectations for his heirs. He pushed his children hard to be great and, more important, to be accomplished. A frequent houseguest remembers Maxwell interrogating the children at the dinner table and quizzing them on history or geopolitics. If they didn't know the answers, he would lose his temper.[12] Sometimes, Elisabeth Maxwell recalled in her autobiography, *A Mind of My Own: My Life with Robert Maxwell,* he would fly into rages and subject the children to "humiliation and harsh treatment" that included corporal punishment.

Growing up Maxwell meant being privy to a life of obscene luxury and dazzling mystery as well as learning lessons about the close relationship between money and power. The children witnessed political leaders, bankers, con men, spies, and accountants zipping in and out of their palatial home at all hours.

The James Bond persona that Maxwell fancied for himself was inescapable. He crisscrossed the world on his Gulfstream private jet. The children were occasionally allowed to accompany him, and Ghislaine racked up more miles than any of the other kids. He doted on her, even naming his 180-foot yacht the *Lady Ghislaine* in her honor. She referred to her father as the Captain, just like his servants and the many groveling investors who sought his favor.

Ghislaine was much like her father, even in appearance. "I have some physical resemblance: my eyebrows, his dark hair, his strong features," Ghislaine said in an interview with *Hello!* magazine. "I thought I have my mummy's nose. Character-wise, my father was ambitious, determined, hard-working, and goal-driven. I like to think I share some of those qualities."[13]

Her mother, Elisabeth, who was known as Betty, would write in her 1994 autobiography that she felt "devastated" when young Ghislaine once told her, "Mummy, I exist."[14] Even if she was her father's favorite, Ghislaine could not escape the ever-present tension and stress inside the Maxwell universe. Behind the façade of planes, cars, and homes were simmering financial issues. The stress of her father's verbal tirades and his relentless self-promotion left Ghislaine with scar tissue.[15] Ghislaine reportedly struggled with anorexia as early as age five.

HAVING DEVELOPED PERGAMON INTO A media empire, Maxwell exploited his publications, most notably the *Daily Mirror,* to corroborate the popular image of him as a man too large for this world. Fleet Street newspapers—like *The Sun,* owned by his archnemesis Rupert Murdoch—lampooned him ruthlessly, casting him as a simpering outsider masquerading as a British tycoon; he was a Jewish refugee, after all, and not a member of the British gentry. His boorish ways sometimes left British society aghast. In his memoirs, former British government minister Gyles Brandreth recalled the scandal of Maxwell's placing his arm around Her Majesty's shoulders at a gathering in Scotland.

Maxwell's obsession with control was particularly consuming when it came to Ghislaine. Dark-haired, glamorous, and polished, Ghislaine was the toast of the wealthy party circuit in which she moved, a circle that included the royal family, the Clintons, and the Kennedys.[16] She was "smart, witty, and charming," according to one interview—but when she went to Oxford, Maxwell forbade her to bring any boyfriends home, and she was given explicit orders never to be seen in public with any possible suitor.[17] Maxwell viewed any love interest as a threat—someone who was after the family fortune, someone who would be privy to their secrets. And so Ghislaine had to remain Daddy's little girl; there were to be no scandals involving her.[18]

LAURA GOLDMAN, A FRIEND OF Ghislaine's sister Isabel, described the youngest Maxwell's allure as a "superpower" that no man could resist. Ghislaine was known to bring up taboo topics of conversation, like talk of sexual prowess and techniques, at inopportune social occasions, and she was well versed in dirty jokes.[19]

Ghislaine's sexuality became a signature part of her persona. She had learned the importance of self-branding from her father, though her ways soon became a nightmare for him. She had her first brush with scandal at twenty-six, when compromising pictures of her and the Duke of Rutland's son were splashed all over the cover of a Fleet Street tabloid. Her father's own tabloid, the *Daily Mirror,* had leaked photos of an affair between a conservative member of Parliament and young males; this, then, was the retaliation.

Ghislaine pursued various ventures that sometimes embarrassed her father. One idea was a business selling branded condoms. She also helped establish a women's club named after the original Kit-Kat Club. "My ambition had always been to work on my own and do my own thing," she said in an interview.[20]

Her partying days were supposed to be over, though, when she met Count Gianfranco Cicogna around 1986. Cicogna came from one of the most legendary Italian noble families; his grandfather was an Italian minister of finance and the governor of North Africa under Mussolini.[21] He was handsome, confident, and an enthusiast of adventure sports—primarily aviation (the latter hobby would prove fatal; he was killed in a crash at an air show in South Africa in 2012). The Italian nobleman had everything Ghislaine lacked: a pedigree, a secure family fortune, and effortless good looks.

Gianfranco was like Robert Maxwell in one way: He had to be in charge at all times, especially as it related to Ghislaine. He, even more than Maxwell, "molded the Ghislaine we now see. He told her where to get her hair cut, and what to wear," journalist Michael Robotham stated.[22]

The relationship ended after four years.

THE VOID IN GHISLAINE'S LIFE after the breakup resulted in friction with her father. Robert Maxwell wanted his daughter out of the tabloids. But Ghislaine began to commute across the Atlantic, enjoying the social scenes in both London and New York, where her father had established a foothold in the American publishing industry. Maxwell's dream was to create a transnational media empire.[23] He invested in publishing houses and dailies in France, Hungary, and Israel. His ultimate target was the United States and the center of the mass media universe: New York City. And in the hope of keeping his daughter out of trouble—and keeping an eye on her—he used her fondness for New York City to his advantage. Ghislaine became her father's sidekick at the obligatory social events the newspaper magnate had to attend to further his business interests.

Maxwell had acquired Macmillan Publishing in 1988 as well as the New York *Daily News* three years later. In New York, Ghislaine would often appear at business functions to work the crowds. She even befriended John F. Kennedy, Jr. For once, her father would have celebrated any sign of flirtation; he had always dreamed that Ghislaine would marry the president's son.[24]

It was also in New York that Ghislaine met Donald Trump. Trump, a young real estate developer who promoted himself with as much fervor as Maxwell, appealed to the Captain to publish a Trump-branded magazine. Maxwell would often receive Trump on the *Lady Ghislaine*. The parties he hosted there were always conducted with style and a classically British elegance, a reporter remembered; Trump was the only guest misbehaving. At one of these gatherings in

1989, the source, who wishes to remain anonymous, said Trump "tried to grope me as I made small talk with the Captain."[25]

Robert Maxwell basked in his newfound glory in the New World. In 1991, the year he acquired the *Daily News,* he was made an honorary grand marshal of the Salute to Israel parade on Fifth Avenue.[26] As her father's emissary to Manhattan, Ghislaine was now a staple of the New York social scene. And New Yorkers seemingly couldn't get enough of the posh English people. New acquaintances loved that Ghislaine could connect them with London's A list.

But the fantasy of the Maxwell media empire was coming to an end almost as soon as it began. Maxwell bought and sold companies on the verge of bankruptcy, seizing assets at a fraction of their worth and then building them back up toward profitability. In his pursuit of cutting corners, he routinely found himself at war with trade unions as he eliminated jobs and reduced benefits. Most troubling of all, Maxwell's American expansion, as well as the day-to-day functioning of his enterprises in Great Britain, relied on pilfered cash. He mandated that close to $600 million from his companies' pension funds pay his debts and acquisitions. Maxwell had created an empire built upon fraud and theft, and it would soon crash.

IN THE FALL OF 1991, as Robert Maxwell's sons Kevin and Ian battled the Bank of England to delay defaulting on close to $75 million in loans, the Captain was off the coast of the Canary Islands on the *Lady Ghislaine*. He was last seen at roughly 4:25 on the morning of November 5. Investigators later theorized that the tycoon had gone on deck to urinate into the ocean and had fallen overboard. Robert Maxwell's body was found twelve hours later in the Atlantic Ocean by Spanish fishermen.[27]

An autopsy revealed no physical signs of foul play. Other than the ship's crew, there had been no one on board. The coroner ruled that the cause of death was a heart attack and accidental drowning. But many of Maxwell's creditors believed it to be suicide: a way out of the debt and disgrace he could no longer hide. "One thing I am sure about is that my father didn't commit suicide," Ghislaine would later say in an interview. "It is not easy to fall off the side of a boat."[28] According to one later report, she would insist that a dark conspiracy of Mossad renegades and Sicilian contract killers was responsible for her father's death.[29]

Maxwell's health had been in decline just as his financial woes deepened. Estranged from his wife, he had even confided in Kira Vladina, his Russian mistress, his hopes for his estate in the event of his death: "My family won't inherit anything when I die. The only ones who deserve anything are Ghislaine and Kevin. I adore both of them. Kevin is so much like me and Ghislaine is a friend."[30]

Ghislaine spoke fluent Spanish, just as her beloved father had, and she was flown to Tenerife to make his final arrangements. Armed with an envelope and £15,000 in cash, she was determined to buy the silence of the yacht's crew.

Robert Maxwell was buried in Israel with the pomp and circumstance usually reserved for a head of state. His funeral was in Jerusalem's Hall of the People and attended by Israeli politicians, including Prime Minister Yitzhak Shamir and President Chaim Herzog. Herzog, a former head of A'man, the Israeli military intelligence service, eulogized Maxwell as "a man cast in a heroic mold."[31]

The reverence for Maxwell raised many eyebrows. A few weeks before his death, Maxwell had sued Seymour Hersh. In his book *The Samson Option: Israel's Nuclear Arsenal and American Foreign Policy,* Hersh had accused Maxwell, as well as the foreign editor of one of Maxwell's tabloids, of brokering arms sales to Iran and betraying the whereabouts of Mordechai Vanunu, an Israeli technician who had revealed secrets of Israel's nuclear program.[32] The Maxwell family maintained that their patriarch had been a good friend to Israel by investing heavily in publishing, pharmaceutical, and computer firms in the country.[33]

• • •

GHISLAINE MAXWELL WAS DEVASTATED BY her father's death. Even once her brothers Kevin and Ian had cleaned up the financial mess their father had left behind, the Maxwell brand was tarnished irreparably. Ghislaine abandoned London to settle in Manhattan.

The trust fund established by her father meant Ghislaine would be entitled to a $100,000 annual allowance. While more than enough to live a nice life at the time in Manhattan, it was a pauper's allowance for a woman accustomed to a fifty-three-room mansion, private jets, and an army of servants. Christina Oxenberg, sister of actress Catherine Oxenberg and a distant cousin to the British royal family, recalls being invited to Ghislaine's new apartment on East Seventy-Ninth Street. Ghislaine had warned her friend that she was "poor," but Oxenberg encountered a light-filled, spacious home. Ghislaine hosted the get-together in a white lace bra, panties, and a lot of expensive jewelry. Present, too, was Ghislaine's Yorkshire terrier, named Max after her father, that she tossed around in an aggressive way.[34]

To observers, these were signs of a troubled and rudderless woman. It was the first time in Ghislaine's life that she was without a controlling and domineering male figure in her life. Robert Maxwell had been known to warn his children: "Confidence is like virginity. You can only lose it once."[35]

# 8

---

# POWER COUPLE

NEW YORK CITY WAS A MAGICAL PLACE TO BE YOUNG AND BEAUTIFUL in the late 1980s and early 1990s. Being wealthy didn't hurt.

On October 19, 1987, the stock market had taken a catastrophic nosedive that eviscerated the global financial system. On Black Monday, the Dow Jones Industrial Average plummeted 508 points, a record fall. Pundits spoke of another depression; tens of thousands of people lost their jobs, their fortunes, or both.

But New York City had already survived urban blight, white flight, blizzards, and bankruptcy. The discos, the nightclubs, and the Michelin-starred eateries would bounce back. The AIDS epidemic had curbed some behavior, but condom usage made others feel invincible. For the nightlife set, cocaine was the drug of choice at dance parties that lasted into the next day.

Keeping up with the scene was a full-time profession—one that Ghislaine Maxwell was made for. Partying was a welcome distraction from her father's death, not to mention the pool of debt he had left behind. If her family's fall was a scarlet letter in London, to the party set of the Upper East Side it meant little—or might even have been a badge of honor.

Maxwell became a staple on the circuit. Her East Seventy-Ninth Street apartment was strategically situated at the epicenter of Gotham's good-time zone, so she could often walk to and from each soiree; mostly, though, people sent town cars. Celebrities, princes, politicians, icons of industry, and old-world money all called the streets of Manhattan's Upper East Side home. They lived in door-man buildings and fortified brownstones, where parties featured free food, booze, and sometimes more illicit substances.

Former Philadelphia stockbroker Laura Goldman, who knew Ghislaine through Ghislaine's sister Isabel, recalled that she was a fixture on the social calendar. "She would be at every event, network-ing. That was her job. No one knew what she did for a living; she kept the details of her trust fund secret. Going to parties and meet-ing people was her thing. She was everywhere."[1] And everywhere she went, she turned heads.

Maxwell was, of course, putting up a brave front. Friends recalled that she continued to struggle with the emotional fallout of her father's death and the breakup with Gianfranco Cicogna. Stuart Pivar, a scientist and friend of Jeffrey Epstein's who founded the New York Academy of Art with Andy Warhol in 1982, described her as the most depressed person he had ever seen. "She was constantly crying," he remembered.[2]

But Pivar remembered something else—an observation that would resonate as Epstein and Maxwell grew closer. "She arrived a dysfunctional wreck from what happened to her on account of her father. And the last thing that should've happened to someone like that is to fall into the care of the likes of Jeffrey. He molded her with his aberrations."[3]

Another friend of Maxwell's during her first days on the New York City social scene remembers a woman shaken with insecurities. "For the daughter of such a powerful man, she seemed insecure," the friend, who requested anonymity, recalled. "It was if she wasn't sure of how to fit in. She always seemed a bit sad to me." At parties, Max-well "never seemed comfortable in her skin," the woman recalled.

"She was trying to find her way in life. That leads me to think the dynamic was she'd lost the strong father and was the kind of woman who might fall under the spell of another strong man."[4]

Laura Goldman remembered Maxwell a bit differently—as a confident creature of the party scene. Everyone enjoyed Ghislaine's company, Goldman recalled—especially members of the opposite sex. "She would say the things most people would never say. Men loved her."[5]

IT ISN'T KNOWN WHEN EXACTLY Ghislaine Maxwell met Jeffrey Epstein. It is believed that Epstein met Robert Maxwell at an event for the latter's New York tabloid, the *Daily News*, and at some point later was introduced to Ghislaine.

Epstein and Maxwell had a lot in common. Both had recently lost their father: Seymour Epstein, Jeffrey's father, had passed away after a long illness in December 1991. Jeffrey Epstein spent much of his adult life profiting from the lies he told about himself; Ghislaine Maxwell profited from the lies her father had told to amass an unbelievable fortune. But they were opposites in many ways, too.

Epstein was shy and reserved. As men go, especially the men Ghislaine had grown up with, he was insecure and insignificant. He didn't have the polish of a man raised in the public schools of the English gentry. With his boorish mannerisms, disregard for formal dress, and lack of social graces, Epstein looked more like one of the servants who collected a paycheck from the Maxwells than a man worth a fortune. No one inside Ghislaine's inner circle, no one she had met vacationing in the Riviera, looked like Epstein—or sounded like him, with his thick Brooklyn accent.

If Maxwell found anything irresistible about Epstein, the consensus among Ghislaine's friends was that Jeffrey Epstein was something of an idiot. A friend remembered, "I would ask him about the markets, and he didn't seem to know anything. He didn't have answers for simple questions like 'What are your favorite stocks?

What's the outlook?' He didn't want to discuss it. Most people who are involved in the markets are obsessed with them. He didn't have an opinion. And it was strange that he didn't. He would be talking to you and looking at some girl's ass."[6]

Epstein's constructed narrative of embellishment and fantasy fanned the attraction between the two. He introduced himself to Ghislaine as an international man of mystery: He had worked for the international arms trade, knew men like her father. He told people that he was a corporate intelligence agent who spied on corporations to find where they hid their money.[7]

WHEN HE MET GHISLAINE MAXWELL, Epstein was already living at 9 East Seventy-First Street, a stone fortress with a medieval-looking wooden door that was half a block from Fifth Avenue and Museum Row and across the street from the Frick Collection, one of the city's most exclusive collections of classical art. The house initially wasn't his, or solely his—an entity notionally controlled by Les Wexner had purchased the building in 1989 for $13.2 million, considered a bargain at the time.[8]

Around 1996, in a move unexplained to this day, Wexner transferred title of the mansion to Epstein for $0. In 2011, a trust controlled by Wexner and Epstein formally transferred the property to an entity based in the Virgin Islands; while transaction records indicate no money was exchanged when the property was transferred to Maple Inc., the Epstein trust in the Virgin Islands, *The New York Times* reported that Epstein paid $20 million.[9] Epstein turned the mansion into his castle. The address was too exclusive even for gangsters. It was where old New York money—the kind earned through marriage and inheritance—lived. The area was so ritzy that policemen from the nearby Nineteenth Precinct used to joke that even the rats and roaches had trust funds.[10]

A Sea Gate rube dropped into high society, Epstein had money but no class or charisma. Ghislaine, on the other hand, knew everyone. "Her Rolodex would blow away almost anyone else's I can think of," wrote journalist Vicky Ward in *Vanity Fair*.[11] An entrepreneur in the same social circles said that Ghislaine Maxwell was on first-name terms with media moguls and bankers: "She was the best-connected person in the city. And she was an easy friend to have. At cocktail parties, she would invariably be speaking with the most interesting people in the room. [So] you wanted to be where she was. We all did."[12]

Once they clicked, Epstein and Maxwell became a kind of perfect, symbiotic creature. The control that her father had exerted over Ghislaine and her behavior and appearance was now directed at Epstein.[13] Ghislaine made sure that Jeffrey dressed right, looked right, and spoke right. She was both nanny and headmistress. "She'd tell Jeffrey what to do in front of people," according to a friend requesting anonymity. "She would say, 'No! You don't do it that way!' But then Ghislaine eventually relented to his casual style. He was like a hoodie guy before tech." The friend claimed that it was Maxwell who told Epstein to get rid of his long fur coat. "She said it made him look like a pimp."[14]

THOUGH THEY WERE IMMEDIATELY INSEPARABLE, to observers Epstein and Maxwell lacked the sexual chemistry that was expected of a high-profile romance. Despite the jokes and sexual bravado in conversational settings, the relationship between Jeffrey and Ghislaine seemed platonic. "He'd put his arm around Ghislaine's neck. It was collegial, affectionate, not a sexual act," the friend remembered. Another insider, who requested anonymity, was never convinced that they dated. "It was more of a partnership," the source said. "They didn't touch like a couple. He'd have his arm around her shoulders, not her waist."[15]

What Maxwell's true desires were in regard to Epstein remain the subject of intense debate. Did she want to marry Epstein, as some believed, or was it all an act?[16] "Ghislaine was starving herself,

I asked her about it," Christina Oxenberg recalled. "She said it's because Jeffrey likes his women thin. And I could see the delusion, because she was his employee, albeit being paid very well. The more she tried to push it that she was having an affair with Jeffrey, I could see with my own eyes that that just wasn't the case."

To Oxenberg, "There was no romance." Maxwell was Epstein's "beard" and the pair were "two grifters trying to outgrift each other."[17]

Other friends believed that Maxwell's talk of settling down with Epstein was a smokescreen to hide the fact that she, as they believed, was bisexual. "I never thought she liked guys. I don't think she ever dated a guy," said one former friend of the couple who requested anonymity. "I thought she was all about control."[18]

# 9

## NO ANGEL

IN 1982, WHEN LES WEXNER'S L BRANDS ACQUIRED THE COMPANY, Victoria's Secret was a fledgling, unfocused retailer, notching just $4 million in annual sales and near bankruptcy. Wexner, inspired by European lingerie trends, had a vision to bring this aesthetic to America. Soon Victoria's Secret was known for affordable versions of elegant and sexy women's lingerie.

Within a decade, the brand had grown into the largest lingerie retailer in the United States, with 350 stores and sales of more than $1 billion annually. The marketing genius behind the brand, however, was just getting started. In 1995, Victoria's Secret inaugurated its now annual fashion show, and in 1999, the show went online for the first time, featuring supermodel Tyra Banks. The "Internet-breaking moment" resulted in the company's website crashing after 1.5 million viewers tuned in hoping to see the latest designs—and the models, who were now known widely as the brand's "angels." Five years later, according to *Business Insider*, Gisele Bündchen walked the runway in the most expensive piece of lingerie ever created, a $15 million diamond-and-ruby-encrusted "Fantasy Bra."[1]

A fringe benefit of Jeffrey Epstein's relationship with Wexner was that Epstein could now claim to be associated with Victoria's Secret, the retail impresario's cash cow, a boast that aspiring models could find irresistible. Wexner had already trusted Epstein with the keys to his vast kingdom, consisting not just of Victoria's Secret but also the retail brands Pink, Bath & Body Works, Henri Bendel, the White Barn Candle Company, and others.[2] Among other wide-ranging duties Epstein performed for Wexner personally and for his company and foundation, Epstein had Wexner's power of attorney. He cut checks, purchased real estate, and had the ability to influence hiring decisions—including, reportedly, the young women who appeared in the catalog, the calendars, and the fashion shows in New York, Los Angeles, Las Vegas, London, and Paris. Epstein's connection to these formidable brands gave a veneer of legitimacy to every sales pitch he made to a young girl.

In these years, Epstein turned the 9 East Seventy-First Street mansion into an address known throughout the city where aspiring models and actresses could find a break. One day in 1993, Amy McClure, known then as Amy Sparks, rang the doorbell of Epstein's mansion. Originally from Oklahoma, Sparks, after modeling in California for a few years, had traveled to New York, hoping to break into the business there. She stayed at the Plaza Hotel—then owned by Donald Trump and managed by his first wife, the Czech-born model Ivana.[3] Sparks made the rounds among various modeling agencies, lugging her portfolio across town. She was invited to a party, and then another party. In an account given to the UK newspaper *The Sun,* Sparks recalled meeting a Frenchman at one of these New York fashion parties who "took a liking" to her. "[He] told me that they knew somebody called Jeffrey Epstein who was in this world and he would love me, that I'm the type of person he would like. I remember thinking he would be someone who could help me or manage me. . . . I remember being so happy."

Sparks recalled Epstein's home as a stately building.[4] After ringing the bell, she was greeted by a young woman, who ushered her inside and then walked her through what looked to Sparks like a palace. Sparks was led to a room where Epstein was on a table receiving a full body massage from what appeared to be a professional masseuse. When Sparks entered, Epstein looked Sparks over and dismissed the woman giving him the body rub. He ordered Sparks to disrobe. Epstein told her, "I just want to see what you look like. It's no big deal." But she said he quickly became annoyed after he asked, "How old are you?" She said, "I [told him I] was twenty-one, that's when he got irritated, almost angry."

Sparks looked younger than her twenty-one years. It was part of her allure, an angle she played up in her shoots. But Epstein erupted in anger when he learned of her age—then threw her to the ground and forced himself on her.

Sparks left Epstein's mansion inwardly destroyed, but she did not report the rape. "I didn't say anything to anyone at the time because I felt like it would come across like it was my fault," she said. "I felt nobody would believe me. I blamed myself for a lot of it. And I didn't know what anyone could do, anyway, these people were from a different world—they were rich, untouchable. Although I didn't know quite how untouchable back then."[5]

Epstein's parting words left no doubt about his intentions. "If you tell anybody anything," he told Sparks, "I'll crush whatever career you might have."[6]

JEFFREY EPSTEIN WAS SO SUCCESSFUL in his predation because he knew how to conceal his crimes behind his wealth. A man of lesser means could never have gotten away with it, but among the many luxuries enjoyed by Epstein was the luxury of washing his sins away, at least in the public eye, with acts of well-publicized generosity.

Like any financial powerhouse keen to assert benevolence, Epstein donated to charities and painted himself as a philanthropist. Though Wexner was reportedly the source of much of Epstein's wealth, Epstein is on the record as giving more than $40 million to one of Wexner's first nonprofit foundations.* He was especially fond of promoting the arts. He had a charity, Gratitude America Ltd., that funded an elite all-girls school in Manhattan, Harvard University's theater group the Hasty Pudding Institute, the Film Society of Lincoln Center, and the Metropolitan Opera. He ran this philanthropic operation out of his office on Madison Avenue, in the heart of midtown.[7]

One of the charities closest to his heart was his own alma mater, the Interlochen Center for the Arts, a refuge for the world's great musical students, isolated in the pine forests of northern Michigan. In spring 1994, Interlochen erected the Jeffrey Epstein Scholarship Lodge in his honor.[8] The benevolence was insidious in nature. The camp was full of young girls, and the gift afforded useful cover for his predatory ways.

IF THERE WAS ANY QUESTION about the extent of Maxwell's knowledge of Epstein's dark arts, it would be answered in the account provided by a thirteen-year-old girl identified in court documents as Jane Doe. She was a student in the camp's voice program in 1994, a year after Epstein had assaulted Sparks. Doe was sitting alone on a bench when she was approached by Epstein and Maxwell. They regaled her with stories of the support they provided to the arts and to the fledgling talents at Interlochen, like her. And they asked for details about her parents, her upbringing, and her residence—even obtaining her address in Florida. Doe was bemused but polite; she figured that as a teenager, she couldn't dismiss the two adults.

Several weeks later, after camp had ended and Jane Doe had returned to Florida, Epstein phoned her at home. He invited her and her mother to his Palm Beach estate and even sent a driver across

---

* Epstein also gave millions over the years to universities, including a $6.5 million gift to Harvard in 2003—part of $30 million in total gifts to Harvard; he donated to more than a hundred organizations after the Florida plea deal in 2008. But some of the alleged recipients of his donations later disputed the size of the gifts or whether they received any donations at all.

town to pick them up. At the house, Epstein suggested that he could become a mentor to the young girl, promising to nurture her musical aspirations and even to pay her way with scholarships. By playing the role of Epstein's love interest, Ghislaine legitimized the deal. The sales pitch seemed innocent, and it hit Jane Doe's mother where she was most vulnerable: her husband had died a short time earlier, and money was in short supply.

Over the following months, Epstein and Maxwell took Doe to movies and the mall. It was a teenager's dream to hang out at a mansion and be lavished with clothing and gifts—even though sex had begun to creep into conversation, according to legal documents. Maxwell told Doe that having sex with ex-boyfriends was easy: Once you slept with them, "they've been grandfathered in and you could go back and fuck them whenever you wanted."[9] When they went shopping, Epstein and Maxwell insisted that Doe pick out children's cotton underwear. To deflect objections from her mother, Epstein would send the girl home with two or three hundred-dollar bills to help things out at home, and he started to pay for Doe's singing lessons, too. Whenever Doe expressed hesitation, Epstein and Maxwell scolded her for being ungrateful.[10]

Several months after their initial meeting, Epstein invited Doe to the pool house of his Palm Beach mansion. He grabbed her forcibly and pulled her onto his lap. He then began to masturbate. He told her this is what "professionals" did. According to court papers, Epstein called himself "Godfather."

Seemingly emboldened by his wealth and enabled by his permissive relationship with Ghislaine, Epstein was establishing a system for his pursuit of young and underage women whose scope seemed to have little precedent. Ghislaine provided Epstein with a most plausible cover—they appeared to the world as a young and carefree couple who couldn't possibly pose a threat to a young girl, when in reality they were a predatory Bonnie and Clyde.

The incident in the pool house inaugurated a hellish period when Doe was repeatedly raped, abused, and pimped out to associates by Epstein.

# 10

## THE PALM BEACH NEIGHBOR

It was impossible to be a plugged-in New Yorker in the 1980s or 1990s and not know who Donald Trump was. The self-promoting developer was everywhere: on television, on radio, on the covers of the city's tabloids, and shuttling between his home and Lower Manhattan's courthouse, where he was the plaintiff and defendant in endless lawsuits. Men driven in stretch limousines spoke of Donald Trump, as did the homeless. City Hall knew who he was; so, too, did the mob. He was larger than life, covered in a gold-plated shine and draped in gaudy red velvet. It didn't matter that he had built a reputation as a cheat, stiffing contractors and referring disputes to Roy Cohn, his bulldog attorney. He was a bestselling author, too, though *The Art of the Deal* seemed a funny title given that Trump had lost money on virtually every deal he made.

To the tabloids, he was known simply as "The Donald," a swipe at his wife's tendency to refer to him in the third person. He lived in Trump Tower, a fifty-eight-story skyscraper of black glass and gold on Fifth Avenue, between Fifty-Sixth and Fifty-Seventh streets. Its bold architecture was designed to overshadow Manhattan icons like Tiffany, on the same block, and Harry Winston, across the street. Trump was a regular on the campy television show *Lifestyles of the Rich and Famous*; the glimpses viewers had of his penthouse apartment evoked the homes of third-world dictators. Everything was gold and marble. The lavish interior looked like a parody of how rich people lived.

The truth was that Trump wasn't a member of Manhattan royalty. He was no Carnegie, Mellon, or Frick. He was a transplant from Queens, the son of a slumlord who would spend his entire life overcompensating for his origin in Jamaica Estates and not on Park Avenue.[1] Donald Trump, like Jeffrey Epstein, was an outer-borough kid.

Trump and Epstein had quite a lot more in common. Both of them had climbed a ladder of lies and luck into high society. Both were fond of women; both had enough money to be above the law, an imperviousness especially enjoyed by Epstein. Their second homes in Palm Beach were a stone's throw from each other. They became fast friends upon first meeting in 1987. They traveled in the same social circle and sometimes flew together from New York to Palm Beach.

Epstein was a regular at Trump's Mar-a-Lago estate, the second-largest mansion in Florida. Trump purchased Mar-a-Lago in 1985 for $8 million ($5 million for the house and $3 million for the furniture) and put Ivana, his then wife, in charge of running the property. (It remained a private residence of Trump's until 1995, when he turned it into a members' club.)

Trump and Epstein's friendship grew with each charity event and gala they attended; it developed behind closed doors, too, at private social gatherings where men of means spoke about money, power, and women—an elite fraternity that operated on the transactional logic that if all its members committed crimes together and were all equally vulnerable, the others inside the inner sanctum would retreat to their protective webs rather than preying on one another.

Epstein knew unsavory details about Trump that could kill a business deal, an acquisition, a gaming license, even a political future. Trump, in turn, was intimately acquainted with Epstein's true nature. "I've known Jeff for fifteen years. Terrific guy. He's a lot of fun to be with. It is even said that he likes beautiful women as much as I do, and many of them are on the younger side. No doubt about it—Jeffrey enjoys his social life," Trump would famously gush to *New York* magazine years later.[2] Attorney Bradley Edwards, who would later sue Epstein on behalf of numerous victims, claimed Trump later told him that the "terrific guy" line was invented by Epstein. According to Edwards's account, Epstein called Trump to ask if he could attribute the "nice words" to him.

Virginia Roberts, who would become one of Epstein's most vocal accusers, told journalist Sharon Churcher that she recalled Donald Trump visiting Epstein's Palm Beach mansion one day during this period when several girls were lounging by the pool.

In 2000, journalist Michael Corcoran trailed Trump around Florida for several days to write a profile on the businessman for the now defunct *Maximum Golf* magazine. According to the article, at one point in Corcoran's reporting, the journalist waited with Trump at a New York airfield for Jeffrey Epstein and Ghislaine Maxwell, who were to accompany Trump and Corcoran on Trump's private 727 to Florida. Epstein and Maxwell are described in the article as a couple who had an evidently chummy relationship with Trump, who "gently chides" the pair for breaking "the cardinal rule"—that is, "never be late for someone else's plane."

In an interview years later with *The Daily Beast*, Corcoran recalled that there was also "a young woman boarding with them"—a detail that did not make it into *Maximum Golf*. "I honestly couldn't guess her age, but she was young made up to look a bit older," Corcoran told the site, adding that he witnessed nothing "untoward."

THE FRIENDSHIP BETWEEN DONALD TRUMP and Jeffrey Epstein lasted almost fifteen years, from the early 1990s into the early 2000s.

It was early in their acquaintance, in November 1992, when Donald Trump hosted a party at Mar-a-Lago, attended by Jeffrey

Epstein. Trump was in the process that year of finalizing his divorce from Ivana but was in an on-again, off-again relationship with Marla Maples, whom he eventually married the next year. The 1992 event at Mar-a-Lago was featured on *A Closer Look,* an NBC talk show hosted by Faith Daniels. Trump agreed to appear on the show only after he kissed Daniels, without her permission, when her husband's back was turned at a charity event.

In the footage, Trump, then forty-six, struts on a dance floor and schmoozes with cheerleaders from the Buffalo Bills and Miami Dolphins. Epstein looks on at the parade of flesh, barely able to contain an approving smile. Of all the guests, Trump seems most at ease standing next to his friend and whispering into his ear. "She's hot," Trump comments, in a moment captured by cameras.[3]

That film crew also caught him groping one woman. Daniels called him on it and asked Trump how he would justify that to his then teenage son, Donald Trump, Jr. Trump responded that his son was "fourteen, and, uh, he could really understand that one. No, that one's all right."[4]

There was another party that year. After his divorce from Ivana and before his marriage to Maples, Trump hosted another event at Mar-a-Lago. Staff at the Palm Beach estate were told that VIPs would be in attendance, but the only arrivals were Epstein and twenty-eight girls. The women had been flown in for Trump by George Houraney, a Florida-based businessman who hosted live events at Trump's casinos for a "Calendar Girls" competition; the organizer called the women "contestants."

Well aware of Epstein's reputation, Houraney expressed reservations about leaving so many women with him. "I said, 'Look, Donald, I know Jeff really well, I can't have him going after younger girls,'" Houraney told reporters for *The New York Times* years later. He felt he had no choice but "to ban Jeff from my events. Trump didn't care about that."[5] Trump responded, "Look, I'm putting my name on this. I wouldn't put my name on it and have a scandal." The party went on as planned with the only males in attendance being Trump and Epstein.

JEFFREY EPSTEIN WAS EAGER TO show off Jane Doe, whom he'd recruited from the Interlochen music camp. Sometime in 1995, Jeffrey took the now fourteen-year-old across the bay to Mar-a-Lago and beamed as he presented her to Trump. Epstein told Trump, "This is a good one, right?" as he elbowed Trump "playfully" during the introduction. The minor continued to be abused by Epstein; she was raped at Epstein's home in New York in 1997 and the assaults continued until she moved to California in 1999. In court papers, she stated that the abuse and exploitation caused her "immeasurable pain and suffering every day."

Trump has faced his own accusations of sexual impropriety with underage girls. According to a 2016 lawsuit, which was later dropped, a woman going by the name Katie Johnson alleged that the future president had raped her at one of numerous parties in Jeffrey Epstein's Manhattan home in 1994 when she was only thirteen.

Like many of Jeffrey Epstein's victims—and, indeed, those who have accused Donald Trump of wrongdoing—Johnson's real name has never been revealed, and neither Trump nor Epstein has been allowed to confront her in court. Through an intermediary, she declined to be interviewed for this book.[6] The pseudonymous Johnson has never offered any corroborating evidence for her claims; she dropped her lawsuits, and the source of her claims has come under media scrutiny.[7]

Although the claims in the abandoned Katie Johnson lawsuit have never been proved, other accounts corroborate the existence of parties Epstein threw that featured women and girls who appeared to be underage. Heather Braden, a model represented by the Elite agency in the late 1990s, described the girls at Epstein's parties as teenagers, some as young as thirteen. As she acknowledged, though, he was far from an anomaly in this social scene of wealthy business-men. "All these men were out trying to lure [models], get with them. It was a predatory world in a predatory market where young girls were preyed upon by these rich men," Braden said. "Trump, these types of men, are predators, exploiters. They are essentially traffick-ers. They're essentially passing girls among themselves. We were used as bargaining chips."[8]

AFTER ENTERING POLITICS, TRUMP WOULD say that he hardly knew Jeffrey Epstein. The claim is hard to take seriously: They were fre-quently photographed at social events in the 1990s and Epstein's phone directory was found to contain fourteen phone numbers for Trump, including emergency numbers, car phone numbers, and numbers for Trump's security guard and houseman.[9]

Lawyer Bradley Edwards said Trump recalled years later "he had seen young women who, Epstein explained, were part of a mentoring-type program that he was involved in. Trump admitted this was odd and then quickly said to me: 'The guy was always strange. Even back when I ran into him more, I never really liked him.'"[10]

In a 2010 deposition, Jeffrey Epstein was asked if he had ever socialized with Donald Trump in the presence of women under the age of eighteen. Without hesitating for a second, Epstein answered, "Though I'd like to answer that question, at least today I'm going to have to assert my Fifth, Sixth, and Fourteenth Amendment rights, sir."[11]

# 11

## ALARM BELLS

THE 1990S WERE A HIGH-FLYING PERIOD FOR JEFFREY EPSTEIN. HE was building his wealth and furthering his connections among powerful individuals in business, media, politics, and science. He was also working to perfect the strategy and tactics of recruiting and grooming women—what would become the "sexual Ponzi scheme" that would take him down more than twenty years later. In a handful of these early incidents with young women, however, Epstein nearly came face-to-face with the prying eyes of law enforcement after courageous victims raised the alarm. Had the outcome of this legal scrutiny proved different, the course of Epstein's life and crimes might have taken a radically different path.

WHEN SHE MET JEFFREY EPSTEIN and Ghislaine Maxwell in the spring of 1995, Maria Farmer was a twenty-five-year-old artist living in New York City, according to a court affidavit. Born in Kentucky, Farmer was a figurative painter who showed real promise, and she was eager for that one lucky handshake that would propel her to big-city success. Blond, with a petite figure and a natural Midwestern beauty, she could have been mistaken for one of Gotham's countless aspiring models or actresses.

Farmer met Epstein and Maxwell at a New York Academy of Art graduation gallery show, where she was showcasing some of her paintings. It was the kind of event where wealthy patrons could hob-nob with the city's artistic up-and-comers while sipping free cham-pagne. Epstein normally did not go to events like this, but because of his friendship with Eileen Guggenheim, then dean and now board chair of the New York Arts Academy, he made an exception.

Farmer worked the room; she knew that artists had to sell them-selves as well as their oeuvre. One of her featured works was inspired by *Interior,* also known as *The Rape,* a well-known Degas painting in the collection of the Philadelphia Museum of Art. Epstein and Max-well hovered around Farmer's piece, seemingly interested. Ever the haggler, Epstein offered to buy it, though there was a catch: If Farmer agreed to sell him the work at half the $12,000 asking price, he would advance her career.

Farmer, who knew that Epstein was a benefactor to the school, accepted the offer. As they signed the paperwork, Epstein asked Farmer if "she had a father."[1] Farmer answered, "Of course I do, but my parents are divorced." Even as she celebrated the sale, Farmer remembers being taken aback by Epstein's questions. Her parents were divorced; her father had left when she was sixteen, and her mother was struggling.

Epstein hired Farmer on the spot—first as an art collector, and then as a receptionist for his East Seventy-First Street townhouse.

To the wide-eyed Farmer, Epstein's mansion might as well have been a castle. The limestone exterior, beautifully maintained, looked as fresh as when the building was completed in 1930. It was guarded by pear trees and fifteen-foot oak doors. Pedestrians who walked by couldn't help but give the location a double look, wondering what mysteries were hidden inside. The block itself was notable for its celebrity resident. Bill Cosby had lived across the street since 1987, a decade before Epstein moved in.

Before Epstein took over the house in 1996, Les Wexner, who considered himself something of an art expert, had filled the townhouse with priceless works, including Picasso originals. When Epstein moved in, though, he added pieces more to his own taste: hundreds of suggestive images of nude and seminude women, and other curious pieces, including paintings of nude African warriors.[2]

Working at the front desk at the Epstein house meant signing the usual stampede of visitors into the logbook. Farmer noted that foot traffic included a steady stream of young girls; most were under the age of eighteen and many wore school uniforms. Once logged in, they would be escorted upstairs, where Maxwell took over. Maxwell, Farmer was told, was a recruiter for Victoria's Secret; the girls were aspiring runway models, auditioning for the catalog. Men visited, too, including Harvard Law School professor and constitutional expert Alan Dershowitz and Donald Trump. (Referring to Farmer, Epstein told Trump that "this one isn't for you.") Farmer remembered whispers that the Secret Service would inspect the location in anticipation of a presidential visit by Bill Clinton.

All the activity in the house seemed odd to Farmer but not illegal. She knew that Ghislaine went on frequent excursions "to go get girls for Jeffrey," young women she referred to as "nubiles," according to an interview Farmer gave about her experiences to *The New York Times*.[3] In the interview, Farmer described Maxwell's scouting operations as "cowboy" in nature. "They had a driver, and he would be driving along, and Ghislaine would say, 'Get that girl.' And they'd stop, and she'd run out and get the girl and talk to her."[4]

AT SOME POINT IN HER time at Epstein's mansion, according to published accounts, Maria Farmer divulged to her employer that she had a sixteen-year-old sister named Annie who lived in Arizona and was hoping to go to college. As a show of benevolence, Epstein flew Annie to New York and offered to mentor her.

Annie remembers Epstein as kind and unpretentious. He wore

sweatpants and drank champagne as he gave her advice about college, rubbing her hands and then her lower leg.[5] He never let her sister see these advances, as Annie recorded in her diary: "It was one of those things that just gave me a weird feeling but wasn't that weird and probably normal."

In the summer of 1996, Jeffrey Epstein offered to take Annie on an all-expenses-paid trip to Thailand. He asked her sister and their mother for permission. He explained that he was mentoring a group of students and the trip to Thailand was part of their experience. Both women gave their approval, convinced of its legitimacy.

Annie's flight to Thailand included a stopover at Zorro Ranch, Epstein's 26,700-square-foot New Mexico mansion. Epstein had bought the property in 1993 from the former state treasurer David King. It sat high on a mesa, overlooking ten thousand acres of desert between Santa Fe and Albuquerque.[6] The main house was similar to a Mexican hacienda, boasting a courtyard with high-ceilinged hallways, stone columns, and a central fountain. The living room measured about 2,100 square feet, larger than the average house in Santa Fe County. The home had an elevator, eight bathrooms, four fireplaces, and three bedrooms. Zorro was not a typical ranch, however. It had an aircraft hangar and a landing strip. Butlers worked in the mansion. Guesthouses dotted the lavish grounds.[7]

Annie had expected to meet her fellow travelers at the ranch, but other than the staff, the only people there were Epstein and Maxwell.

She wasn't the first teenager lured to the location. A few years earlier, Santa Fe real estate agent Pat French was hired by Epstein to find a property in the area suitable for a major ranch development. Before leaving town, she stopped at the tony Rancho Encantado resort, where Epstein was staying. "I went to the door where he was staying, it was filled with teenage girls," French recalled. "I just assumed they were his daughters. I didn't think much about it at the time."[8]

During Annie Farmer's visit, the weekend's agenda at Zorro was rigidly planned and completely inappropriate for the sixteen-year-old.

The three went to a movie, during which Epstein petted Farmer. But it was Ghislaine who allegedly became aggressive, persuading the reluctant Annie to give Epstein a foot massage and giving her pointers on how to touch him. And she relentlessly pressured the sixteen-year-old into receiving a full body massage. When Annie relented, Maxwell placed her facedown on a massage table and commanded her to remove her bra and panties. At first Annie was shielded by a sheet as Maxwell massaged and fondled her. But then Maxwell ordered the girl to turn over and began fondling her breasts. According to her account in *The New York Times,* Annie Farmer was convinced that Epstein was nearby, watching it all.

When the weekend concluded, Annie Farmer was confused and alone. "I don't think there was any reason for [Ghislaine] to be touching me that way," she wrote in her journal.[9]

Annie Farmer had been flown to New Mexico to be molested. She made Epstein honor his promise to pay for her to travel to Thailand. She flew on to Thailand, taking her secret with her across the Pacific—a secret she would keep for well over a decade.

IN THE SUMMER OF 1996, Maria Farmer found herself in New Albany, Ohio, a guest of Jeffrey Epstein on the sprawling country estate of Les Wexner. Still employed by Epstein after a year, she was at the time an artist in residence and had been commissioned to create two works for the film set of *As Good as It Gets.* Besides her artwork, she was also tasked with picking up Epstein and Maxwell when they flew in to nearby John Glenn Columbus International Airport on their private jet.[10] She was staying in the 10,600-square-foot guesthouse at Les Wexner's mansion that had been deeded over to Jeffrey Epstein four years earlier. According to an interview she gave to CBS News, Epstein used to tell anyone who'd listen, including Maria, that Wexner would do anything for him.[11]

Farmer worked mainly in the garage, not entirely by choice. She was sequestered there to keep her out of sight. She wasn't allowed to wander the grounds—for a walk, a jog, a grocery run, or a trip into town—unless Abigail Wexner, Les's wife, gave her the okay. Farmer claims that she never personally met Abigail.[12] An avid runner, Farmer was forced to exercise inside Epstein's spacious house; the grounds were patrolled by Wexner's private security staff, many of them members of local and nearby police departments.[13] The situation was unbearable, but starving artists usually had few choices to keep their dreams alive. But there was always a breaking point.

Toward the end of Farmer's stay in Ohio, Epstein and Maxwell visited Wexner's estate. One evening, Farmer was asked to give Epstein a foot massage, according to her interview with *The New York Times*. She had been hired as an artist, not a private masseuse, but eventually she briefly capitulated and rubbed Epstein's feet before the three of them watched a PBS documentary on math. It was then that Epstein and Maxwell attacked her. Over the course of several minutes, they started groping Farmer over her clothing.

Farmer fled the room, crying, and barricaded herself in another bedroom. Alone and surrounded, she telephoned the Franklin County Sheriff's Office to file a criminal complaint and request a patrol car. A police operator kept her on hold and then hung up on her. Later, she learned that sheriff's deputies were already on the Wexner grounds.[14] (According to their records retention policy, the Franklin County Sheriff's Office does not retain records of the type of calls Farmer says she made for longer than two years.)

The compound's security detail refused to let Maria leave the property for close to twelve hours.[15] Farmer pleaded with Epstein to let her go. But the security team was determined to keep her quiet and on the grounds. One of Wexner's security guards appeared at the house and told her, "You aren't leaving. You are not going anywhere."[16] Later that morning, another security guard asked Farmer to come out; when she did, he took her arm and she had to fight him off. She was left with a bruise on her arm.

Maria Farmer was saved only when her father drove from

Kentucky to Ohio to rescue her. Fearing a public scandal, Wexner's security staff let her leave with him.[17]

The incident in Ohio was the breaking point for Farmer. She wanted to press charges. Back in New York, she tried to file a complaint with the NYPD's Sixth Precinct in Greenwich Village. There was nothing the detective squad could do for her—the crime had been committed out of state. But the detectives suggested that she reach out to the FBI. Her resolve, sapped by the trauma she had just endured, ended there.

Maria Farmer did inform several friends of her ordeal. According to her account in the *Times,* she told Eileen Guggenheim, then dean of the New York Arts Academy, about the assault. Guggenheim would state that she didn't believe the case warranted intervention.[*18]

Other people were more sympathetic. When Farmer told Eric Fischl, a fellow painter, about the incident, he told her, "You've got to get out of there." She also confided in Stuart Pivar, an art maven and personal friend of Epstein who had promised to watch over Maxwell after her father's death. Pivar ended his friendship of twenty years with Epstein over Maria Farmer's account; Pivar would later describe Farmer's treatment at the hands of Epstein and Maxwell as "too terrible to repeat."[19]

(Pivar contends that Epstein was afflicted with male nymphomania, or satyriasis, and that Epstein was intellectually curious about his "ailment."[20] Pivar remembered that Epstein "had a very inquiring mind and he was uneducated but he would ask questions about what he thought was going on. He was sort of an idiot savant. I gave him three books he wanted—*Psychopathia Sexualis* by Richard Freiherr

---

* In June 2020, the New York Academy of Art issued a report, produced by the law firm Walden, Macht & Haran, that said Guggenheim played "no role" in introducing Maria Farmer and her younger sister, Annie, to Epstein. Additionally, the report said: "[Maria] Farmer alleged that she reported her abuse . . . to Guggenheim, but that Guggenheim did nothing to assist her. A number of these allegations are contradicted by Farmer's own sworn statements, as well as by other witness testimony." After the report was issued, Annie Farmer accused the New York Academy of Art of "victim blaming."

von Krafft-Ebing; an edition of Stephen Jay Gould's *Ontogeny and Phylogeny;* and an American edition of Otto Weininger's *Sex and Character* that was banned.")

THE ALARM HAD BEEN SOUNDED, but no one acted on the warnings. Maria and Annie had been abandoned by indifferent—or, worse yet, corrupt—law enforcement agencies and by their friends. And theirs were not the only cries to fall on deaf ears.

Alicia Arden, a model and actress who had appeared on the hit television series *Baywatch,* met Jeffrey Epstein at the Shutters on the Beach Hotel in Santa Monica, California, on May 12, 1997. She was twenty-seven. Arden had been referred to Epstein through a mutual friend who worked in finance. Hopeful that Epstein could get her into the Victoria's Secret catalog, she placed her modeling portfolio inside a FedEx box and sent it to Epstein's Manhattan office. Epstein, who sometimes led others to believe that he acted as a talent scout for Victoria's Secret, arranged to meet Arden for an audition to be in the catalog—one of the most prestigious and lucrative opportunities in the modeling world.

The two agreed to meet in his hotel room for Arden's audition. "I was nervous to pick an evening appointment to come see him," she remembered in an interview for this book conducted in 2020. Epstein's request to meet in a hotel room struck Arden as unusual. But she trusted her friend and tried to push her doubts out of her mind. "I talked to his secretary and I thought, 'Okay, I'll just, you know, go and show him my book,'" Arden recalled. "I wouldn't have to be like in an audition with a sea of girls. I'm just going to get one picture in the catalog because he already has seen my picture."

Arden was wearing a skirt and top over a swimsuit. As Epstein opened the door, she remembered being struck by his casual attire. "Sometimes people are dressed more professionally at auditions. But he was like in a USA sweatshirt, had a hat on, sweatpants, and no shoes," Arden said. As Epstein paged through Arden's portfolio, he made comments about the images. "'Well, Alicia, you look a little bustier in some of these photos.' And I said, 'What? I'm very athletic, Jeffrey. I work out. I play tennis. And I was a gymnast and I'm in great shape.' And he goes, 'You look too busty in person, too.' And so I said, 'I could look, however, you know, you want me to look.'"

Arden sensed that Epstein wasn't impressed by her, a thought she recalled later when she learned about his abuse of young girls. "He thought I looked busty and he didn't like that, which makes me think now like, Oh my God. That's why he's like running after these underage girls. He's attracted to fifteen-year-olds. And they're not developing yet."

Epstein told Arden he wanted to evaluate her. He lifted Arden's shirt and skirt and proceeded to touch Arden's butt and hips. "He was making me spin like the girls would do, modeling on the runway. 'And then, oh, let me manhandle you for a second. Let me manhandle you.' And that word is so horrifying to me. I never heard that word before and I never heard it again. No one has ever said that word to me in my entire life."

Arden tried to remove Epstein's hands, but he persisted in touching her. Arden remembered feeling intimidated by his size. Finally she was able to collect her belongings and prepared to leave. As she did so, Epstein placed $100 on the table. "I said, 'I don't want that,'" Arden recalled. "I said, 'I'm not like a prostitute or anything. I don't know why you're doing that. I want to be in the catalog.' I left that."

Confused, Arden didn't know where to turn. She called a friend who knew where she had gone. "I was crying the whole way to the car in the hallway, telling her I'm not going to get Victoria's Secret. It was going badly. He was touching me. I didn't know what was happening. And he was lifting my shirt and my skirt and saying these things about my body. And he didn't like the padding in the bra. I was telling her all this on her cellphone, which she recorded in because she was at home."[21]

The psychological ramifications of Epstein's attack intensified in the hours and then days that followed. At work at Spago, a restaurant in Beverly Hills, Arden kept replaying the events in her mind. "And I was thinking it's wrong to have this person say he could get me in the Victoria's Secret catalog and end up touching me the way he did. And I thought I should file a police report because what if he's doing this to other girls."

A WEEK AFTER THE ASSAULT, Alicia Arden drove once again to Santa Monica—this time to Olympic Drive and the Santa Monica Police Department headquarters. When she announced that she wanted to file a criminal complaint, the police were less than receptive. "I just felt distraught about the whole thing, and I didn't know he was doing this to other girls," Arden remembered. "And I went there, but I was told to kind of leave and maybe think about filing this report. I was really discouraged by the police officers."[22]

Arden's family, like the police, resisted her determination to file a criminal complaint. "My family always thought, if you do that kind of thing and you file police reports, some people [will] come after you. I just kind of went back to work after that. And thought about [the fact] that even the police had told me to think about it."[23]

The more she reflected, though, the angrier she became. A week later, Arden returned to the Santa Monica Police HQ to file an official complaint. The police report was a routine "sexual battery" case. The suspect was noted as "Epstein, Jeffrey"; a notation was made on the report that Epstein was barefoot. The recording officer noted that Epstein's vehicle was a large four-door Mercedes, color: "Black." The trademarks of the suspect included "Posing as or representing Victoria's Secret Company: Gropes during the interview." Type of weapon: "Hands."[24]

The Santa Monica Police Department detective who took Arden's report expressed skepticism.[25] A male detective noted that she had willingly gone to Epstein's room, even though the purpose of the encounter was business; Arden later said she was frustrated that she wasn't able to speak to a female detective instead.[26]

Despite their apparent doubts, the police did question Epstein soon after Arden's complaint. His statement didn't match Arden's accusation. Jeffrey Epstein said he called his friend who had arranged the meeting and denied ever assaulting Arden.[27] Arden got the impression that Epstein and his attorneys had undertaken an effort to discredit her. "I was very discouraged. I came out of the police department crying."[28]

Arden never heard back from investigators. No charges ever came out of it—and in a dispute, detectives wrote that Arden did not want to press charges but wanted police to issue a warning to Epstein, a claim she vehemently denies. The Santa Monica Police Department claimed to have closed the case because the victim was not "desirous of prosecution."[29]

Arden has sworn that this is also a lie.

YEARS LATER, WHEN THE EXTENT of Jeffrey Epstein's crimes became clearer, Les Wexner and his wife, Abigail, would deny knowledge of the Farmer sisters' abuse—even though Epstein's behavior had been flagged to Wexner again and again. "[The Wexners] had no knowledge of her, never met her, never spoke with her, and never spoke with Mr. Epstein or anyone else about her," a Wexner spokesman said in a statement given to media in 2019.[30] But Wexner was well aware of Epstein's activities. Two senior Victoria's Secret executives had alerted Wexner that Epstein was passing himself off as a recruiter for the company, but there is no record that Epstein was ever reprimanded, according to reporting in The New York Times.[31]

Maxwell, on the other hand, was no bystander. She was a co-conspirator, and she knew very well the damage that her partnership with Epstein was wreaking on innocent lives. In 1997, Maxwell invited her old friend Christina Oxenberg to celebrate the success of Oxenberg's novel Royal Blue.[32] At some point during the meeting, the conversation turned to Maxwell's relationship with Epstein. "Jeffrey is very important to me and I need him to marry me," Oxenberg recalled Maxwell saying. Maxwell, said Oxenberg, confided that she was unable to "keep up" with Epstein's "sexual appetite." Because Epstein's needs were "impossible to meet," Maxwell felt obliged to "bring him young girls to fulfill his sexual needs," according to Oxenberg's account of the conversation. Oxenberg says she was horrified by what Maxwell was telling her and tried to change the subject. Maxwell went on, saying, "They're nothing, these girls. They are trash."

Oxenberg said she had no specific knowledge of Maria or Annie Farmer, nor Alicia Arden, at the time.

DID EPSTEIN'S NEAR BRUSHES WITH the law in the mid-1990s give him reason to worry? His next real estate move may have been an effort to create an environment that would be far from the prying eyes of law enforcement—or anyone else, for that matter.

In 1998, having gotten free of those entanglements with law enforcement, Jeffrey Epstein bought a seventy-two-acre private island in the U.S. Virgin Islands named Little St. James.[33]

On his very own island, he would be king.

# PART THREE

# BREAKING BAD

I am every girl he did this to, and they're all me.
—Anouska De Georgiou

They're nothing, these girls.
—Ghislaine Maxwell

# 12

# THE RUNAWAY

DONALD TRUMP, THE SELF-APPOINTED MASTER OF DEAL MAKING, WAS a frequent visitor in bankruptcy court in the early 1990s, with four of his properties in Atlantic City and New York seeking Chapter 11 bankruptcy protection just between 1991 and 1992. Reportedly worried about the $3 million annual upkeep on Mar-a-Lago, the historic Florida dream home that Trump had purchased at a bargain a decade earlier, the developer hit upon an idea: He would transform the property into a resort and private club. The Palm Beach town council initially shot down Trump's scheme, but after suing the council, Trump got the go-ahead in August 1993 to proceed with his latest moneymaking venture.[1]

Mar-a-Lago wouldn't be just any hotel: Trump vowed to turn it into the most exclusive address in the world. To ensure membership was limited to the wealthiest and most prominent people, Trump set the club's initiation fee at $200,000. Annual dues were another $14,000 a year; guests eager to stay at the hotel had to pony up $2,000 a night. To cater to its moneyed members and keep the place running, Mar-a-Lago employed an army of menial workers. There were cooks and waiters to serve the hungry guests, and chambermaids and groundskeepers to clean rooms and tend the estate. One of these, a maintenance manager, was a man named Sky Roberts, and he had a daughter named Virginia.

Virginia Roberts was born on August 9, 1983, in Sacramento, California. Her parents relocated to the small community of Loxahatchee, a rural stretch of Palm Beach County, when she was four years old. Roberts described herself as coming from a "broken home."[2] When she was seven, she ran away after a family friend molested her. She lived in foster homes and on the street. In 1996, at the age of thirteen, she was picked up by a sixty-five-year-old sex trafficker named Ron Eppinger. Eppinger ran a model agency, Perfect Ten, that provided prostitutes to clients in Miami. Between 1997 and 1999, Eppinger lured women from Eastern Europe with the prospect of a modeling career, only to put them to work as prostitutes.[3] Virginia lived with Eppinger for six months. At the time, his modeling agency was coming under scrutiny from law enforcement. He ended up being raided by the FBI and subsequently pleaded guilty to money laundering, alien smuggling for prostitution, and interstate travel for prostitution.

Virginia Roberts eventually reunited with her father and returned to Palm Beach County. After the horrific experiences of her early teen years, her life looked as though it was on a better track. She attended Royal Palm Beach High and had a boyfriend named Tony Figueroa. Virginia loved animals and dreamed of one day becoming a veterinarian.[4] In the meantime, to earn some extra cash, she started working at Mar-a-Lago as a spa attendant.

JEFFREY EPSTEIN AND GHISLAINE MAXWELL were frequent visitors at the club—one of the perks of living a mile and a quarter away and of their friendship with Donald Trump. During one visit to the club in the summer of 2000, Ghislaine Maxwell noticed the young Mar-a-Lago worker reading a book on massage techniques while at her post in the spa. She was wearing a white polo shirt and miniskirt and a name tag that said JENN.

With an accent out of *Masterpiece Theatre*, Maxwell had been schooled in the art of charm all her life. She walked over to Virginia, smiling, and struck up a conversation. As Roberts later recalled in a legal document in a suit against Ghislaine Maxwell, including an unsealed 139-page draft of an unpublished memoir she wrote titled "The Billionaire's Playboy Club," she responded politely to the older woman, who began to "chat a bit about this rich guy that she worked for and she knew offhand that he was looking for a massage therapist." Noting Roberts's evident interest in massage therapy, Maxwell offered to introduce the Trump employee to her wealthy friend for a possible position as masseuse in training.

"I declined her first proposition, thinking out loud, told her I didn't know the body well enough to even attempt an interview," Roberts recalled. "She didn't seem worried at all by my fear of incompetence, saying that if he liked me enough, he would get me the best training in the industry." Maxwell told Roberts that she liked the girl's "cheery persona" and that she "fit the quota for what he was looking for."

Roberts took down Maxwell's phone number and a house address she provided. After Maxwell departed, Roberts raced over to the club's tennis courts where her father was working. The father and daughter agreed Maxwell's proposition "could be a wonderful opportunity" for Roberts to get her accreditation in massage.

Given the clientele of the club, Roberts and her father saw little reason to hesitate. Maxwell had struck Roberts more as a "nurturer than procurer," as she later put it.

Later that day, around five o'clock, Sky Roberts drove his daughter over to Epstein's house at the end of El Brillo Way off the Palm Beach Intracoastal. They pulled in to a driveway in front of a large pink mansion with heavy wooden doors, at which point the elder hugged his daughter and wished her success in the "interview." He walked Virginia to the front door, where they were greeted by an older man dressed in what appeared to be a casual butler uniform. Virginia told the butler that she was there to "meet Ms. Maxwell for a massage trial."

Soon Maxwell appeared, taking Sky Roberts's hand and kissing both father and daughter on the cheeks. As the trio made small talk, Virginia thought she could sense impatience on the part of Maxwell. "She was in a hurry, you could tell, to end the conversation and say goodbye to my dad," Roberts recalled.[5]

Soon Sky Roberts departed, the heavy wooden doors closing behind him. Virginia, he believed, was in good hands.

As Ghislaine Maxwell led Virginia Roberts upstairs to the estate's master suite, they whisked passed other employees and an array of rooms. The suite contained a sauna and steam rooms with tinted windows and was lit by a gigantic chandelier. Through French doors, Roberts could see a spiral staircase and a swimming pool. They passed a chest of drawers, in which, Roberts would learn later, Epstein's sex toys were stored in neat rows. The walls of another room were plastered with floor-to-ceiling photos of nude girls and young women.

As Roberts stepped inside the sauna room, Epstein was already lying facedown on a massage table, his head resting on his folded arms. Roberts's first thought was that he was athletic-looking despite his silver hair. Maxwell introduced him as "Mr. Jeffrey Epstein," but he told her to call him "Jeffrey" and thanked her for taking the time to visit.[6] If she was good, he promised, she would see the world as Epstein's traveling masseuse.

In 2011, Roberts, breaking her silence for the first time, would relate the exchange to *Mail on Sunday* journalist Sharon Churcher, whose extensive notes from the interview are a source for this book.

In the sauna room, Epstein proceeded to pepper Roberts with questions about her sexual history. "Did I have any diseases? How many people had I slept with? Within the first hour, he knew my life story." As Roberts recounted her troubled early life, Epstein seemed pleased by her answers.

"So, you're a bad girl in a good girl's body," Roberts recalled Epstein saying, before telling her a little bit about his own early life in New York.

At some point, Roberts understood that the conversation part of the meeting was ending, and that she would now be expected to touch Epstein. Throughout the exchange, Maxwell had been hovering nearby. It became clear to Roberts that she was expected to follow Maxwell's lead.

"She had me put oil on my hands and then she grabbed one of his feet and started to massage it and she told me to take his other foot," Roberts said.

When Epstein flipped over, Roberts was surprised to see that he had an erection. "Ghislaine took off her shirt and starts rubbing her nipples on him and she rubbed her breasts over his torso, and she told me to get undressed. I'm thinking, 'This is wrong. This is not a legitimate massage. I know they don't do this at Mar-a-Lago,'" Roberts said.

Standing behind Roberts, Maxwell began to fondle the girl, and she instructed Roberts to straddle Epstein. He then said, "Put your mouth around Daddy's cock. You're such a good little girl." Roberts performed oral sex until Epstein climaxed. "Ghislaine said I'd got a knack for it," Roberts recalled.

When the encounter ended, Maxwell paid Roberts $200. Another employee drove her back to her father's house.

The "massages" became routine. Over the course of two years, the sexual abuse of a sixteen-year-old girl became a professional arrangement.

"After I did those things for Epstein, he and Maxwell said they were going to have me travel and were going to get an education for me. They were promising me the world," Roberts stated later. Epstein told Roberts that he would find a wealthy suitor so that Roberts would be "set up for life."[7] She felt that her dream of becoming a veterinarian might actually materialize.

· · ·

EPSTEIN'S ABUSE OF VIRGINIA ROBERTS continued in Palm Beach and soon extended to his home in Manhattan. Roberts was no longer a $9-an-hour changing-room assistant at Donald Trump's resort. She was now virtually a full-time employee of Epstein's, frequently flying between the financier's homes on his private jet.

Roberts would later write in the draft of her unpublished memoir, which was submitted in a legal action against Maxwell and unsealed by the court in 2019, that before Epstein took her on the first trip to New York, Roberts's father, Sky, came by Epstein's house. Sky said he would take on the task of informing Mar-a-Lago that she wasn't returning to the job there. She wrote: "We said our good-byes outside in the driveway, Jeffrey even coming outside to meet with my father to shake his hand and assure him that his daughter will be more than looked after. I hugged my dad tightly, feeling like I was on the verge of a steep cliff." (In interviews years later, Sky Roberts said that he did not know about Epstein's abuse. "I wish I had known all this stuff was going on, but I didn't," he said.)[8]

Epstein guaranteed Virginia Roberts a minimum of $200 each time she gave him what he called an "erotic massage" and $200 an hour for her other chores: "I would always receive the money immediately. He would give me the cash from a wad he carried in a black leather duffel bag or an assistant paid me," she said.

Roberts became a regular at Epstein's mansion on East Seventy-First Street in New York, where she recalled her first visit. "I was shown to my room, a very luxurious room. The mansion was huge. I got scared because it was so big." As in Palm Beach, Epstein's Manhattan home also had a room that contained a massage table, where he would abuse Roberts. To Roberts, the room resembled an "S&M parlor."

The sexual abuse was virtually nonstop, Roberts recalled. "I had sex with him four to eight times a day. I never put up a fight. I complied even if it was the middle of the night. I was on call twenty-four seven. There was an intercom. Ghislaine, him, or a maid would come on and say Jeffrey needed me."[9]

Epstein and Maxwell molded Roberts into the perfect Jeffrey Epstein servant. She received instruction on how to properly use sex toys on men and women, but Roberts's "training" wasn't limited to sex. "They wanted me to be able to cater to all the needs of the men they were going to send to me," Roberts recalled, which included knowing "how to keep my mouth shut."[10]

Maxwell was the enforcer, the madam, and the schoolmistress. But, according to Roberts's statements in court filings, she was also an abuser. Roberts's employment included having sex with Maxwell, which began at the Palm Beach mansion when Roberts was just sixteen and continued on a regular basis thereafter. "Maxwell was all about sex all the time. She had sex with underage girls virtually every day when I was around her and she was very forceful," Roberts said in court papers. "I had sex with Maxwell in the Virgin Islands, New Mexico, New York, as well as France and many other locations. I also observed Maxwell have sex with dozens of underage girls."[11]

The underage girls who passed through Epstein's and Maxwell's hands were always documented. Maxwell took sexually explicit photos of them for display in Epstein's homes. Sometimes, Roberts recalls, Maxwell instructed Roberts to perform sex acts in conjunction with Maxwell's photo taking.[12]

Soon even more would be expected of Roberts.

EPSTEIN AND MAXWELL BELIEVED THAT Roberts could play an integral role in procuring new girls. The criminal enterprise required a steady flow of "talent" coming in and out of Epstein's mansions. One day Epstein came to Roberts with a proposition: If she could procure additional girls for him, he would double her salary.

"I asked him how does one [actually] propose such a thing to a complete stranger?" Roberts recalled in her memoir draft, submitted in a legal action against Maxwell and unsealed by the court in 2019.

"'Well,' he said in a build-up to another kind of lesson. 'If I were you I would use your charm to entice them and my money to bring them, I would tell them you work for a multibillionaire who has a taste for young, beautiful girls and with his contacts in the acting, modeling, or rich husband world, your boss could help them. All they have to do is come meet me first.'"

Maxwell told Roberts that Epstein preferred white girls. If the girl was non-white, she had to be "a knockout beauty." Under no circumstances was she to bring in a girl who was addicted to drugs. Tattoos and piercings were frowned upon.

Once a young girl was brought to Epstein's mansion, Maxwell would set the trap. "She would say, 'We'll pay you two hundred dollars an hour, it's lots of money. It's a very nice mansion. Check it out. Swim in the pool for the day,'" Roberts recalled.

At first Maxwell would give the recruits mundane tasks, like answering the phone. At a certain point, Maxwell would then explain that part of the job as an Epstein "assistant" involved giving him massages. "You wouldn't know who that girl was or what she about until that peak moment," Roberts explained.[13]

Not all of the young girls could be trapped. In one instance, according to Roberts, a girl named Clarissa that Roberts had recruited "got halfway into it" with Epstein before abruptly stopping. "She grabbed her top and said, 'I can't do this. Don't worry about money' and walked out."[14]

Johanna Sjoberg, who was recruited in 2001, when she was a college student, has said Maxwell's job was to ensure that Epstein had three orgasms a day: "It was biological, like eating." Sjoberg was reprimanded when Epstein failed to climax during a massage that she gave him.

Epstein rented two apartments for Virginia Roberts: one in Royal Palm Beach, where she lived with her boyfriend, and one in New

York. She often would stay at Epstein's residences or accompany him and Ghislaine Maxwell on trips.

The relationship between the two predators and Roberts was difficult for a teenager to process. Early on in her "employment," Roberts told her mother that she was working for a rich guy. Her mother said, "Go, go far away."[15] But Roberts was worried about what might happen to her. "I knew these people were powerful. I didn't know what would happen if I said no."[16]

Roberts recalled once asking Maxwell about the nature of her own relationship with Epstein. The teenager wondered what the older woman got out of her seemingly one-sided relationship with Epstein. "It takes the pressure off me to have sex with him," Roberts said Maxwell responded. She told Roberts that she had "hit hard times" and was "disgraced," and Epstein had offered her a job.[17]

As for Roberts, even though they frequently shared a bed, Epstein would sometimes introduce her as his daughter. At other times, Epstein referring to Roberts as his "traveling masseuse."

Roberts was tasked with washing Epstein behind his ears and between his toes, scrubbing his back in the shower, rubbing lotion on his feet, and dressing him afterward. "It was like everything you would do for your four-year-old child," Roberts recalled.

Epstein and Maxwell ordered Roberts to take part in role-playing games. Sometimes she had to dress as a young German maid. Or she would be a schoolgirl in knee socks and pleated miniskirts. "Ghislaine sent me to a dentist to have my teeth whitened and I went for Brazilian waxes. He wanted me to look prepubescent," she said. Other times, she would have to wear high boots for sadomasochistic scenes that included Maxwell and other girls. "He loved to watch a girl choke me with a leather collar with studs and I had to do that to her."

In an interview with journalist Sharon Churcher, Roberts recalled one instance—previously unpublished—in which a girl's thighs became bloody during an S&M encounter. When the girl asked

Roberts to drink her blood, Roberts was disgusted. "I said, 'Jeffrey, it's getting too weird.' He drew the line after that, and he got rid of her."[18]

The mixed messages were confusing to the teenager. "I felt that he and Ghislaine [really] cared for me. We'd do family things. We'd watch *Sex and the City*. We'd pop popcorn. Have normal dinners. Drink normal drinks. But all of a sudden it ends up in a gigantic foursome with Jeffrey and Ghislaine and other girls," Roberts told Churcher. "It was a very sick and twisted family."[19]

WHAT WAS A TEENAGER SUPPOSED to do under such circumstances?

Years later, in court papers, Roberts would record her fears: "I knew that if I left I would be in big trouble. I also knew that I was a witness to a lot of illegal [activity] and very bad behavior by Epstein and his friends. If I left Epstein, he knew all kinds of powerful people. He could have had me killed or abducted, and I always knew he was capable of that if I did not obey him."[20]

# 13

## 24-KARAT PRISON

THE STOCK MARKET WAS BOOMING IN EARLY 2001, AND AFTER A contested election, George W. Bush, the son of forty-first president George H. W. Bush, was inheriting a strong economy and a relatively peaceful geopolitical stage.

The optimism of the year came crashing down in September, however, with the al-Qaeda terrorist attack. The televised destruction of the World Trade Center changed American politics overnight.

While the rest of the country grappled with the new reality of terrorism and war in the Bush era, Jeffrey Epstein seemed to be taking his cues from Bush's predecessor, Bill Clinton, who, much to the amazement of some observers, had just survived a scandal-plagued two terms with his popularity among the American people largely intact.

In the early 2000s, Epstein seemed to be doubling down on his abuse of young girls. For Virginia Roberts that meant she was no longer merely a companion to Epstein and Ghislaine Maxwell. Epstein would now be ordering Virginia Roberts to "entertain" other men—men that he would personally select, according to an interview Roberts gave to Sharon Churcher.[1]

Roberts would be paid up to $10,000 for a weekend spent with these "clients." At first Roberts was shocked by the new dynamic, but she told herself that it was a badge of honor: Epstein was sharing her with his "friends" because he trusted her. "I would do anything to keep Jeffrey happy and to keep my place as his number one girl." Roberts kept telling herself she was lucky to be making good money.

Epstein's social circle included politicians and titans of industry—men who traveled with bodyguards and whose indiscretions were shielded from public scrutiny. And if they did get into trouble, there were always attorneys.

Donald Trump had his legal pit bull in Roy Cohn. O. J. Simpson had Alan Dershowitz, a Harvard professor and frequent legal commentator on TV. Dershowitz would become Epstein's guard dog, too. According to Roberts, he was also one of the first men that Virginia Roberts entertained at the behest of Epstein—an accusation that Dershowitz has vehemently denied.

ALAN DERSHOWITZ WAS EQUAL PARTS lawyer, legal scholar, and media star. He had joined the faculty of Harvard Law School in 1964 when he was just twenty-five years old, and he rose to fame with his defense of socialite Claus von Bülow, who had been accused of the attempted murder of his wife. Dershowitz had a long list of notorious and notable celebrity clients that included Mike Tyson, O. J. Simpson, and the TV evangelist Jim Bakker. Dershowitz became something of a household name, thanks to publishing dozens of books and his prolific, combative TV appearances. Like Epstein, Dershowitz was Brooklyn born, and Dershowitz's father had founded a synagogue near the family home in the ultra-orthodox bastion of Borough Park.

Dershowitz has stated that he met Epstein through businesswoman and political donor Lynn Forester de Rothschild, who "suggested that he would enjoy getting to know Epstein, an 'interesting autodidact,'" according to an account in *The New Yorker* by Connie Bruck. Epstein reportedly flew to Martha's Vineyard and met

Dershowitz. The two hit it off. "We talked about science, we talked about academia, we talked about Harvard," Dershowitz said.[2]

Dershowitz was also allegedly a frequent guest at Epstein's homes over a period of years, and Roberts remembered Dershowitz as being seemingly unfazed by the house's sexually charged atmosphere. "Dershowitz was so comfortable with the sex that was going on that he would even come and chat with Epstein while I was giving oral sex to Epstein," Roberts stated in court documents.[3]

Roberts recalled one instance when Dershowitz knocked on Epstein's bedroom door in the middle of Epstein's abusing her. To her astonishment, Epstein answered the door and in walked Dershowitz. "They began to converse about business immediately, right in front of me," Roberts said in a legal filing. "How else am I going to make a million dollars while I'm sleeping?" she says Epstein remarked.[4]

Roberts has claimed that she went on to have sex with Alan Dershowitz at least six times, alleging that the first instance took place when she was "about sixteen" and the final instance when she was nineteen. The alleged encounters took place at Epstein's homes in New York and Palm Beach, as well as at his ranch in New Mexico and on Little St. James Island in the U.S. Virgin Islands. During an alleged encounter on Little St. James, Roberts said she was asked to "give Dershowitz a massage on the beach." The lawyer later requested that they go "somewhere more private," according to Roberts's account, where the pair "had intercourse." Another sexual encounter between Roberts and Dershowitz allegedly took place on Epstein's airplane, during which time another girl was present.[5]

As THIS BOOK WENT TO press, Alan Dershowitz was continuing a multiyear fight to clear his name for what he's maintained are false allegations lodged against him by Virginia Roberts (now known as Virginia Roberts Giuffre).[6]

In 2020 he threatened to file a defamation suit against Netflix for airing Giuffre's accusation in its documentary series *Jeffrey Epstein: Filthy Rich* (based on the James Patterson book of the same name) that she was trafficked by Epstein to have sex with Dershowitz. Dershowitz also appeared in the documentary, asserting, "Let me state categorically: I never had sex with an underage person in my life."[7]

His latest legal action follows a chain of ongoing defamation lawsuits and countersuits that began after the accusations against Dershowitz first appeared in a 2014 legal motion filed by Florida attorney Bradley Edwards, who has represented Epstein victims. Dershowitz has maintained that he has never met Giuffre. "She's made this whole story up out of whole cloth." He has said that it may be a case of "mistaken identification."

In 2016, Edwards and attorney Paul Cassell issued a joint statement to acknowledge "that it was a mistake to have filed sexual misconduct accusations against Dershowitz; and the sexual misconduct accusations made in all court filings (including all exhibits) are hereby withdrawn." The claims were in response to a 2014 filing in which they questioned the validity of Epstein's non-prosecution agreement.

Dershowitz has claimed Giuffre's allegations were part of a broader extortion plot aimed at billionaire Leslie Wexner and orchestrated by Giuffre's lawyers. "The decision to name me publicly," Dershowitz alleged in a 2019 court filing, "was calculated to send the following message to Wexner: If you don't want to have happen to you what happened to Alan Dershowitz, you should settle the complaint against you, even though the statute of limitations has long expired."

In December 2018, two years after reaching a settlement in a previous defamation case, a second accusation against Dershowitz spilled into the news via a defamation case brought by Giuffre against Ghislaine Maxwell. Maxwell settled with Giuffre for an undisclosed sum, and the court documents had been sealed. But in a public transcript of the court proceedings, Maxwell's attorney mentioned offhand that Sarah Ransome, a South African woman who was also trafficked by Epstein, stated in a sworn affidavit that she had also been lent out to Dershowitz for sex. The story was published by the New York *Daily News,* with the headline SECOND WOMAN CLAIMS BILLIONAIRE PERV JEFFREY EPSTEIN "DIRECTED" HER TO HAVE SEX WITH ALAN DERSHOWITZ.

Dershowitz again denied everything. He said he had never even met Ransome and called her "delusional." In April 2019, Giuffre sued Dershowitz for defamation.[8] He told the *Daily News* he welcomed the suit. He had been egging her on to make her claims in public for years. "This is the opportunity I've been looking for," he told the *Daily News.*

In July 2019, Dershowitz took to Twitter, saying that the "smoking gun emails and unpublished manuscript" of a book written by Giuffre would "prove I was framed for financial reasons and that I'm totally innocent, as I've consistently asserted since the day I was falsely accused."* The emails in question were an exchange between Giuffre and *Mail on Sunday* journalist Sharon Churcher. Giuffre had begun writing a book about her experiences and had asked Churcher for help making a list of men she had previously identified in photographs.

"Don't forget Alan Dershowitz," Churcher wrote in an email. "We all suspect Alan is a pedo and though no proof of that, you probably met him when he was hanging out with Jeffrey Epstein." Giuffre told *The New Yorker,* "I can't say what she was thinking, but I think she threw Alan into it forgetting that I had already mentioned him."

---

* Virginia Roberts Giuffre stated her book manuscript draft was "99 percent true," according to the UK's *Sun* in a November 16, 2019, report. Giuffre's lawyers said she used a fictional narrative style to tell the truth of her experiences. According to a legal document—the Plaintiff's Statement of Contested Fact and Plaintiff's Undisputed Facts—submitted by Giuffre's lawyer Sigrid McCawley, "Ms. Giuffre began to draft a fictionalized account of what happened to her. It was against this backdrop of the trauma being unearthed, her steps to seek psychological counseling for it, that she drafted this manuscript. Doing so was an act of empowerment and a way of reframing and taking control over the narrative of her past abuse that haunts her."

Dershowitz countersued Giuffre for defamation and harassment. He asserted once again that Giuffre was pressured by her lawyers, including David Boies, to make knowingly false accusations against him. He also published a book about his saga, *Guilt by Accusation: The Challenge of Proving Innocence in the Age of #MeToo.*

Boies turned around and filed a defamation suit against Dershowitz, saying, "In an effort to distract attention from his own misconduct, [Dershowitz] has engaged in a campaign to attack and vilify each of the lawyers who have represented his victims."[9]

In April 2020, Giuffre filed an amended complaint to include battery, since New York had by then passed the Child Victims Act, which provided a one-year "look-back window" to reopen the statute of limitations for victims of child sexual abuse to bring new claims.[10] The legal battle was ongoing as this book went to press.

For the record, Dershowitz said he received one massage at Epstein's home administered by "a fifty-year-old Russian woman named Olga," adding that he kept his underwear on during the session.[11]

BY THE EARLY 2000S JEFFREY Epstein was extremely wealthy. He owned luxurious homes, vast stretches of real estate, a private jet, and even an island in the Caribbean. Just how wealthy has been the subject of immense speculation. In an October 2002 *New York* magazine story, Landon Thomas, Jr., wrote that "Epstein is said to run $15 billion for wealthy clients." A July 2019 *New York Times* story noted a 2002 court filing from his company, Financial Trust Company, which said he had twenty employees and Financial Trust had $88 million in contributions from shareholders at the time. Epstein seemed to measure his worth, however, not just in dollars but in people.

Epstein collected contacts the way some boys collect baseball cards, mingling with the wealthy and powerful.

One of these men was *Simpsons* creator Matt Groening,

according to Roberts's account in an interview with Sharon Churcher. Roberts met the TV legend while he was accompanying Epstein on his private jet from Carmel, California, to Los Angeles in 2001, according to the account, which has also been described in unsealed court papers in the lawsuit Roberts later filed against Ghislaine Maxwell. "Matt Groening was the most disgusting man I have ever had to be with because of his feet and his stench," Roberts stated. "I could have taken a grinder to his toenails and it wouldn't have cut them. It was just disgusting, and he was laughing at me, having to touch his feet, everyone was laughing at me. Jeffrey was laughing. Everyone was laughing at me. It was like Shrek. It looked like an ogre's foot."[12]

Another contact was hedge fund billionaire Glenn Dubin, who was both Epstein's financial rival and the husband of his former girlfriend, Eva Andersson. According to Roberts, Epstein "still had a lot of feelings for Eva" and had decorated his house with pictures of her. Roberts first gave the pregnant Eva a nonsexual massage and then, after Eva had fallen asleep, had intercourse with Glenn.[13] (This account, which also appears in unsealed court papers, was met by outrage from a Dubin spokesperson, who called it "demonstrably false and defamatory.")

Jeffrey Epstein had a fascination—some would even go as far as to say obsession—with Harvard University. In the memoir draft that was submitted as part of the legal case against Ghislaine Maxwell and unsealed by the court in 2019, Roberts wrote that Epstein was giving her "a new client." She wrote: "He is a Harvard professor, named Stephen." The man's last name was redacted when the document was unsealed. Roberts added, "Without Jeffrey even verbalizing the need to have sex with him, he told me to keep him happy."

Also named by Roberts in the unsealed legal file were former New Mexico governor Bill Richardson, former Democratic Senate majority leader George Mitchell, and MIT computer scientist Marvin Minsky. They were all business and social associates of Epstein.

Richardson claimed he never met Roberts, had never been to Epstein's island, and never saw Epstein in the presence of young girls; Mitchell also denied having any contact with Roberts or ever being aware that Epstein, during their association, was involved in inappropriate conduct; Minsky died in 2016, three years before Roberts's allegations became public.

ANOTHER ONE OF EPSTEIN'S CLOSE friends and business partners around 2005 was the Frenchman Jean-Luc Brunel. Brunel had started as a talent scout but now owned and ran Karin Models, later called MC2 Model Management, based in Miami, Florida; Epstein financed the relaunch.[14] Epstein, according to Maritza Vasquez, a bookkeeper for the agency, invested $1 million in Jean-Luc Brunel's MC2.[15]

Brunel had often worked with Eastern European models, even when the Iron Curtain was still up, and did a brisk business with special clients in the Middle East in places like Kuwait and Saudi Arabia.[16] Favoring women from poor backgrounds with little education, he was skilled at securing travel documents and visas for his models so that they could enter the United States.[17]

In some circles, Brunel was known for discovering Danish supermodel Helena Christensen; in others, for forcing himself upon the young models in his agency.[18] In 1988, some of them went on *60 Minutes* to describe the abuse that proliferated behind the catwalk.[19] According to the models, Brunel pressured them into having sex to advance their careers. Two women claimed that Brunel had drugged and raped them.

Beyond Epstein's financial investment in Brunel's business, the friendship was built on a steady pipeline of underage girls whom Brunel sent to Epstein's homes in New York City or Palm Beach, according to Virginia Roberts. Roberts said Epstein would fly to locations where Brunel's models were working. Flight records indicate Epstein's jets stopped all over the world—Morocco, Paris, London, Mexico, Slovakia—for only hours at a time.[20] Air traffic controllers in

St. Thomas observed Epstein accompanying children from his jet to his island.

Roberts remembers Epstein bragging to her that he had slept with more than a thousand of Brunel's models—many of whom were teenage girls.[21] The models were often very young—thirteen, fourteen, and fifteen years of age—and in New York some were housed in apartments at 301 East Sixty-Sixth Street in New York, a building purportedly owned by Epstein.[22]

Epstein shared his women with Brunel, too, according to legal filings. Roberts stated that she was assigned to have sex with Brunel at Little St. James and in Palm Beach, New York City, New Mexico, Paris, the South of France, and California.[23] Often these encounters would include others. Roberts recalled that as many as ten underage girls would be forced to participate, some of whom did not speak English.[24]

JEFFREY EPSTEIN NEVER FLEW COMMERCIAL. Like other wealthy men, including Donald Trump, Epstein maintained his own fleet of aircraft that could be summoned on a whim to chart a course to the Caribbean, to South America, or across the Atlantic Ocean.

The Epstein Air Force consisted of a black Gulfstream, a private helicopter, and a twin-engine Cessna 421. The fleet's flagship was a Boeing 727-200, a passenger jet with a seating capacity of nearly two hundred that was modified for private use.[25] The aircraft even had what's known as a Bloomberg terminal on board so that Epstein could monitor international financial markets from 30,000 feet above sea level. The aircraft was headquartered at Teterboro, New Jersey, a small airport in the Meadowlands that is a mere twelve miles from the Upper East Side. The young women seen entering and exiting the aircraft prompted local mechanics to refer to the aircraft, with its white and blue livery, as the Lolita Express, a term that was embraced by tabloids.[26]

During one trip to London in 2001, Epstein, Roberts, Maxwell, and his entourage of young women stayed in a townhouse owned by Maxwell. Maxwell took Roberts shopping for a £5,000 designer bag, numerous dresses, a pink singlet, and perfume.[27] She told Roberts that she would be meeting a prince later that day. The prince, Roberts was informed, was to receive whatever he wanted.[28]

# 14

## THE "NEGATIVE CHARISMA" PRINCE

UNTIL 2015, TWO ARMED UNITS OF THE LONDON METROPOLITAN Police were responsible for dignitary protection assignments. SO1, or Special Operations 1, protected ministers and public officials from terrorist threats and assassins' bullets. Like the U.S. Secret Service, they provided round-the-clock protection to the prime minister, as well as to visiting heads of state. SO14, or Special Operations 14, was the armed squad tasked with protecting the queen and the rest of the royal family.

SO14, like all the specialized units of the London Metropolitan Police, is a volunteer force. Applicants are handpicked and subjected to a rigorous background check. Hopefuls endured months of highly specialized firearms instruction, followed by tactical training scenarios meant to replicate an all-out terrorist assault on a member of the royal family; in the past, after all, the Provisional IRA had killed Lord Louis Mountbatten, a cousin of the queen, and had come within an inch of assassinating Prime Minister Margaret Thatcher.[1] "Members of the unit are expected to protect the very fabric of British history," as one former member put it, and few pass the training course.

Even then, there was no guarantee you would last inside the

unit. "The royals," a former officer explained, "treated the protection force like they did most others—as mere commoners, and in this case servants. These men and women were born into privilege and raised to believe that they were above reproach. If a royal didn't like the way you looked, or something you said, that was it. You were out."[2]

Members of SO14, on the other hand, reserved judgment at all times. Their job was not to weigh in on the royal family's dalliances; instead, they were to investigate each location, scout out hidden threats, and then wait in the Jaguar until summoned—potentially many hours later. As far as the royals were concerned, discretion was always the better part of valor. Fleet Street newspapers paid a king's ransom for any morsel of royal scandal, but as a former unit member remembers, "What happened to any one of the royals remained between them and their conscience and we were never to breathe a word to another soul."[3]

The size of an SO14 detail depended on the role of the principal and the threat level reported. Queen Elizabeth and Prince Philip warranted the largest detail: SO14 officers assigned to Buckingham Palace were older and more experienced than the others. The lesser royals received smaller teams. The unlucky ones received Prince Andrew.

PRINCE ANDREW LIKED TO PARTY, and this caused a world of headache for his SO14 detail. He ran them ragged at times, sneaking into exclusive addresses and the homes of female friends. He was always trailed by writers and paparazzi hungry for a good story. Often they were rewarded; he had always been known as something of a scoundrel. Before he married Fergie, he and his female companions were known as Randy Andy and His Web of Arm Candy; after his divorce, he became known as the Playboy Prince.[4] The SO14 members assigned to him had little choice but to turn a blind eye to any questionable behavior.

Born in 1960, Prince Andrew is the Duke of York and the younger brother of Prince Charles. Never the proximate heir to the throne, he trained with the elite Royal Marines, completing the All Arms Commando Course, for which he earned a coveted Green Beret. He later went on to serve in the Royal Navy as a helicopter pilot; during the 1982 Falklands War, he flew combat missions as a copilot on a Sea King chopper off the H.M.S. *Invincible*. In 1986 Andrew married Sarah Ferguson, a fiercely independent redhead who Buckingham Palace had hoped would win the couple the adoration that Prince Charles and Diana Spencer had garnered five years earlier. The marriage dissolved in 1996.

THE BODYGUARDS ARRIVED FIRST, OF course.

The specialists from SO14 had been to Ghislaine Maxwell's London townhouse before. They knew that the prince was friends with both her and Epstein, who had in turn introduced Andrew to another playboy: Donald Trump.[5] (A source told Sharon Churcher that in 1999, Maxwell phoned Trump and said that Prince Andrew wanted to play golf at Mar-a-Lago. Trump obliged. The following February, Andrew, Maxwell, and Epstein flew to Palm Beach for a house party.)

It was March 9, 2001, and Virginia Roberts had flown to London with Epstein and Maxwell. Earlier in the day, Maxwell had taken her shopping to prepare Roberts for the arrival that evening of a special visitor, a "prince."

Roberts, in a 2011 interview with journalist Sharon Churcher, recalled the bodyguards bringing Prince Andrew inside Ghislaine's townhouse and leaving only once they were satisfied that the young blond American girl posed no threat. Andrew knocked at the door just after 6:00 P.M., and Maxwell greeted him. Maxwell served Andrew biscuits and tea from a porcelain pot.[6]

Maxwell and Epstein introduced Roberts to Andrew, who kissed her formally, on each cheek. Roberts was starstruck in front of the royal, while Maxwell seemed to beam with satisfaction. "Guess how old she is?" Maxwell asked Prince Andrew; Maxwell, Roberts remembered, loved asking that question among her friends. Prince Andrew took a stab at it, and said, "Seventeen." Epstein smiled. Ghislaine chuckled, according to Roberts's account to journalist Sharon Churcher, and said, "She'll be too old soon," revealing to the prince that Roberts was just sixteen, the age of consent in the United Kingdom.[7]

The four went to a nearby Chinese restaurant and then Andrew's motorcade, followed by Ghislaine, Roberts, and Maxwell, processed to Club Tramp on Jermyn Street. Situated between the exclusive Mayfair neighborhood and Pall Mall and Buckingham Palace, Tramp is known as one of the most exclusive members' clubs in the world. Photography is forbidden and the use of cellphones is tightly controlled. The group was immediately shown to a secluded table.

The atmosphere inside dazzled Roberts. The fog of Cuban cigars was punctuated by hypnotic flashing lights. Waiters rushed bottles of top-shelf booze to thirsty club members, while £200 plates of Iranian Beluga caviar were devoured as if they were French fries.[8]

Prince Andrew had pulled out all the stops to impress his companions. Even though Roberts was only sixteen, she was served alcohol.

At some point during the group's hourlong visit to the club, the Duke of York asked Roberts onto the dance floor. "He was the most incredibly hideous dancer I had ever seen and couldn't help but laugh." After an hour or so of "pelvic smashing" on the dance floor, Roberts stated in her unpublished memoir draft, submitted in a legal suit against Ghislaine Maxwell and unsealed in 2019, that she and the prince "finally exited the floor," the royal "dripping with sweat." To Roberts, the prince's forward behavior was an obvious sign that he "wanted to intimately get acquainted" with her.[9]

After Maxwell signed the check, the group headed back to Maxwell's townhouse in two vehicles, with Andrew's SO14 detail in tow.

Roberts knew what was required of her that night. She had asked for only one thing in return: a photograph with His Royal Highness.

Epstein did the honors. Prince Andrew stood next to the teenager, placed his arm around her waist, and smiled; Ghislaine, off to the left, was beaming, too.

The photo was a cue. Epstein and Maxwell kissed Roberts good night and headed upstairs, telling Roberts and Prince Andrew to "have fun," leaving Roberts alone with the forty-one-year-old royal.[10]

"It was sexual intercourse and everything in between. It was disgusting," Roberts would later write in an unpublished memoir that would become part of the court record in her defamation suit against Maxwell. Roberts wrote that she tried to "put on a good show for" Andrew and was fearful of letting down Epstein and Maxwell. In a bathroom, Roberts slowly undressed and started to pour a bath. As the room filled with steam, the prince began to touch and kiss Roberts, at one point even licking her toes. After a while, the pair moved to a bedroom in the townhouse, where they had sex.*[11] When the encounter was over, the prince dressed and left.[12]

Roberts says that she retreated under her covers after taking a Xanax. Drugs like marijuana and speed were strictly forbidden inside the Epstein universe—he had fired a girl who was caught using cocaine—but for some reason, he had no objection to prescription drugs. "It was an escape drug," Roberts explained. She was already up to eight pills a day.

Years later, Prince Andrew denied meeting Roberts that night in London, claiming that he had simply gone out for pizza with his daughters. But a member of SO14, who spoke to the *New York Post* on the condition of anonymity, later undercut the prince's alibi, telling the paper that the prince had returned to Buckingham Palace late at night.[13]

---

* In her encounter with Prince Andrew, Roberts said that the prince did not use a condom; none of Epstein's friends ever did when they had sex with her, she has stated. Early on in her time with Epstein and Maxwell, Roberts has claimed that she suffered a miscarriage. She had not known she was pregnant and did not know whose baby it was. She has stated that Epstein and Maxwell made her agree not to tell anyone.

· · ·

JEFFREY EPSTEIN WANTED TO HEAR all about her night with the prince and was thrilled that Roberts had done as she was told.[14] Back in New York, he paid her a whopping $15,000 for the trip—a small price, in retrospect, for her silence.

Less than two months later, Roberts saw Prince Andrew again. He had come to New York City, his SO14 detail buttressed by a small contingent of DSS special agents and a plainclothes member of the NYPD. Andrew had come to see Roberts. This time, their sexual encounter took place in Epstein's massage room, and in the presence of Ghislaine Maxwell.

According to an account Roberts gave to Sharon Churcher, Epstein summoned Roberts to New York. When she arrived at Epstein's mansion, she found Andrew sitting in the library in a leather armchair. Behind him, on a desk, were nude photos of girls and young women, including one of her. "I don't think Andrew could have missed seeing it when he walked in," Roberts recalled. "Ghislaine had just given him a present, some kind of big blow-up toy that was his spitting image puppet. Mr. Prince was smiling ear to ear. It was like a kid going to Disney World."[15]

Johanna Sjoberg, the college student who was employed as an assistant to Maxwell, was perched on Andrew's lap.[16] "He recognized me though I don't know if he remembered my name," Virginia told Churcher. "We kissed each other on the cheek and Ghislaine placed me on his other knee. Ghislaine told me I should take him upstairs for a massage." In the massage room, classical music was playing softly on the speaker system. It was dark in the room, but Roberts noticed the presence of a painting, a six-foot oil canvas that depicted Roberts in a sexual position with another girl. "Andrew couldn't have missed it," Roberts recalled. "I was so embarrassed."

Just as she had been taught by Epstein and Maxwell, Roberts proceeded to give Andrew a massage that ended with oral sex.

•  •  •

THE RELATIONSHIP BETWEEN THE JEWISH boy from Brooklyn and the
Duke of York was mysterious and, to many, confusing. "Epstein had
a reputation as a mysterious wheeler-dealer and Ghislaine was his
constant companion in the demimonde," journalist Sharon Churcher
would later comment. "One pal of Fergie's told me Andrew was so
'innocent and naive' that he didn't realize he probably was being used
by the pair for his name and access to potential investors."[17]

Royal advisers should have warned Prince Andrew of the potential harm of cavorting with Epstein and Maxwell, the child of the
notorious Robert Maxwell. But Andrew had always had odd tastes in
friends and acquaintances—he was drawn to Middle Eastern oilmen
of dubious reputations, Kazakh oligarchs, and even the son of Libyan
strongman Muammar Gaddafi.[18]

Months before Andrew met Roberts, a contact of Churcher's
snapped a picture of a disheveled, sweaty Duke of York with Ghislaine at a hookers-and-pimps-themed party thrown by supermodel
Heidi Klum.* A year later, Andrew was photographed on a yacht with
Epstein in Thailand, surrounded by topless women.[19] Epstein also
arranged for him to make a midnight visit to a Miami club notorious
for its "theme" evenings that featured sadomasochistic scenes and
performers in cages. According to the club's greeter, Epstein phoned
to warn them that he was "sending over a friend, Andrew York, Prince
Charles's brother."[20] A friend of both Epstein's and Maxwell's remembered a dinner party in the East Seventy-First Street mansion that
was packed with women "clearly there to be their playthings."

According to that friend, who spoke on the condition of anonymity, Epstein and the prince were well matched—in their arrogance
and lack of charm, or what might be called "negative charisma":

---

* Prince Andrew has tried to suggest the picture was somehow faked, but years
later the original was handed to the FBI. The agency never has questioned the
photo's authenticity.

"They came across as bored billionaires trying to amuse themselves." The observer was put off by Epstein's seemingly obsequious behavior around Andrew: "I've been around royals enough times to know how you should behave around them and how most people do, and this was the opposite. It was like he wanted to prove he could do what he wanted and was so friendly with the prince that he could speak in this way. He was like, 'Oh, Andy, Andy.' He kept calling him Andy. It made me really uneasy."[21]

THE FOLLOWING YEAR, IN 2002 before the month of August, Roberts encountered Prince Andrew once again. This time the rendezvous took place at Epstein's Virgin Islands hideaway, and, unlike Roberts's previous encounters with the royal, it wasn't a small affair.[*]

The house party included seven or eight Russian girls brought by a modeling agent, Roberts told Sharon Churcher. "Jeffrey was so excited. He said, 'We're going to do a big photoshoot with you and the girls,'" said Roberts. "We were topless, and he had us in sexual positions. Then we're told to assemble in a big cabana. When I walked in, Andrew and Jeffrey were seated in chairs. 'Why don't you girls start kissing and having some fun!' Jeffrey and the prince were just sitting back, laughing."[22]

The next day, Andrew was gone—whisked back to the real world by his SO14 protective detail, which had spent the night aboard a small private boat.

---

* While Buckingham Palace has declined to confirm or deny that Andrew stopped off at Epstein's island on this trip to the Bahamas, the royal family has denied that the Duke of York had any form of sexual contact or relationship with Virginia Roberts and maintains that any claim to the contrary is false and without foundation. Additionally, Roberts Giuffre's allegations against Andrew were struck from the U.S. federal court record in 2015. In doing so, Judge Kenneth Marra denied her attempt to join a lawsuit against the U.S. government that challenged Epstein's non-prosecution agreement. "At this juncture in the proceedings, these lurid details are unnecessary," Judge Marra wrote in his order, issued in U.S. District Court in Florida, and concluded, "These unnecessary details shall be stricken."

Roberts's family, though in the dark, were less pleased. Her parents had initially supported her taking on a job with Epstein, but they were always wary of the billionaire. Tony Figueroa, on the other hand, hadn't suspected a thing: He used to drive her to Epstein's Palm Beach estate. But upon her return to the United States, Roberts implied that her stay in London had involved sex. Figueroa was devastated. "I was getting serious with Jenna [his nickname for Virginia]," he told Sharon Churcher years later. "I tried to get her to stop the trips with Jeffrey, but she didn't. I think she was scared."[23]

Scared was only part of the equation. As Roberts puts it, "Jeffrey was my master. I was totally in his power. He said that it was good for me to be set up with his rich friends. . . . He said that one day he'd marry me off to a billionaire. He said, 'You'll make a good mom one day.' I remember thinking I would never have a normal life again but, as sick as it sounds, I never thought of trying to escape."[24]

# 15

## FRIENDS IN HIGH PLACES

POLITICIANS NEED MONEY. TO WIN A POPULAR ELECTION, YOU NEED vast sums for travel, staff, opposition research, and advertising. Which is to say, you need donors. The political action committees, lobbyists, and billionaires who facilitate large-scale donations can mean the difference between political hopes and election day despair.

It comes at a cost, of course. The six- and seven-figure amounts poured into campaigns and political party slush funds are down payments for future favors. Politicians kiss babies to convince the public of their benevolence; they kiss the rings of the financiers and moneymen to turn cold hard cash into terms in office.

Politicians don't stop needing money just because they have served their time in office. It's surprisingly easy to get accustomed to being waited on hand and foot. A former federal agent described this as "open-the-door syndrome": once someone reaches the pinnacle of power, they no longer want to open a door for themselves—they expect doors to be held open for them.

Jeffrey Epstein liked to hold open doors. Collecting famous friends was integral to his business model. The more success he found as a financier to the A list, the more intimate he became with them. He wasn't invited to their mansions for a Sunday dinner or to meet the wife and kids. Rather, he hosted parties in Manhattan, in Palm Beach, or on Little St. James, where these men could get away from their families and perhaps participate in activities their loved ones would find distasteful, if not wholly shocking.[1]

Virginia Roberts remembered how Epstein would joke about all the favors he was owed. "He's got everybody in his pocket, and he would laugh about [that]."[2] Key to Epstein's control were the secrets he kept in his black address book, the names and numbers of politicians and decision makers from all over the world. More important, his black book included aides and office chiefs—the gatekeepers who filtered communications with men of power to make sure that only the most important calls came through. President Bill Clinton was prominently represented in Epstein's book, which listed twenty-one different ways to contact Clinton, from cellphone numbers to his home number in Chappaqua, a suburb of New York City.[3]

JUST HOW JEFFREY EPSTEIN AND Bill Clinton became friends remains a mystery. It is known that on September 28, 1993, Bill and Hillary Clinton invited to the White House a group of donors who had contributed funds to the building's renovation.[4] The reception culminated in an intimate tour of the refurbished 1600 Pennsylvania Avenue, followed by dessert and an address from the president and the First Lady. Among those being thanked that evening were Jeffrey Epstein and Ghislaine Maxwell.

Over the years Epstein had donated to both the Democratic and Republican parties. Years later, after Bill Clinton had left office and established the Clinton Global Initiative in 2005, Maxwell persuaded Epstein to write a six-figure check to the foundation.

According to one source, Clinton and Ghislaine became "super close," though there was never any indication that the two were sexually involved, despite published reports.[5] It has been suggested that she first introduced Clinton to Epstein.

Virginia Roberts met Bill Clinton in 2002, when she was seventeen, a year older than she was when she met Prince Andrew. According to an account by journalist Sharon Churcher, Roberts was in the Dominican Republic with Epstein and Maxwell when Maxwell—for whom Epstein had provided flying lessons and purchased a helicopter—picked up the former president. Roberts recalled Clinton arriving with the Secret Service in tow. At some point, Epstein informed Roberts that he and the former president were "good friends." When Roberts inquired further, Epstein laughed and told Roberts that Clinton "owes me some favors."[6]

On the night of Clinton's arrival, the group dined together. "Jeffrey was at the head of the table. Bill was at his left. I sat across from him. Emmy Tayler, Ghislaine's blond British assistant, sat at my right. Ghislaine was at Bill's left and at the left of Ghislaine two olive-skinned brunettes who had flown in with us from New York. I'd never met them before. I'd say they were no older than seventeen, very innocent-looking."

Clinton did not seem interested in the brunettes, according to Roberts.

For all the media speculation about Clinton's friendship with Epstein, Roberts says that she never had sex with the ex-president—though, she says, it would have been hard for Clinton to overlook the seedier aspects of Epstein's life, considering the "photos of naked girls" that covered "three desks in the living area of the villa." Clinton would downplay his relationship with Epstein. In a 2002 interview with *New York* magazine, Clinton described Epstein as "a highly successful financier and a committed philanthropist with a keen sense of global markets and an in-depth knowledge of twenty-first-century science. I especially appreciated his insights and generosity during the recent trip to Africa to work on democratization, empowering the poor, citizen service, and combating HIV/AIDS."[7] That trip, undertaken in 2002 with actor Kevin Spacey and comedian

Chris Tucker, was one of the flights Clinton took on Epstein's private plane.[8]

Another world leader with ties to Epstein is former Israeli prime minister Ehud Barak.

Epstein had access to Israel's leaders through the major Jewish organizations and philanthropies with which he was affiliated, including UJA-Federation of New York, Hillel International, National Council of Jewish Women, Friends of Israel Defense Forces, Jewish National Fund, and YIVO Institute for Jewish Research.

In 1998, some twenty of America's most significant Jewish businessmen met to create the Mega Group, a collective aimed at defining Judaism for a new century and funding causes like Holocaust education and Zionism. The Mega Group included Steven Spielberg, Charles Bronfman, and Ronald Lauder; Les Wexner was a founding member.[9]

Out of public service for the first time in his life, Barak entered the world of large-scale projects and high-paying investments—a world in which Jeffrey Epstein featured prominently. According to *The Times of Israel*, Shimon Peres, another former Israeli prime minister with ties to the Mega Group, introduced Ehud Barak to Jeffrey Epstein sometime in 2001 after being voted out of office.[10] *The New York Times* has reported that he received some $2.3 million in grants from Leslie Wexner's foundation between 2004 to 2006.

Barak's ties to Epstein received attention in January 2016 when a photographer for the UK tabloid the *Daily Mail* captured an image of Barak entering Epstein's townhouse while seeming to cover his face with what appeared to be a scarf.

Barak's Epstein connection reared its head again in 2020, during a legal case involving Alan Dershowitz, who identified Barak and Les Wexner as two men to whom Virginia Roberts alleged Epstein had trafficked her. The claims were made in previously sealed depositions that were collected in a 2016 defamation suit, according to Dershowitz lawyer Howard Cooper.

While Barak has acknowledged visiting Epstein's homes in New

York and Little St. James, he insisted, in a statement provided for this book, that he has never met Roberts. Barak said that Roberts was already in Australia by the time Barak met Epstein. Barak said he visited the island only once, in 2016, for lunch, where he says he was accompanied by his wife and a security detail and stayed only for a few hours.

# 16

## THE SPIDER

THE WORLD OF JEFFREY EPSTEIN WAS ONE OF BREATHTAKING WEALTH and power. There weren't many men in the world who entertained former presidents and prime ministers in lavish homes on private islands. Fewer still could fly those VIPs out on a fleet of aircraft that rivaled the armadas owned by Third World dictators; indeed, more money traveled through Jeffrey Epstein's hands daily than were in the national treasuries of many developing nations.

Many aspects of Epstein's life were extraordinary and unusual, starting with his and Maxwell's efforts to recruit a stream of young girls, brainwash them into servitude, and conceal the whole reprehensible operation from the outside world. It took scores of assistants, servants, pilots, and coconspirators to keep this apparatus running smoothly; any one of them could be a liability. Keeping the demented machine working was a full-time endeavor. It's remarkable that both Epstein and Ghislaine believed that it was a sustainable lifestyle and that they were above the law even while they knew the risk involved.

Epstein had always likened himself to a spy, or at the very least an international man of mystery. He had an Austrian passport with a fake name that listed a residence in Saudi Arabia. Possession of a false passport is a felony under 18 U.S. Code 1543, but ostensibly the passport was given to Epstein for his personal protection when traveling in the Middle East, to be used if he was ever kidnapped by terrorists.[1] A former girlfriend reported that he slept with a holstered gun by the side of his bed.[2]

Doubtful as it may be that Epstein was really an intelligence officer, he did develop a surveillance apparatus that would make any John le Carré spymaster proud. He recorded his closest friends and possibly his future adversaries perpetrating crimes against children. As long as he kept this damning archive, Epstein was confident that no one would turn against him.

According to Virginia Roberts, every single room in Epstein's several properties was wired for sound and visuals.[3] There were images, printed and secured; there were video rooms where the incriminating acts were filmed and safeguarded.[4] Epstein did little to hide the fact that anyone who passed through his doors could be added to his treasure trove. Ghislaine even bragged about it to her friend Christina Oxenberg.[5] Years earlier, Epstein had warned Maria Farmer, whom he molested along with her sixteen-year-old sister Annie in separate incidents in 1996, that the whole house was wired with pinhole cameras, and he even took her into the TV-filled room where they were monitored. "I looked on the cameras, and I saw toilet, toilet, bed, bed, toilet, bed. I'm like 'I am never going to use the restroom here, and I'm never going to sleep here,'" Maria Farmer remembered. At one point, she asked what he did with the footage; he responded, "I keep it. I keep everything in my safe."[6] He showed another young woman the camera room that he had in the mansion in New York and told her, "This is where I can make tapes that will protect me in the future."[7]

The abuse had become systematized.


A STUDENT AT THE SCHOOL near Epstein's Palm Beach home, Courtney Wild fit all the criteria of an Epstein target: She was pretty, white, and fourteen years old. She still had braces on her teeth. Like Roberts, she came from a troubled home.[8]

Wild was recruited in 2002 by a friend and told she could make good money hanging out with an old rich guy in Palm Beach. Wild visited Epstein at his home, arriving in a taxi by herself, and told him she was eighteen; that initial visit soon turned into regular visits. She was taught to give him massages, which, as with other recruits, turned sexual.[9]

Wild soon began to recruit others to bring into Epstein's web, eventually totaling seventy to eighty girls. Some, ranging in age from fourteen to sixteen, were lured to Epstein's Palm Beach mansion by word of mouth. Each girl was promised $200 to $300 per massage.[10] It was a fortune for a Florida teen from lower-middle-class and broken home circumstances; it was even a fortune for many of their parents.

Most parents of Epstein victims didn't ask many questions, and the girls were too ashamed or too frightened to tell anyone. Who would have believed them anyway? Jeffrey Epstein was rich. His friends included presidents and professors. He was above suspicion.

The problem, though, was that as more and more girls entered his web, the older girls became expendable.

By the time fourteen-year-old Courtney Wild met Epstein in 2002, Virginia Roberts was nearing her eighteenth birthday. Roberts was no longer of a desirable age for Epstein, but he had found new uses for her.

Epstein was nearing his fiftieth birthday, and it was becoming clear that he was destined to be a bachelor: No matter how many underage girls he could pay for sex, he was alone. Ghislaine was his partner in crime—not his wife. Suddenly, the man who hated kids became obsessed with having offspring.

Epstein made Roberts an offer he was certain she wouldn't

refuse—he'd furnish her with a mansion and a monthly stipend if she'd bear his child. There was, of course, a catch. Roberts would sign all parental rights away to Jeffrey and Ghislaine. She could help with childcare, but only as long as Epstein decided to maintain a relationship with her.[11]

The proposition disgusted Roberts, who told journalist Sharon Churcher, "It was a smack in the face." It became the overdue wake-up call she needed to plan an escape.

Six months later, Epstein sent Roberts to Thailand, purportedly to locate a supply of young girls who could be imported to New York, Palm Beach, and the Virgin Islands. Roberts had no intention of doing any such thing. Instead, she convinced Epstein that she could justify the cost of the trip by getting advanced massage training. She was buying time.

During her time in Thailand, a friend from a massage class Roberts enrolled in there invited her to watch a martial arts competition, a Muay Thai fight. One of the fighters, an Australian martial arts trainer named Robert Giuffre, caught her eye. It was love at first sight. They were married seven days later at a Buddhist temple.[12]

Roberts wondered how she'd break the news to Epstein. She knew he could hunt her down and harm the couple if he wanted. But she simply told him that she wouldn't be returning, and moved to Australia as Virginia Roberts Giuffre.

Roberts was relieved to be rid of Epstein, Maxwell, Prince Andrew, and the mansions and private jets that came with them.

She hoped never to hear from them again.


A HUMAN BEING IN EPSTEIN'S universe was worth only what he or she could offer him. Since Virginia Roberts had outlived her usefulness, her defection caused little concern.

Roberts was swiftly replaced by others. One was Michelle Licata, a sixteen-year-old from Palm Beach County who had been lured to Epstein's mansion by a school friend. When she first met him, Licata recalled, Epstein made her uncomfortable by calling her "beautiful and sexy and gorgeous." That turned into a back rub, which of course turned into something more.

No matter how many beautiful girls he had, though, he wasn't satisfied. "He wanted as many girls as I could get him," Licata said. "It was never enough."[13]

# 17

## BURN EVERYTHING

JEFFREY EPSTEIN DID NOT TRUST THE MEDIA. UNLIKE SOME POWERFUL people, Epstein knew that drawing attention in the press would only serve to jeopardize his criminal enterprise. He was agoraphobic, avoiding New York and Palm Beach's charity gala scene. He even avoided dining in public, where he'd be easy prey for the paparazzi. Instead, he brought New York's elite to his East Seventy-First Street home for lavish dinners, where he could control everything from the menu—leafy greens, protein, grains, no carbs—to the thermostat. He liked the house to be cold.[1]

Despite his best efforts to avoid the press, however, he landed in the public eye in 2003 after his trip to Africa with Bill Clinton, which included stops in Nigeria, Ghana, Mozambique, and Rwanda. Suddenly he was a target for tabloid journalists.

British-born Vicky Ward was among the journalists who wanted to find out the truth about the mystery man. As she would write in *Vanity Fair*, "He makes it sound as though his job combines the roles of real estate agent, accountant, lawyer, money manager, trustee, and confidant. But as with Jay Gatsby, myths and rumor swirl around Epstein."[2]

She noted, among her details, that Epstein had a paperback copy of the Marquis de Sade's *The Misfortunes of Virtue* on his desk. She did not mention the author's perverse sadism and sex crimes against children.

Ward's article for *Vanity Fair* wasn't the usual puff piece on Epstein, like the story that *New York* magazine had published months earlier under the headline JEFFREY EPSTEIN: INTERNATIONAL MONEY-MAN OF MYSTERY. Ward's article, by contrast, explored some of Epstein's opaque financial transactions, including hints about insider trading and stock manipulation, and described him as "a man who loves women—lots of them, mostly young."[3] But other material from Ward's reporting effort never made it into the final draft.

Following the trail of rumors, Ward managed to track down Maria and Annie Farmer in 2003. When Epstein learned that the Farmer sisters, his former employees, had spoken to *Vanity Fair,* he and Maxwell reportedly embarked on a campaign of terror: They called art clients of Maria and others seeking to destroy her professional reputation. According to her civil complaint years later, Maxwell called on behalf of Epstein and threatened "to burn all your art. . . . Your career is burned." Soon, Maxwell was threatening Farmer's life, too, saying, "I know you go to the West Side Highway all the time. While you're out there, just be really careful because there are a lot of ways to die there."

But the threats weren't enough to halt Ward's progress on the article, and Epstein had to take matters into his own hands. He traveled to the headquarters of Condé Nast, *Vanity Fair*'s publisher, on Forty-Second Street near Times Square to talk to Graydon Carter, the magazine's legendary editor.[4]

It was as easy as that. The passages about the Farmer sisters were duly removed from the final version of the article, leaving Ward livid; the Farmers had "very bravely" decided "to go on the record," after all. Years later, in 2019, Carter would tell *The New York Times* that he "respected the work Vicky Ward did at *Vanity Fair,* but unfortunately her recounting of the facts around the Epstein article is inaccurate. There were not three sources on the record, and therefore this aspect of the story did not meet our legal and editorial standards."[5]

Ward had little choice but to accept the cuts; Carter had been a fixture at the magazine for over a decade, and his word was law. She didn't raise the issue again until years later, when Epstein was unmasked.

Once again, Epstein had skirted exposure, thanks to his influence.


WITHOUT MEDIA SCRUTINY, JEFFREY EPSTEIN was effectively unstoppable—until the stepmother of one young victim finally dialed Palm Beach police two years later, in March 2005.

There was no end in sight for the young women caught inside his web. A.H., who does not want her identity to be made public, was one such girl—and one of the first to tell her story to Palm Beach detectives in 2005. She was one of Epstein's favorites: "I was in about as deep as you can get," she would recall.

When A.H. was sixteen, she needed money for a camping trip in Maine that summer. A friend knew how A.H. could earn enough in two hours to buy a plane ticket: Give some old guy a massage. Two hundred bucks for forty-five minutes. "I wasn't naive enough to think that he was going to pay me $200 just for nothing," A.H. told detectives, but she didn't know what exactly would happen. She decided she would go and "feel it out." If she didn't like it, she figured, she'd just leave.

A.H. and her friend drove to Epstein's mansion a few nights later. When the two girls entered the kitchen through the service entrance, they found that the staff already knew their names. "Oh, we're so happy to see you," she recalled them saying. "Jeff will be ready in a second."

A.H. met several young women there, including Sarah Kellen, one of Epstein's assistants. A.H. also encountered another girl, who she later realized was "one of the girls that he bought to have sex with him."

The two teens went upstairs, where Epstein paid the friend $400 for bringing A.H. The friend then told A.H. she'd be waiting downstairs.

The massage started with Epstein wearing only a towel and A.H. fully clothed. Epstein coaxed her into partially undressing. Epstein removed his towel and touched A.H. and masturbated as she continued to massage him. It was over when he "finished," she said.

"I had a problem with it," she said of that first instance of abuse. "But $200 for forty minutes? That was a lot for a sixteen-year-old girl making six bucks an hour."

A.H. never did go to Maine. Instead, she started "working" for Epstein "every single day he was in the country." She went to his Palm Beach mansion hundreds of times over the next two years. Epstein assistant Sarah Kellen called her to coordinate the appointments.

Little by little, Epstein convinced A.H. to go further sexually. And the more she did, or allowed Epstein to do to her, the more A.H. got paid. Not only money but gifts like movie tickets, lingerie, a trip to New York City—even a bright blue Dodge Neon.

Epstein once asked A.H. to perform a sex act on Nadia Marcinkova, one of Epstein's victims who was later called "a potential co-conspirator" by Palm Beach police. A.H. refused. When she said no, "he flashed $200 in front of me. He said, 'Do it for five minutes and you get this.'" A.H. acquiesced. At times the sessions left A.H. so physically worn out that she'd hardly be able to walk afterward. "It was disgusting what I did for money," she told police later.

She was adamant, however, that Epstein never penetrate her with his penis. He did anyway. At the end of a session that included Nadia, Epstein pushed A.H. down onto a massage table and entered her. The teenager yelled, "What are you doing?" Epstein stopped and replied nonchalantly, "Oh, I just wanted Nadia to see this." A.H. was paid $1,000 for the act.

A.H.'s visits to the Palm Beach villa did not always involve sex. Epstein seemed to enjoy simply having naked teenagers in his house. "Sometimes he just asked me to take off my clothes and he'd have work to do. He'd be sitting at his desk or something and I'd just be naked there watching television or reading a book," she told Palm Beach detective Joe Recarey during their extensive taped interview, according to transcripts. "Sometimes he wanted to just watch TV or read, and he'd lay in his bed and he asked me to take my clothes off and lay with him. And that's it, not touch him or anything. And I'd get paid $300 for taking a nap for twenty minutes. Sometimes he just invited me over for breakfast or dinner or to use the swimming pool and I'd get paid for that, too."

A.H. said in all the time she "worked" for Epstein, she never reciprocated his sexual touches. But that didn't stop him from asking. Toward the end of her senior year, A.H. returned the car and stopped seeing Epstein. She said she ended it because he continued to push her for sex. She began to fear for her safety. "I wanted to be able to walk away from this thing saying that I never did that, and I'm glad that I did." She was tracked down by Palm Beach detectives and cooperated with their investigation.

In a police raid on Epstein's mansion in Palm Beach, A.H.'s high school transcript was discovered, along with disturbing items, like an Amazon receipt for a book called *SlaveCraft: Roadmaps for Erotic Servitude*.


IN THE CASES OF YOUNG women like Virginia Roberts and A.H., Jeffrey Epstein's abuse took place over months or even years; in other cases Epstein knew victims in concentrated periods, though the trauma would be lasting.

"Jane Doe 15" encountered Epstein only over a single five-day period, but she would spell out the horror in testimony years later in a 2019 civil suit.

It was on a high school field trip to New York City in 2004 that Jane Doe 15 became ensnared in Epstein's web. Doe's sister, an eighteen-year-old model who lived in the city, already knew Epstein. Doe was invited to the financier's Manhattan townhouse. Though Epstein was not present, the grooming nonetheless began on his behalf: She was greeted by one of his secretaries, "a woman approximately in her mid-twenties with light-brown hair," who then showed the teen around the mansion, took photos of her, and gave her an iPod. Epstein liked her sister, the secretary said, and he wanted to meet her, too.

The secretary later contacted her and said that Epstein was "excited by the photos," and that he liked helping girls from "difficult circumstances," just like her.

Jane Doe 15 had not had many breaks in her life. According to court documents, "Jane Doe 15 had grown up poor. Her parents divorced when she was young, and her mother had moved from place to place numerous times during Jane Doe 15's childhood. When she first met Epstein, she was living in a very small town in the Midwest."[6]

Catching the attention of a person of wealth and power seemed like a lucky break. Epstein's secretary invited Doe and her sister to a magic show in Las Vegas, followed by a stay at Zorro Ranch. Enticed by the "thrilling opportunity," as recounted in her legal complaint, the fifteen-year-old talked her mother into letting her go.

The two girls attended the show in Las Vegas, along with an undetermined number of other young girls invited by Epstein, and even got to meet the performer backstage. "For a girl from the Midwest, all of this was like a dream come true," she would later state in her legal complaint. It was a thrilling taste of a world filled with private jets, meet and greets with celebrities, and beautiful girls.

But the dream was soon to turn into a nightmare. When Doe 15 finally met Epstein at his ranch, the first thing he did was show her the bedroom and tell her to get on the floor. "Feel it," he commanded, according to the complaint. He boasted that the entire floor was covered by Tempur-Pedic mattresses. Doe 15 was uncomfortable and laughed nervously; she didn't even know what a Tempur-Pedic mattress was. Epstein then explained to her that "he liked to have women sleep at his feet." Jane Doe 15 did not understand what he was saying or why, but it "made her immediately think of slaves."

Although her instincts told her that no good could come of this, other factors were working to normalize the situation. Epstein told her that the seat she chose on the plane was the very seat favored by his "good friend Bill Clinton." And there was a young model on the same plane who had just that month been on the cover of a magazine, which Jane Doe 15 found reassuring. She thought, "If she's here, it must be okay."

Then again, a red-haired woman working for Epstein "told Jane Doe 15 that the water jets in the hot tub were positioned so that many girls could use them to masturbate at the same time," according to the complaint. And sure enough, there were other young girls around, who could also ride horses and ATVs or use the pool and that same hot tub at their leisure.

Jane Doe 15 had not packed a swimsuit for the trip, so when she used the pool she wore her underwear. While she was swimming, Epstein approached the pool and demanded Doe 15 hug him—only to criticize her undergarments, saying they would have to get her new ones. Later, Doe 15 said she was "deeply embarrassed" when the red-haired woman asked her about her sexual experience. She had none.

The following day, Doe 15 reported to the main house, where the red-haired woman announced she would be giving Doe a massage. Doe was ordered to strip naked and lie on a table. According to the complaint, Doe was "deeply uncomfortable" to see cameras poking from the ceiling. But everything and everyone around her told her this was normal.

The massage that followed was anything but. According to the complaint, the red-haired woman "massaged" Doe's genitals with her tongue without asking permission, causing Doe "great discomfort." After "what felt like a substantial amount of time, the red-haired woman stopped, and apologetically told Jane Doe 15 that she could tell Jane Doe 15 had not enjoyed the contact." But, she continued, Epstein wanted to give Jane Doe an orgasm.

The next day, Doe 15 was again called to the main house. She was led to an upstairs bedroom, where Epstein was lying on a bed in nothing but a bathrobe. He commanded her to give him a massage. As soon as she began the body rub, he opened his robe and exposed himself. Epstein became frustrated, the complaint states, when Doe

15, an inexperienced minor, didn't know what he expected her to do. Instead, he pushed her to the floor and pressed a very large vibrator against her, "for what felt like an eternity," according to the complaint, causing Doe pain and confusion. Eventually, she realized he was expecting some kind of reaction, so she faked an orgasm.

Seemingly satisfied, Epstein brought her over to the window, saying that first orgasms are "amazing" and that "he wanted to show her how beautiful the world is." He also told her to take time for herself that night to cry, that it "would be beneficial for her growth." Instead, she went out alone on an ATV and drove it into a tree, "realizing that she could die out there and no one would care."

The abuse was still not over. The next day, Epstein gave Doe 15 a "gift"—new underwear—and forced her to model it so he could take photographs of her. Doe 15 was "terrified," according to the complaint, and she began having trouble breathing. Epstein "led her through breathing exercises" to calm her down and then changed the subject, asking her about her plans for the future. She told him she wanted to study biochemistry. Epstein asked Doe how much money she thought he should give her. "I had no idea how to respond to a billionaire who had just raped me," Doe's legal complaint stated. "I was being asked to quantify in monetary terms what had been taken from me." Epstein ended up writing Doe a check for $5,000 made out to the college she wanted to attend, and he also sent her off with several hundred dollars in cash.

The life-shattering experience happened over a course of just a few days. Doe never saw Epstein again—although he did later invite her to Little St. James, according to the complaint. She made up excuses to avoid going.

"It was clear from the time I spent with Epstein that something was very wrong with his lifestyle," she said. "We were not hidden."

# 18

## WEIRD SCIENCE

OF COURSE, JEFFREY EPSTEIN WOULDN'T BE CONTENT WITH THE TYPE of midlife crisis that plagues men of lesser means or more conventional interests. He didn't have to reach into his IRA to buy a Harley-Davidson or pursue a romantic affair in a doomed attempt to recapture his youth. Jeffrey Epstein's midlife funk took the form of nostalgia—a longing for his Brooklyn roots.

In 2002, New York historian Charles Denson published *Coney Island: Lost and Found,* a three-hundred-page coffee table book about the iconic neighborhood in Brooklyn. Denson had grown up around Coney Island, experiencing such legendary attractions as the Cyclone and Thunderbolt roller coasters, the Parachute Jump, and Steeplechase Park. The book was a tribute to those memories, illustrated with archival photos, maps, and images of memorabilia. The book caught Epstein's eye and tugged at his heart.

Authors often receive letters and calls from adoring fans or angry readers, but in 2004, Denson received several calls from a phone number with a 340—U.S. Virgin Islands—area code. A woman with a British accent—believed to have been Ghislaine—called and said, "Mr. Epstein would like to know about whether you remember an

Epstein on West Thirty-First Street." The name didn't ring a bell with Denson, but he told the caller that he'd check on it. When he tried to call back, though, he received an error message stating that the number was nonexistent.

Epstein, it seemed, was starting to wonder about who would remember him—and whether he would leave behind a legacy.[1]

THERE WERE NO HEIRS ON Jeffrey Epstein's horizon. Virginia Roberts had spurned his offer to carry a child, and Ghislaine Maxwell was out of the question. There was no one to whom he could leave his fortune—no one, potentially, who would even remember him.

He had a vision, though. Science had always been a passion of Epstein's, and he had given enough money to various academics and universities to feel that they owed him something. Reportedly, he told one scientist that he was financing efforts to identify a mysterious particle that would trigger the sensation that someone was observing you.

Other experiments were more mundane, like financing a neuroscientist to examine the heart rate effects of playing music to premature babies. In a 2017 interview with a writer from *Science* magazine, Epstein said, "I'm not more than a hobbyist in science but money I understand, [and] I'm a pretty good mathematician." He added that what interested him was science's "rarefied peaks."

Epstein's idea for his legacy was even more fanciful. Beginning around 2001, Epstein started confiding to acquaintances that he wanted to seed the human race with his DNA by impregnating women at his vast New Mexico ranch. He would recruit some of the world's top biochemists, physicists, and others to turn his dream of a vast baby farm into reality.[2] The wild idea was revealed in a July 2019 article in *The New York Times* published shortly after Epstein's arrest.

According to the piece, Epstein even had a site picked out for his "baby farm." Zorro Ranch, his 33,000-acre New Mexico lair purchased in 1993, was the obvious location to serve as a laboratory for a strange and secretive project. It was equipped with ample outbuildings to serve as dormitory space. An underground room reportedly used as a private strip club could be transformed into a clinic for natural and caesarean births.[3]

He scoured his black book to see who in the world of research owed him a favor.


THE LIST OF SCIENTISTS THAT Epstein mingled with read like a who's who of intellectual heavy hitters. It included Nobel Prize–winning physicist Murray Gell-Mann, paleontologist and evolutionary biologist Stephen Jay Gould, and Oliver Sacks, the world-renowned neurologist and bestselling author. Epstein also had access to George M. Church, a molecular engineer who has worked to identify genes that could be altered to create superior humans; Nobel laureate and MIT theoretical physicist Frank Wilczek; and even the one and only Stephen Hawking.

To lure these brilliant minds into his scheme, Epstein invited them to lavish dinner parties at his East Seventy-First Street mansion, where Dom Pérignon was served by the bucket and meals were prepared by Michelin-starred chefs. He even flew the scientists, with whom he had established friendships over the course of several years, to Little St. James, where he took them on a submarine he had hired for the occasion.[4] And he hosted gourmet lunches at Harvard University's Program for Evolutionary Dynamics, known as the PED.[5] Jeffrey Epstein had helped launch the PED in 2003 with a $6.5 million donation; the center focused on the study of the fundamental mathematical principles that guide evolution, including the evolution of cancer, viruses, and economics.[6]

The lofty goal of the PED was to rid the world of such diverse ailments as cancer and "selfishness," though Jeffrey Epstein hoped the dividends from his investment would focus on his project; everything about him was transactional and quid pro quo. He believed there was something extraordinary in his gene pool; Dershowitz

recalled that he talked about it a lot at Harvard. As guests were mingling over lunch, Dershowitz remembered, Epstein hijacked the
conversation to talk about how humankind could be improved genet-
ically.[7] His goal, one scientist remembered, was to impregnate twenty
women at a time. Some expressed surprise that Epstein, whose
extended family had perished in pogroms and later in the Nazi gas
chambers, could embrace the idea of improving the human population through genetic engineering and controlled breeding.[8] But in
another sense, it was entirely in character: his desire to build a birth-
ing facility in the New Mexican desert was just his latest bid for
pure, unadulterated power.[9]

Epstein had one strictly enforced rule for his cabal of pet scientists: Dissent was forbidden. Punishment for disagreeing with
Epstein, or, worse, ridiculing one of his notions, was banishment.
According to *The New York Times,* Steven Pinker, a noted Harvard
cognitive psychologist, was reportedly kicked out of the club when
he contested Epstein's theory that global starvation relief efforts and
better medical care were dangerous since they would lead to
overpopulation.

Most of Epstein's friends in the science world, perhaps placated
by his open wallet, seemingly kept their mouths shut about the financier's strange ideas and what they observed of his unorthodox lifestyle until much later.[10]


EPSTEIN, LIKE OTHER PREDATORS, SEEMED to have a sixth sense for
danger.

In the mid-2000s, it is believed that Epstein received a tipoff
about local Florida authorities ramping up an investigation into his
activities with young girls. Epstein retained a private investigative
firm to find out what he might expect; they in turn reached out to
Stephen Davis, a retired NYPD captain who had a boutique private
detective shop of his own. He was asked to do a "countersurveillance
job" on Epstein's East Seventy-First Street home "to see if anyone

was watching the place." In an interview for this book with journalist Philip Messing, Davis said that the request raised red flags. He was concerned that an authorized court-ordered investigative effort was already under way by a police or federal agency, since Epstein's "reputation for liking young girls was already out there. I said to myself, 'This is not a personal [matter], or a corporate, or a marital sort of thing,'" Davis recalled.

He didn't take the job.[11]

# PART FOUR

# THE EMPERORS HAVE NO CLOTHES

I was told Epstein "belonged to intelligence"
and to leave it alone.
—ALEX ACOSTA

# 19

## ROYAL PALM HIGH

IN 1877 A POST OFFICE WAS OPENED IN THE SLEEPY SETTLEMENT OF
Palm Beach, on a narrow sandy island off the Florida mainland, and
the first resort, the Coconut Grove, opened a few years later. Over
the years the former swamp grew in size and prominence as a preferred destination for the rich and famous. By the turn of the twenty-
first century, the town boasted one of the richest zip codes in the
United States. The median income for the eight-thousand-plus residents of Palm Beach was nearly twice as high as that of the remain-
der of the Sunshine State.

The town's wealthiest denizens tended to live on Palm Beach
Island. The 3.75-square-mile slice of land is dotted with mansions,
most famously Mar-a-Lago, built by the cereal heiress Marjorie Mer-
riweather Post in 1927, but many other estates as well, often designed
with Mediterranean themes, with grounds covered with fauna and
hidden behind high fences. It was where the rich came to live and
play, and it still is. In 2007, seafront estates started at close to $5 mil-
lion.[1] Condos were slightly less expensive.

Protecting this affluent community was the job of the Palm
Beach Police Department, or PBPD, which numbered around a

hundred employees. There were more than seven officers per thousand residents—more than three times the state average; the department made twice as many arrests as the state average. The PBPD's organizational chart included a uniformed patrol force, and the department fielded several specialized units, including a motorcycle unit, a special operations and hostage rescue unit, a dive team, an all-terrain vehicle squad, and a business relations team. The detective bureau investigated serious crimes, including reports of sexual abuse and exploitation. The special investigations unit consisted of the department's top detectives, tasked with handling the town's most delicate law enforcement matters.

JEFFREY EPSTEIN'S TWO-STORY HOUSE AT 358 El Brillo Way was built in 1950 on a lot measuring nearly three-quarters of an acre, according to county property records. Designed by noted Florida architect John L. Volk, the five-bedroom, seven-and-a-half-bath home is located on the opposite end of the Estate Section from Mar-a-Lago on one of the area's famous "El" streets. Just a third of a mile in length, the street stretches between the Intracoastal Waterway and the Atlantic Ocean.[2]

The house, which Epstein had purchased in 1990 under a limited liability corporation called Laurel Inc., contains a generous 14,223 square feet of living space, records showed.[3] There were a pool and a boat deck out back with a view of "the lake," as locals called it. In Epstein's time, the garage was packed with three Mercedes sedans, along with a light green Harley-Davidson motorcycle, leaving no room for Epstein's black Suburban and black Escalade that he was forced to park in the driveway.[4] The interior of the five-bedroom house looked like a combination of a bordello, man cave, and medical office. It contained four massage tables, as well as, inexplicably, a fully equipped dentist's chair and cart, which was stocked with drills and other instruments, as well as a dentist's lamp. He had pictures with quotes from Ralph Waldo Emerson and *Star Trek*'s Mr.

Spock hanging on the walls, in addition to the ever-present images of nude or partially clothed females.[5]

How Epstein's serial abuse of underage girls could continue for so long without a parent, doctor, member of the clergy, or even a boyfriend walking into police headquarters to file a complaint is difficult for us to fathom, but the social mores of Palm Beach may be part of the explanation. Epstein's fondness for young girls was the town's worst-kept secret. Yet people in Palm Beach tended to keep to themselves. Wealth demanded privacy, and what happened inside the Mediterranean-styled mansions was a matter of discretion. Roger Stone was one neighbor. The notorious political fixer for Richard Nixon and Donald Trump would later write in his 2016 book *The Clintons' War on Women* that after Trump once visited Epstein's Palm Beach home, the future president looked at the girls hanging around the pool and said, "The swimming pool was filled with beautiful young girls. 'How nice,' I thought. 'He let the neighborhood kids use his pool.'"[6]

Epstein's address was known to many girls who attended Royal Palm Beach Community High School, known locally as Royal Palm. The student body of Royal Palm was diverse, including many students from lower-income and single-parent homes. In 2020, more than 80 percent of the student body was non-white, and almost 70 percent of students were considered "economically disadvantaged."[7] Children of Palm Beach's wealthy families tended to go elsewhere—to exclusive private schools.

Word got around to girls at Royal Palm that Epstein was an easy source of cash. If you needed money to buy clothes at the mall or to help pay the bills at home, you knew where to go.

Epstein's estate, fourteen miles east of Royal Palm, was a universe away, and it was a challenge to get to if you weren't old enough to drive. It took three buses, with often irregular schedules, and the trip could take hours. Nonetheless, many made the journey. The traffic of girls coming in and out of Epstein's house was nonstop in the early 2000s.

In 2003, the Palm Beach Police Department received reports from some concerned neighbors that strange young women were coming in and out of 358 El Brillo Way at odd hours. In response, marked and unmarked police cruisers began patrolling the area. According to an account from Palm Beach police chief Michael Reiter, when officers approached "three or four" of the women they discovered that they were over the age of eighteen. The women explained that they were employed to do office work for Epstein. Without observing evidence of a crime or even probable cause to escalate the matter, police decided against further action.[8] Epstein's activities continued.

Two years later, however, a new call to police would set in motion a chain of events—a law enforcement and media saga with numerous twists and turns—that would play out over the next fifteen years and ultimately lead to Epstein's undoing.

In early March 2005, two female students at Royal Palm were involved in a fistfight on school grounds. S.G.* was a fourteen-year-old girl of Cuban descent whose family's low income qualified her for school-provided meals. One day S.G. was called a "whore" by another girl. S.G's teacher searched her purse and found $300 in brand-new twenty-dollar bills. Suspecting the girl was selling drugs, the teacher phoned the girl's mother. S.G. refused to explain the source of the money. The school summoned a psychologist. S.G. eventually broke down and told the doctor about what was happening at El Brillo Way.[9]

Accounts differ on what happened next. According to *The Palm Beach Post,* on March 15, 2005, Palm Beach Police Department detective Michele Pagan received a call from a woman who refused to leave her name or a callback number but told the detective that S.G., her fourteen-year-old stepdaughter, had told a friend that she'd had sex with a middle-aged man who had paid her.[10] (In a differing account, it was Royal Palm assistant principal Carolyn Brown who

---

* Name withheld.

telephoned the police and not the girl's guardian.) The man, the caller told Pagan, had a long face and bushy eyebrows and lived in a mansion at the end of a cul-de-sac.[11] Pagan immediately knew that the caller was talking about Jeffrey Epstein.

Epstein was well known to the PBPD. A nine-year veteran of the force, Detective Pagan knew that she was entering a minefield—one small mistake in the investigation could offer a powerful attorney an opening to shoot down the allegations. Moreover, the man who lived at the end of the cul-de-sac was powerful enough to make the rest of her professional existence miserable. In addition to the patrols instituted two years prior based on neighbor complaints, the department had coordinated security at Epstein's home when dignitaries, including Prince Andrew, had visited. Epstein was also known to the department for another reason. On December 14, 2004, he donated a $90,000 firearms training simulator, which he had delivered personally.[12] (Around the same time, Epstein had also donated $100,000 to the local ballet company so that the dancers could receive massage therapy.)

Detective Pagan's first step was to interview the girl in question, S.G. Working alongside Pagan was Detective Joseph Recarey, a Queens, New York, native and a fourteen-year veteran, who would serve as one of the lead investigators. Recarey was considered one of the top detectives in the PBPD; he was one of the most decorated police officers in the department's history, with more than 150 commendations to his name.[13]

Pagan and Recarey also called in Sergeant George Frick and Palm Beach police chief Michael Reiter to listen in on the interview. Reiter, who would bear ultimate responsibility for the investigation, was no stranger to high-profile, potentially politically charged cases; he was one of the lead detectives assigned to the probing of David Kennedy's overdose in 1984, and he worked on the investigation of William Kennedy Smith, nephew of President Kennedy, who had been charged with rape a decade earlier. Reiter's professionalism and leadership were recognized throughout Florida and beyond; he had

taken management courses at Harvard as well as with the Federal
Bureau of Investigation in Quantico, Virginia. As a police officer,
Reiter was known as a worker—someone who got the job done.

Chief Reiter also knew Jeffrey Epstein. As Reiter explained in
the 2020 *Filthy Rich* documentary, he first encountered Epstein
around 2001 when the financier visited the chief's office to discuss
a possible donation to the department. "It was just a little bit of chit-
chat," Reiter said. "My impression was that he was just a wealthy,
very private guy." Two years later, Reiter's department received the
first reports from neighbors about the girls seen coming and going
from Epstein's residence, resulting in the initial investigation that
was later dropped.


IN HER INTERVIEW WITH Palm Beach police, S.G. described the incident that had taken place on February 6, 2005. S.G. said she was
picked up by the girl who recruited her for the rendezvous, and identified the girl as Haley Robson, who was a teenager herself. Although
S.G. was only fourteen, she was told to say she was eighteen and in
her senior year if anyone asked.

S.G. described Epstein's house as a two-story pink house with a
Cadillac Escalade parked in the driveway outside the gate. Upon
arriving, she was escorted up a driveway and past a small security
guard station. A guard emerged to ask what she was doing there. S.G.
and Robson said, "We are here to see Epstein" and the guard let
them in. Epstein, they were told, was not at home, but the two girls
were ushered into the house through a kitchen. They were offered a
soft drink while they waited. The girls looked around at the kitchen.[14]
It was neat and air-conditioned. It looked to them like a home that
would be featured in a magazine.

According to police reports and court documents, Epstein arrived
with a blond woman later identified as his longtime assistant Sarah
Kellen.[15] He looked at the waiting girls and then disappeared into a
back room with Robson. Both returned a short time later.

S.G. was then told to follow Kellen upstairs. They walked up a flight of stairs, past framed photographs of nude females, and entered a room with a large massage table in its center. The room's setup struck S.G. as bizarre. A bathroom was situated to the right, with a green and pink couch to the left. The room was decorated with a large mural of a naked woman. Kellen told S.G. that Epstein would join her in a minute and then left the room.

Epstein entered the room wearing nothing but a small towel. In a stern tone, Epstein instructed the fourteen-year-old to take off her clothes and start working on him. He removed the towel and positioned himself on his stomach; he told S.G. which lotions to use. S.G. stripped to her bra and underwear. Epstein ordered S.G. to climb on top of him and straddle him as he rubbed his buttocks against her. He directed her body movements, telling her when they needed to be clockwise and when counterclockwise.

At some point, Epstein turned over to lie on his back. He ordered S.G. to rub his chest and shoulders, which she did. He then turned on his side and began to masturbate. He also pulled out a purple vibrator and pressed it against the outside of S.G.'s underwear. Epstein eventually ejaculated and used the towel to clean himself up. He then left the room.

S.G. got dressed and walked back downstairs to the kitchen, where Robson was waiting. S.G. told police she was then given $300. Robson received a $200 finder's fee.[16]

Before leaving the police station, S.G. picked out Epstein as the perpetrator from photos the detectives showed her.

THE SAME DAY, MARCH 15, as police completed paperwork to launch a sexual battery investigation, Epstein and Maxwell were in Manhattan to attend the 2005 Wall Street Concert Series Benefiting Wall Street Rising, at the famed Cipriani Wall Street eatery.[17]

Police would conduct much of the 2005 Florida investigation—including interviews—across the waterway separating Palm Beach

Island from the rest of the county. The drab mainland subdivisions where many of Epstein's young victims lived were a far cry from the Mediterranean villas near the ocean, where the existence of a high-profile investigation into a member of the Palm Beach elite would be hard to keep under wraps for long. Police attempted to shield their work from prying eyes, but Epstein eventually received a tip that he was under police scrutiny.[18]

THE PBPD INVESTIGATION CENTERED ON three individuals: Epstein, his longtime assistant Sarah Kellen, and Haley Robson, the teen who received financial compensation for each underage girl she brought to the Epstein home. Ghislaine Maxwell was never a target of the 2005 criminal probe.

Robson had first encountered Epstein just after her seventeenth birthday when a classmate at Royal Palm named Molly asked her if she'd like to earn extra cash by giving a massage to a rich man. Like many of Epstein's victims, Robson was young-looking and pretty and had grown up in a lower-income home.

Just like what would take place later with her friend S.G., Robson had been taken by Kellen to a room with a massage table where Epstein, wearing only a towel, was waiting. Epstein paid Robson $200 for the massage, but it was clear that Robson was uncomfortable letting the older man touch her, so he offered her a different role: She would scout for him and be paid for every girl she brought to El Brillo Way.

Sarah Kellen, also known as Kensington, was by this time a trusted member of Epstein's inner circle, the detectives would learn.[19] She was a designer by trade who had first entered Epstein's world as an employee of his financial services business. Kellen, who flew on Epstein's jet with him and Bill Clinton at least eleven times, was sometimes referred to as Ghislaine Maxwell's lieutenant.[20] In Palm Beach, she was responsible for handling the young girls who arrived at the mansion alone, or who were driven there by Haley

Robson. Kellen made it a point to jot down the names and telephone numbers of girls who passed through. Kellen allegedly told girls not to speak about Epstein.

THE PBPD PLACED 358 EL Brillo Way under surveillance. Epstein's three black Mercedes sedans were in his garage, parked alongside a green Harley-Davidson. Detectives noted each time one of the vehicles left the compound and who was inside. Staff at Epstein's home also included a private chef and a small group of assistants identified by the detectives through license plate numbers.

As police would learn, the entire staff at 358 El Brillo Way was mobilized to serve Epstein's perverted enterprise. Some girls needed to be driven home; some were given rental cars. The chef was on hand to feed them. Alfredo Rodriguez, a worker at the house, told police that at Epstein's direction, he brought a pail of roses to a girl to congratulate her on her performance in a high school play.

Detectives also staked out Palm Beach International Airport, five miles from El Brillo Drive, where Epstein would park his private jet when he was in town. On one occasion, detectives reported that Les Wexner's private plane landed at the airport, where it was met by Escalades sent from Epstein's home.[21]

Detectives even arranged with the Town of Palm Beach Sanitation Bureau to sift through Epstein's garbage. The long-shot strategy revealed amazing tidbits of evidence, including the phone numbers of girls who had been summoned to El Brillo Way for interviews. They also found papers with names and phone numbers, sex toys, and feminine hygiene products. Police also found receipts for S&M books, including *SM101: A Realistic Introduction*; *SlaveCraft: Roadmaps for Erotic Servitude: Principles, Skills and Tools*; and *Training with Miss Abernathy: A Workbook for Erotic Slaves and Their Owners*.

One note discovered by detectives was a message stating that a certain female could not come over at seven o'clock because of soccer. Another said a girl had to work Sunday—seemingly suggesting

"Monday after school?" as an alternative. And still another note contained the work hours of a girl, saying she left school at 11:30 A.M. and would come over the next day at 10:30 A.M.[22]

THE DETECTIVES PURSUED LEAD AFTER lead over the next seven months. The police interviewed Sarah Kellen and a few other Epstein estate employees. They spoke to more than a dozen underage girls whom Epstein had abused in exchange for money. One girl said that when she had sex with Epstein she closed her eyes and thought about cash. "In my mind, I'm like, 'Oh my God, when this is over you're getting so much money.'"[23] Reports of what happened in the massage room varied. Sometimes the encounter involved Epstein masturbating while the girl rubbed his body down with lotion. Other times, the abuse involved penetrative sex. One girl, police records show, described Epstein's penis as "Egg Shaped."[24]

Some girls refused to return after a single instance of abuse at Epstein's hands. Others said they went back more than a hundred times. Epstein, detectives learned, received as many as three massages a day. His staff was always told to have at least $2,000 on hand.[25] Epstein paid between $200 and $1,000 for an encounter—the higher amounts might involve travel to Little St. James. Juan P. Alessi, one of Epstein's aides in Palm Beach, swore under oath that "girls were always coming and going. Twenty-two girls traveled with him as massage therapists."[26]

If Epstein feared that a girl might contact the authorities, he also paid more. In cases where Epstein forced himself on a victim, entering her against her will, he sometimes paid $1,000 or more. He was quoted as complimenting some of the girls on their physical attributes, even telling one fourteen-year-old he raped that "she had a hard clit."[27]

Sometimes Epstein ordered victims to have sex with one another. One such instance was with one of Epstein's assistants, a girl named Nadia Marcinkova. Epstein was very fond of Marcinkova and, according to one victim interviewed by Detective Joseph Recarey, "had purchased her from her family in Yugoslavia."[28] (Marcinkova, who was actually born in what is now Slovakia before moving to Yugoslavia as a child, has put forward the narrative in other media outlets covering her later career in aviation that she was "discovered by a modeling agency in her native Slovakia" and that she "modeled internationally for Chanel, Dior, Vogue, and MTV" before her modeling agency moved her to New York.)[29]

One victim told police that on one occasion Marcinkova entered the massage room from the adjoining steam room area and was already naked. Epstein instructed the victim to perform oral sex on Marcinkova; the victim refused. Epstein offered an additional $200 for her to perform oral sex on Marcinkova for five minutes. The victim eventually gave in.[30]

THE EPSTEIN INVESTIGATION DRAGGED ON through the summer and fall of 2005. Each clue the Palm Beach police found—a new phone number, surveillance of a license plate—revealed additional clues and new witnesses. Detective Recarcy later told the *Miami Herald*: "I was surprised at how quickly it snowballed. I thought at some point there would be a last interview, but the next victim would supply me with three or four more names and the next one had three or four names and it just kept getting bigger and bigger." The detectives were eager to make this case, but they knew Epstein had friends in the department—and powerful friends across the state. They were determined to do everything by the book.

For Epstein's part, he showed no signs of being concerned about the criminal probe. On December 12, 2005, while police were wrapping up their investigation, Epstein hosted Harvard president Larry Summers and his new wife, Lisa. They traveled on board the "Lolita Express."[31] Flight logs show the flight was from Bedford, Massachusetts, to the Virgin Islands. Ghislaine Maxwell accompanied them on board, but not Epstein.[32]

After more than a year of interviews, evidence gathering, and relentless police detective work, the Palm Beach Police Department believed that they had all they needed to secure a search warrant and tee up a strong case for Palm Beach County state attorney Barry Krischer to prosecute. But this, after all, was Florida.

A few weeks after the PBPD handed Krischer their disturbing report, Epstein dispatched Alan Dershowitz into the fray.[33]

# 20

## FLORIDA JUSTICE

IN 2000, FIVE YEARS BEFORE AN ANONYMOUS PHONE CALL TIPPED THE
Palm Beach Police Department off to the predatory crimes of Jeffrey
Epstein, Palm Beach County state attorney Barry Krischer made
national news for a very difference case. Krischer, who branded himself as a tireless protector of law and order, had persuaded a grand
jury to indict a thirteen-year-old black boy on first-degree murder
charges for shooting a white teacher.[1] The controversial case sparked
great debate in Florida, but it was just one instance of a tough-on-
juveniles strategy that had given Krischer "a national profile," according to an assessment in the *South Florida Sun-Sentinel*.

The citizens of Palm Beach County had first elected Krischer
state attorney in 1992 and he had remained popular, running unop-
posed in the election that preceded the onset of the 2005 Epstein
investigation. The four-term incumbent was neat looking, with
slicked-back hair highlighting stern wire-rimmed glasses. Krischer
looked every part of the no-nonsense lawman. Although he was a
Democrat, his no-mercy style of policing was well received by wealthy
conservatives in Palm Beach and the other resort communities in the
county. For many prosecutors in Krischer's shoes, leading the Epstein

case—the prospect of taking down a twisted criminal preying upon the underprivileged girls of Palm Beach County—was a slam dunk political golden ticket.

On October 20, 2005, the PBPD's Special Investigations Unit executed a search warrant at 358 El Brillo Way. Detectives and uniformed personnel entered the gates and parked in the driveway, which was flanked by two large gargoyles.

The police carted off massage tables and boxes of photographs, many seized from Ghislaine Maxwell's office on the ground floor next to the kitchen.[2] Police also discovered unusual items, such as soap shaped like male and female genitalia in his showers. The search warrant was served "right under the noses of New York decorator Mark Zeff and architect Douglas Schoettle, who were there planning a renovation," though NBC News had managed to hear about the raid ahead of time, with a crew arriving before the police.[3]

Epstein's possessions were cataloged into a police inventory sheet. More than twenty vehicles were registered to him, including a Rolls-Royce and a Bentley. According to a deposition police took with Epstein staffer Alfredo Rodriguez, there were fifteen telephones in the house. Police found computers, but in some cases the hard drives had already been removed and systems had been scrubbed. Epstein had indeed been tipped off ahead of the police action.[4]

Despite the missing computer hard drives, the Palm Beach Police Department was certain that there was probable cause to charge Epstein with unlawful sex acts with a minor, and lewd and lascivious molestation. When Chief Reiter first enlisted Barry Krischer on the case in January 2006, Reiter said that the state attorney was very enthusiastic, saying, "This is somebody we have to stop."

It appeared that Florida justice was laying the groundwork to eviscerate Jeffrey Epstein.[5]

FOR A MAN FACING THE possibility of being charged as a sexual predator and spending time in county lockup as a child molester, Jeffrey

Epstein seemed to show little fear as to his fate. Initially, he confided in friends that he believed the investigation—and the subsequent allegations—were a conspiracy of state-sponsored anti-Semitism. It was true that the Town of Palm Beach was historically known as a bastion of gentile privilege, with private clubs known for keeping Jewish members out.[6]

Epstein, however, was no victim of anti-Semitism.

With the indictment sticking, Epstein assembled a legal team. Names of some of the best attorneys in the world were typed inside Epstein's 92-page little black book, which contained 1,749 entries. Jeffrey Epstein's dream team of lawyers read like a who's who of the legal world. They included Jay Lefkowitz, a senior partner at the famed firm Kirkland and Ellis, who had also served in the George W. Bush administration as general counsel in the Office of Management and Budget; Jack Goldberg, a noted Palm Beach criminal defense lawyer; Roy Black, who had worked to acquit William Kennedy Smith of a rape charge; eminent defense attorney Gerald Lefcourt; and former U.S. attorney Guy Lewis. Rounding out the team was Epstein's friend Alan Dershowitz.

Dershowitz was the pit bull, the driving force, in a go-for-broke defense. About Dershowitz, fellow Harvard professor and lawyer Laurence Tribe had once said, "He revels in taking positions that ultimately are not just controversial but pretty close to indefensible."[7] This tendency was on full display in the Epstein defense. Dershowitz was quoted by *The New Yorker* years later as saying, "I think of myself like a doctor or a priest. If they wheel Jeffrey Epstein into the emergency ward, the doctor is going to take care of him."

Shortly after Dershowitz assumed command as lead attorney, the defense team embarked on a campaign to discredit everyone associated with the investigation, from law enforcement to the accusers. Private investigators followed members of the PBPD investigation team. Chief Reiter stated in a deposition that both he and Detective Recarey were under constant surveillance for months. Their backgrounds were examined, and their movements were followed; even their trash was searched.[8] Rumors began to circulate that Reiter was involved in a messy divorce; the chief was indeed going through a divorce, but no aspect of it was considered out of the ordinary.[9]

Dershowitz and his team sought information to expose Epstein's victims as delinquents and sexually promiscuous teenagers. Dershowitz provided the PBPD with a dossier on several of the victims, showing the underage girls engaging in alcohol and drug use and insinuating that their behavioral history made them unreliable. One of the girls interviewed by police had run away from home. Another had lied about a narcotics arrest.

There were also threats to the victims and their families. Private investigators hired by Epstein began a campaign of intimidation against anyone who might testify against the financier. According to police reports, one of the girls raped by Epstein phoned another victim and said, "Those who help [Epstein] will be compensated and those who hurt him will be dealt with."[10] Dershowitz has denied he had anything to do with gathering background on the girls or in directing anyone to follow or intimidate the police, the girls, or their families. "I'm not an investigator," Dershowitz told the *Miami Herald,* "My only job is to negotiate and try the case when it comes to trial."

THE INVESTIGATIVE TEAM AT PBPD wanted charges filed against Sarah Kellen and Haley Robson, as well as others who worked at the estate. The police had assembled an impressive witness list of thirteen underage girls. They provided the police with near-identical first-person accounts of how the owner of the mansion at 358 El Brillo Way had raped or abused them, and the actions of Kellen and Robson in facilitating these attacks.

Despite the investigators' confidence in the strength of their case, Barry Krischer gave the impression that he believed the victims to be guilty of poor judgment, or, worse, to be prostitutes. He signaled that he didn't have confidence in his case even as he referred it to a grand jury in May 2006.[11] "Krischer's reasoning was that, had he taken the case to trial, jurors would consider the victims to be whores and wouldn't convict Epstein of human trafficking," the veteran Florida journalist Jose Lambiet remembered.[12]

"Here you had a guy who had Monopoly money to play with, hundreds of millions of dollars, and he used all this cash not to better the world, but to make it even worse for people who never had his luck. Some history books would have us believe that in sixteenth-century Europe, some lords gave themselves the right to take the virginity of some of their subjects. This is how I've always thought of the Epstein saga. It was a modern *droit de cuissage*. Epstein was a guy who lived in Palm Beach and dared to send envoys across the Intracoastal to find young girls in the poorest parts of suburbia, neighborhoods ten miles west of Mar-a-Lago where they had not even bothered paving the roads, streets where you could smell desperation."[13]

IN APRIL 2006, KRISCHER'S OFFICE offered Epstein a sweet deal: He'd plead guilty to felony aggravated assault; he wouldn't be incarcerated; if he complied with terms of probation, his criminal record would be expunged; and he wouldn't have to register as a sex offender.[14] Despite the advantageous terms for Epstein, the deal fell apart.

In the end, Barry Krischer went to the grand jury with just a single victim. The grand jury convened in Palm Beach County represented Florida justice at its worst. One of the three victims called was not in Palm Beach County, but 270 miles away in Jacksonville, and she failed to testify. One of the victims, then in college, never received the subpoena. Another victim, who told the PBPD that Jeffrey Epstein had penetrated her, never showed—a no-show that the legal team would use to highlight their claims that the girls were lying and only looking for a payday. Detective Recarey would later theorize that some of the girls received payouts to recant or forget their claims.[15]

In June 2006, the grand jury returned an indictment of one count of solicitation of prostitution. Nowhere was it mentioned that Jeffrey Epstein had had sex with a minor. Epstein argued to anyone who'd listen that in his hometown of New York City, the act of solicitation for prostitution was a Class D misdemeanor punishable by a $100 fine.[16] Epstein likened his offense to that of "a person who steals a bagel."*[17]

ON A QUIET SUNDAY, JULY 23, 2006, *Palm Beach Post* staff writer Nicole Janok sat down at her computer and filed an eleven-paragraph story for Monday's newspaper. A tiny mug shot of Epstein accompanied the six-word headline MYSTERY MONEY MAN FACES SOLICITING CHARGE.

Janok described Epstein in her story as "a part-time Palm Beach resident who has socialized with Donald Trump, Bill Clinton and Kevin Spacey" who was now "jailed . . . with accused drug dealers, drunken drivers and wife beaters after he was charged with soliciting a prostitute."

Epstein, now fifty-three, had been picked up by police at his home on El Brillo Way at 1:45 A.M. Hours later, he was back on the street—after posting bond of just $3,000.

CHIEF MICHAEL REITER WAS NO stranger to the two worlds that existed within Palm Beach County, though that intimate knowledge did not lessen his feeling that his department—and the victims— had been abandoned. In a May 1, 2006, memo to Krischer, Reiter wrote, "I must urge you to examine the unusual course that your

---

* More than a decade later, Florida newspapers and lawmakers fought to get the sealed Epstein grand jury transcripts released. As of June 2020, a judge denied the request. State Senator Lauren Book, a sexual abuse survivor, said of Krischer years later: "It's a disgusting and deplorable state of affairs. He revictimized these young girls."

office's handling of this matter [is taking]." He continued, asking whether "good and sufficient reason exists to require your disqualification from the prosecution of these cases."[18]

Reiter would later say that the Epstein case was the first time in his lengthy law enforcement career when he felt that he "could not really protect the victim."[19] Frustrated, Reiter decided on a drastic course of action: He would bring the case to the attention of the Federal Bureau of Investigation.

IN 2006, WHILE HIS ATTORNEYS and police and prosecutors battled behind the scenes, Epstein was free to carry on with his life as usual. He was introduced to a twenty-two-year-old modeling hopeful named Sarah Ransome. Born in South Africa to British parents, Ransome was introduced to Epstein and Maxwell through a friend. Epstein, she was told, could help her get into and help finance her studies at the Fashion Institute of Technology.[20] Tall, slender, and beautiful, Ransome soon found herself sitting on board Epstein's 727 flying from Teterboro to the Virgin Islands.[21] On the flight, she witnessed Epstein have sex with another girl.[22]

Ransome was older than most of the girls in Epstein's orbit. But in her case, it didn't matter. Epstein raped her as many as three times a day. The abuse was both physical and psychological. Trapped far from home in the hellish prison of "Little St. Jeff's," Ransome contemplated swimming from the island in a last-ditch escape attempt.[23]

# 21

## OPERATION LEAP YEAR

Tension between local law enforcement and "the feds" is a hallmark of the American justice system. As the national law enforcement agency—a powerful and all-knowing force that was thirty-five thousand strong—the FBI has a culture of taking over in high-profile cases, and, of course, taking the credit for investigative work that others had done when it pans out. Many police officers, and indeed police agencies, didn't like working with the bureau specifically because FBI supervisors and their special agents were secretive and uncooperative and often snatched cases handed to them as if they were their own. A retired New York City Police Department officer who went on to work for a federal law enforcement agency put it this way: "The FBI doesn't play well with others."[1]

The case against Jeffrey Epstein was one such instance.

The FBI field office in Miami has historically been one of the busiest in the bureau. The division is responsible for addressing serious federal criminal violations throughout nine counties in the southern half of the Sunshine State, as well as addressing extraterritorial violations of American citizens in Mexico, the Caribbean, and Central and South America. In addition to criminal investigations of some of the nation's most serious criminals who operate in Florida, the field office has always had more than its share of workload thanks to Miami's role as an ever-vibrant illegal hub of the narcotics trade. Four smaller offices, known as resident agencies, act as satellites. The one in West Palm Beach serves as a busy shop for the handful of agents assigned to work Palm Beach County and vicinity.

In July 2006, Palm Beach police chief Michael Reiter went behind the back of the state's attorney and drove one mile across the Royal Park Bridge connecting Palm Beach with the mainland, carrying with him a box of evidence and affidavits. After Reiter's initial call, the FBI's investigation of Jeffrey Epstein was assigned to Special Agent E. Nesbitt Kuyrkendall. The case was codenamed Operation Leap Year.[2]

The FBI was very interested in the case. High-profile criminal investigations that could bring national headlines were just the kind of cases senior special agents were encouraged to accept. But the FBI and the U.S. attorneys who prosecute federal crimes prefer the slam dunks that never make it to trial—cases with such overwhelming evidence that a suspect has little choice but to plead guilty and beg for leniency.

Despite local law enforcement's wariness of cooperating with the feds, the FBI had resources that were simply unavailable to a small agency like the PBPD. (Detective Recarey later likened the FBI to "white knights" coming to the rescue.)[3] They also could expand the scope of the investigation that Reiter and the detectives of the Special Investigations Unit had started. State law in Florida addressed specific crimes like rape and assault. Federal statutes, however, could apply to a broader web of criminal activity involving the exploitation of minors. Proving that someone crossed state lines to engage in criminal enterprises, especially those involving children and sex trafficking, could mean a life sentence in a federal penitentiary. The hope was that when faced with the prospect of a life behind bars in a maximum security federal prison, Epstein would at least sit down at the negotiating table. Assistant U.S.

attorneys were often willing to play ball with a lawyered-up defendant if it meant avoiding the costly resources needed for a protracted criminal trial.

Special Agent Kuyrkendall and his team reviewed the entire Epstein file, revisiting witnesses and the evidence seized. By November 2006, Operation Leap Year had grown in scope; it was now a national and international investigation. FBI agents interviewed potential witnesses and victims in New Mexico and New York. Flight logs overseas were reviewed; so, too, were passenger manifests and immigration forms filled out by girls that Epstein had brought over from France courtesy of his friend the modeling agent Jean-Luc Brunel.

Epstein's lead defense attorney, Alan Dershowitz, brought on another star attorney to thwart the federal investigation—Kenneth Starr. A graduate of the Duke University Law School, Starr was a federal judge nominated by President Ronald Reagan and had served as solicitor general during the George H. W. Bush administration before reaching national prominence as the special counsel who, in the course of investigating President Bill and First Lady Hillary Clinton over the Whitewater business deal, had uncovered Bill's extramarital affair with Monica Lewinsky. "I proposed to bring in Ken Starr because Jeffrey deserves the best representation possible," Dershowitz said.[4]

It was, of course, the ultimate irony that a man who played a key role in the impeachment of a president over an inappropriate relationship with a young—though not underage—intern would become one of the lead defenders of another powerful man, this one accused of raping underage girls.

IN THEIR PURSUIT OF EPSTEIN, federal agents interviewed more than forty girls in multiple jurisdictions.[5] Law enforcement had always believed that there were many more victims out there who couldn't be located or who kept silent about the abuse they experienced. Yet while the FBI worked its case interviewing girls who had been victimized by Jeffrey Epstein, once again Epstein's formidable defense team went into overdrive. Their goal would be to delegitimize the girls who were coming forward to speak to the federal agents, raising questions about the credibility of the prosecution's key witnesses.

West Palm Beach attorney Spencer Kuvin represented three of Epstein's victims. He recalled the character assassination tactics of Epstein's legal team both in the state's investigation and later with the FBI. "They were trying to portray these young girls as money-grubbing, opportunistic, from poor neighborhoods, just going after this poor old rich guy to try and get money," Kuvin explained. According to the lawyer, Epstein's defense team sought Planned Parenthood records to see if any girls had terminated pregnancies, as well as looking for medical records that could reveal the use of antidepressants. "They would go out and interview ex-boyfriends of these young girls to see what type of sex acts they would have been involved in in the past, what they did, and whether they were loose girls or users of drugs or alcohol, those things," Kuvin said.

The investigators hired on behalf of Epstein would, according to Kuvin, seek out interviews with family members of the accusers, sometimes under the guise of being "officials." "They would come up to people and say, 'Hi. We're investigators looking into this claim. Would you talk to us?' They never elaborated if they were the ones hired by Epstein to defend him. They wouldn't lie, but they certainly would skirt the truth."[6]

Accusers were also followed, Kuvin added. "A lot of my clients mentioned that they would have black-tinted-windowed Tahoes outside their house for days on end, following them and their friends to school." For Kuvin's clients, the intimidation tactics became overwhelming. "Some of them said, 'I'm tired of it. I want this over with,'" he explained. "'Just settle my case. Be done with it.' And that was [Epstein's] intent from the beginning: to intimidate these young girls into submission."[7]

The FBI's behavior was not above reproach either. One victim,

Dainya Nida, was introduced to Epstein in June 2003 when she was a sixteen-year-old student at John I. Leonard High School, ten miles from Epstein's Palm Beach mansion. Nida would later comment that neither FBI agents nor federal prosecutors seemed interested in her plight. The agents would come to where she was working to question her, making it appear as if she was the one who had done something wrong.[8]

Investigators working for Epstein attempted to speak to Nida's friends, her acquaintances, and even her employers. The private investigators that she believed were hired by Epstein's legal team even contacted Nida's parents about what had taken place, framing the situation in a way that implied their daughter was in the wrong on account of having taken the cash offered to her by Epstein.[9]

On some level, it's possible Epstein had convinced himself that he was the victim—that he'd never done anything wrong. Even while he was being placed under the microscope of law enforcement, in the crosshairs of a large-scale operation, he told journalist Michael Wolff from *New York* magazine, "What can I say, I like young girls," making it sound as though his serial abuse was merely an eccentric hobby.[10]

IN JUNE 2007, THE U.S. Attorney's Office in Miami drafted but never filed a fifty-three-page indictment against Epstein that in essence took over the case from State Attorney Barry Krischer.[11] The next month, federal grand jury subpoenas were issued for Epstein's computers, but those hard drives had long since disappeared.

Still, Epstein's defense team, led by Alan Dershowitz, was becoming nervous, according to a source close to the investigation. The FBI investigation had rapidly progressed from a nuisance to a possible full-blown federal indictment. Epstein's attorneys now maneuvered to seek an outcome that would protect his assets, shield his celebrity, and allow him to evade the long arm of the law. If he went to trial and lost, he was facing a mandatory minimum sentence of ten years on just the one charge. And more federal charges were likely to follow.

On September 24, 2007, according to federal records, Epstein's attorney Jay Lefkowitz sent a one-line email regarding the possible indictment to the U.S. Attorney's Office in Miami, saying, "Please do whatever you can to keep this from becoming public."[12]

# 22

## ACOSTA: THE INSIDE MAN

THE BLUEPRINT FOR A DEAL BETWEEN THE U.S. GOVERNMENT AND Jeffrey Epstein was reached on September 24, 2007. Assistant U.S. Attorney Ann Marie Villafaña, one of the prosecutors in the Southern District of Florida, worked feverishly to coordinate the fine print with Epstein's lawyers. On October 3, 2007, Villafaña emailed Jay Lefkowitz, one of Jeffrey Epstein's lawyers, laying out the government's contention that "Epstein, through his assistants, would recruit underage females to travel to his home in Palm Beach to engage in lewd conduct in exchange for money." Villafaña stated that the investigation has turned up forty "young women who can be characterized as victims" and that "some of those women went to Mr. Epstein's home only once, some went there as much as 100 times or more."[1] During the local investigation, Detective Joe Recarey would identify an even higher number—an astounding forty-seven girls who had fallen prey to Epstein in Palm Beach.

The courtroom testimony of any one of these girls should have been enough to send Jeffrey Epstein to prison for life. This wasn't the type of case that was plea-bargained. Local and state prosecutors typically lived to put pedophiles and sex traffickers behind bars for life. Yet there would be no trial of *People v. Jeffrey Edward Epstein* in a United States federal courtroom.

Rene Alexander Acosta was the U.S. attorney for the Southern District of Miami, and the lawyer ultimately responsible for how the federal prosecution of the Epstein charge would play out. The Miami-born son of Cuban immigrants, Acosta was the first member of his family to graduate college. He earned his B.A. from Harvard, attended Harvard Law School, and clerked for future Supreme Court justice Samuel Alito, then a judge on the United States Court of Appeals for the Third Circuit, before taking a position at Kirkland and Ellis, where both Jay Lefkowitz and Kenneth Starr worked. Being Cuban and Republican helped catapult Acosta to President George W. Bush's Justice Department. In 2005, he was appointed the U.S. attorney for the Southern District of Florida.

In their own ways, both Acosta and Alan Dershowitz—two Harvard alumni—went to work to make Epstein's entire ordeal disappear. As Dershowitz later told *New Yorker* writer Connie Bruck in 2019 about representing Epstein, "Every honest criminal lawyer will tell you that he defends the guilty *and* the innocent."[2]

From the onset, Dershowitz tried to dilute Epstein's actions, making them appear to be nothing more than overblown charges by an overzealous police department. In the state case, Dershowitz provided Krischer's office with a detailed dossier on other men in South Florida who had been charged with similar crimes and who received probation. To Dershowitz, the PBPD and then even the Palm Beach State Attorney's Office were overacting and overreaching.

When it became apparent that the case could not be swept under a county—or a federal—rug, Epstein's legal team would play long ball, attempting to delay matters as much as possible to drag the process out. Their strategy was to exhaust prosecutors, exposing them to claims of investigative mistakes and bad press.

Epstein's lawyers engaged Acosta's office in exhaustive negotiations. Their goal was securing what is known in the federal courts as a non-prosecution agreement, or NPA—a contractual arrangement between the U.S. Department of Justice and an individual facing a criminal charge that defers prosecution in exchange for compliance, cooperation, and some sort of adherence to ground rules for compensating victims.

While NPAs were "fairly common" within the Department of Justice overall, for a U.S. attorney to agree to an NPA in a child sex trafficking case "was not common at all," according to former U.S. prosecutor Berit Berger. "In fact," Berger explained in a 2019 interview with NPR about the Epstein case, "I would say they're almost unheard of."

Epstein's dream team negotiated the terms of the NPA with Acosta's office in chambers, and it did so in secret—in hotel rooms and in other places where discretion was guaranteed. Some of the meetings were held clandestinely at the Marriott Hotel in West Palm Beach—an eight-minute drive from 358 El Brillo Way.[3] Ann Marie Villafaña even communicated with Epstein's attorneys on her private Gmail account to keep sensitive communications off the Department of Justice servers.[4]

To his attorneys, Epstein laid out a set of expectations: He didn't want to have to register as a sex offender, and he didn't want to be in a position where he'd have to settle what was bound to be a relentless wave of lawsuits. And he certainly did not want to go to prison.

NINE DAYS AFTER VILLAFAÑA SENT the email laying out the prosecutors' position on the facts of the case to Jay Lefkowitz, U.S. Attorney Acosta drove the seventy miles to Palm Beach to meet Epstein's lawyer face-to-face at the Marriott Hotel. This in itself is remarkable. U.S. attorneys personally appointed by the president of the United States typically did not travel to meet defense lawyers—defense lawyers were grateful if the U.S. attorney agreed to a brief sit-down.

The negotiations between Acosta's office and Epstein's attorneys were conducted far from the public's view—and even without the knowledge of the attorneys representing Epstein's victims. One of

the most important stipulations for Epstein was that the NPA protect his employees from being charged as coconspirators. The agreement secured immunity for Sarah Kellen, Ghislaine Maxwell's
"lieutenant"; Adriana Ross, Epstein's scheduler; Lesley Groff, an
assistant; and Nadia Marcinkova.[5] The agreement hammered out
between the parties provided immunity to all named and unnamed
coconspirators from future state and federal charges.[6] There was no
mention of Ghislaine Maxwell in the agreement, though the wording
of the NPA was fluid and allowed for additions at a later date.

The negotiations dragged on for nine long months. Epstein's lawyers provided the state attorney with a five-thousand-word testimonial
tracing Epstein's life from early childhood through adulthood, along
with a note that read: "Enjoy some fun reading on your defendant."

Astonishingly, the first person Epstein lawyer Jack Goldberger
offered to give a testimonial in support of Epstein was none other
than Kathy Suter, his former junior high school crush, whose words,
at least as recorded by the defense, indicated that she still felt positive about Epstein more than forty years after they had first met.

Kathy Suter was now married—she went by the name Kathleen
Lindman—and her observations, written up by an attorney working
on Epstein's behalf, depict a woman who not only harbored no
grudges against her onetime flame but remembered him with affection. That ugly scene outside the movie theater in Brooklyn back in
1979, after she'd broken up with Epstein and had gone on a date
with lawyer Bernard Laffer, when Epstein surprised them both by
confronting them publicly? It was as if the incident never happened.
Kathleen Lindman wrote a 165-word paean to her former friend:

> It's difficult to express how much Jeffrey's friendship has
> meant to me over the course of my life, but he is nothing
> short of being my guardian angel. I have been blessed with a
> lifelong friend who regardless of the stresses of his own work
> and life, always makes time to listen and talk to me with
> gentleness, wisdom, and humor.

I've watched Jeffrey grow from boyhood into one of the hardest working, responsible, and generous men I know. For instance, when the time came to send my son to kindergarten, I wanted him to get the best possible education, but our local public school was a failure and my husband and I couldn't afford to send him to an independent school. Jeffrey understood how much I valued education, and empathetically volunteered to cover the costs of our son's education. This past June, our son graduated from Columbia University with honors, and it would not have been possible without Jeffrey's long-term commitment and generosity.[7]

Other friends and acquaintances, including others who had been the recipients of Epstein's financial support, also wrote letters that extolled his kind spirit.

BY THIS POINT, EPSTEIN WAS facing legal threats from multiple quarters. In addition to the pending criminal charge, some of the girls investigated by Palm Beach police filed suits against him; other victims were also beginning to come forward.

In February 2008, an anonymous woman who claimed that she had been recruited by Jeffrey Epstein when she was sixteen years old and serially abused filed a $50 million lawsuit against him. The following month, attorneys for a second woman filed a separate civil action. Epstein's defenders appeared to be following the same playbook in the civil cases as they had in the criminal defense effort. The father of one of the victims told the FBI that mysterious men were photographing his family and chasing visitors who came to the house. He also claimed that he was followed by men in a car. In one case, Epstein's private eyes almost forced another car off the road as they attempted to keep up with the girl's father as he went to work.

Then, in May, federal prosecutors threatened to add the charge of sexual tourism—which carried a significant potential prison sentence—to the list of crimes he would have to answer to in court if he didn't settle the NPA once and for all.[8] The NPA for Jeffrey Epstein was filed with the Department of Justice. The State Attorney's Office was not a party to those meetings or negotiations.

Even after Epstein and his attorneys signed the provisions, there was hesitancy on Epstein's part to acquiesce to the provisions of the deal. Such obstinacy in the face of federal favoritism was baffling to the U.S. Attorney's Office—it was the definition of arrogance. As *Washington Post* columnist Helaine Olen pointed out later in a scathing review of the legal process as it pertained to Epstein, the case revealed "the empty and sickening bromides used to justify obscene wealth and power and [the] privilege that they really are."[9]

By June 2008, all sides were ready to end the nightmare. Once the NPA was signed and the provisions agreed to, Epstein was kicked back to the responsibility of the Palm Beach County State Attorney's Office, who would now be responsible for the terms of his jail sentence.

On June 30, 2008, more than three years after Palm Beach detectives began staking out his gated mansion on El Brillo Way, Epstein walked into the Daniel T. K. Hurley Courthouse on North Dixie Highway in West Palm Beach. He wore a blue blazer and blue jeans; his light blue button-down shirt was open at the collar, revealing tanned skin. His attire was more suited to a Ralph Lauren ad than a courtroom. He walked with a confident gait, like a man with no worries in the world. Epstein had in fact spent time at Little St. James in the prior weeks.

Sitting alongside three of his attorneys, Epstein, as per the NPA, pleaded guilty to one count of solicitation of prostitution and one count of procuring a person under the age of eighteen for prostitution. Epstein had demanded—unsuccessfully—that his attorneys stipulate that any deal with the government shield him from being classified as a sex offender. Here, for the first time in the entire process, he lost. He would also not escape jail time. He was sentenced to eighteen months behind bars in the county lockup. Upon his release from jail, he would have to register as a sex offender wherever he traveled in the United States.[10] Once in the hands of the county department of corrections, Epstein would have to submit to an HIV test, with the results provided to the victims and their parents.[11]

The discussions between circuit judge Deborah Dale Pucillo and Epstein's attorneys were held quietly, away from the bench. He was fingerprinted; a DNA swab was taken.[12] Palm Beach County sheriff deputies then led him away.

THE CRIME VICTIMS' RIGHTS ACT, 18 U.S.C. § 3771, was signed into law in 2004 to protect victims in federal criminal cases. The act granted victims eight rights, including the right to be reasonably protected from the accused; the right to reasonable, accurate, and timely notice of any public court proceeding, or any parole proceeding, involving the crime, or of any release or escape of the accused; the right not to be excluded from any such public court proceeding unless the court, after receiving clear and convincing evidence, determines that testimony by the victim would be materially altered if the victim heard other testimony at that proceeding; the right to be reasonably heard at any public proceeding in the district court involving release, plea, sentencing, or any parole proceeding; the reasonable right to confer with the attorney for the government in the case; the right to full and timely restitution as provided in law; the right to proceedings free from unreasonable delay; and the right to be treated with fairness and with respect for the victim's dignity and privacy.[13]

Virtually every one of those tenets was violated by U.S. Attorney Acosta and Epstein's attorneys. The press received advance word of the last-minute scheduling of the Epstein hearing—not the attorneys for the victims and not even Palm Beach police chief Michael Reiter. The affair was meant to be covert and handled far from the watchful eye of the police and Epstein's victims. "Unfortunately, the way I've seen our system work for twenty-five years, money buys a lot," Spencer Kuvin, an attorney representing some of Epstein's victims, said. "And it's sad, but it's true. You take the ordinary guy off the street, a gardener, a plumber, an electrician, he gets charged with something like this, he goes away for ninety years. You see someone like Epstein charged with the crimes he was charged with, and he ends up with a slap on the wrist."

When the NPA was announced, the victims began a yearlong court fight to get the details, and an emergency petition was filed to force prosecutors to comply with the national Crime Victims' Rights Act. By September 2009, when the federal NPA had finally been made public, Epstein was facing at least a dozen civil suits from victims. He began settling them out of court.

FOR SOME OBSERVERS, THE QUESTION remained: Why had Alex Acosta agreed to this outcome? Even for an ambitious U.S. attorney who had additional political goals ahead of him and was smooth in front of the news cameras, Acosta found it difficult to justify the preferential treatment that Epstein had received from his office. At first he claimed that the prosecution was anything but a sure thing; any trial, he hinted, was a roll of the dice and the outcome uncertain. By forcing Epstein to sign the NPA and adhere to its rules and stipulations, the U.S. Attorney's Office for the Southern District of Florida guaranteed his going to jail—even if for a short sentence.[14]

Acosta would later backtrack on the basis for his decision. He later claimed he had received instructions from higher-ups at the Justice Department in Washington that he was to go easy on Epstein because the financier "belonged to intelligence" and that the decision was above Acosta's "pay grade."[15] It's true that Acosta wasn't alone in this miscarriage of justice. According to Alan Dershowitz, the NPA with Jeffrey Epstein required that the assistant attorney general in charge of the Criminal Division at the U.S. Department of Justice and the attorney general himself sign off on the arrangement.[16]

Perhaps Acosta was being truthful. Several months after the signing and implementation of the NPA, FBI HQ sent a memo to the Miami Field Division about Jeffrey Epstein. The memo, dated September 11, 2008, dealt with the issue of asset forfeiture—routine in such cases as a measure by which the government can recoup investigation expenses—but issued a directive that no further action was needed at this time. The memo indicated that a case agent had advised that "Epstein is complying with all conditions of his pleas with the State of Florida. Epstein has also provided information to the FBI as agreed upon."[17]

The identity of Epstein's case agent remains classified, as does whatever information Jeffrey Epstein provided to the FBI.

"I'm going to be rich when I grow up," Epstein boasted to classmates before his graduation from Brooklyn's Lafayette High School in 1969. (*Lafayette High School, Brooklyn, New York, 1969*)

Exterior of Epstein's boyhood home in Sea Gate, Brooklyn, where his family lived in a modest two-bedroom apartment on the second floor. (*Barry Levine*)

Interior of Epstein's old bedroom in Sea Gate, where a painting of Jesus Christ and a crucifix hang from the walls. (*Barry Levine*)

Epstein's school crush was Kathleen (Kathy) Suter. Years after they dated, the woman's then boyfriend accused Epstein of following them and provoking a confrontation. Suter later defended Epstein before his sentencing in Florida. Here, she and Epstein stand together in a June 1966 ninth-grade picture. (*Mark Twain Junior High School, Brooklyn, 1966*)

**KATHLEEN SUTER**

Kathy Suter in her 1969 high school yearbook photo. (*Abraham Lincoln High School, 1969*)

Epstein, then twenty-seven, featured in *Cosmopolitan* magazine's July 1980 issue as "Bachelor of the Month," inviting women to write to him at Bear Stearns. (Cosmopolitan *magazine, July 1980*)

The 1975 Dalton School yearbook showed Epstein teaching. In a legal deposition, he refused to say whether he had sex with any of his students after he left the private school. (*The Dalton School Yearbook, New York, New York, 1975*)

Epstein and his first serious girlfriend, Eva Andersson, in the early 1980s. The former Miss Sweden later vouched for him to his parole officer. (*Stefan Lindblom / HBG-Picture*)

Eva Andersson-Dubin; her husband, billionaire hedge fund manager Glenn Dubin; and their daughter Celina, whom Epstein expressed a wish to marry in 2014, when she was nineteen. (*Lars Niki / Getty Images for the Museum of Modern Art*)

Epstein and Ghislaine Maxwell attend a Givenchy fashion show in Paris in January 1992. Both had just lost their fathers in consecutive months. (*Bertrand Rindoff / BESTIMAGE*)

Before his death in 1991, Ghislaine attends an event in England with her father, press baron Robert Maxwell. She called him "the Captain," as did many of his employees. (*News UK Ltd / Shutterstock*)

Epstein with Donald Trump and his children Eric and Ivanka, then nine and twelve, at the NYC Harley-Davidson Cafe opening in 1993. (*Dafydd Jones*)

An NBC crew caught Donald Trump telling Epstein "Look at her, back there. She's hot," singling out an NFL cheerleader at a 1992 Mar-a-Lago party. (*Still from NBC Archive*)

In 2014, Epstein with then New York Academy of Art dean of students Eileen Guggenheim. Epstein met victim Maria Farmer when he bought a painting of hers at one of the academy's events. (*Joe Schildhorn / BFA*)

L Brands CEO Les Wexner with model Stella Maxwell in 2016. Maria Farmer said her assault occurred on Wexner's property in 1996; Wexner denied knowledge of the incident. (*Astrid Stawiarz / Getty Images for Fragrance Foundation*)

Victim Alicia Arden around the time she claims Epstein assaulted her in 1997. Epstein pretended to be a modeling scout for Wexner's Victoria's Secret brand to lure the then twenty-six-year-old. (*Courtesy Alicia Arden*)

(*L–R*) Donald Trump, Melania Knauss, Prince Andrew, Epstein, and Ghislaine Maxwell at Mar-a-Lago in 2000. (*Davidoff Studios / Getty Images*)

The controversial March 13, 2001, photo showing Prince Andrew, Virginia Roberts, and Ghislaine Maxwell at Maxwell's home in London. Andrew questioned its authenticity, claiming "That's me, but whether that's my hand . . ." (*Backgrid*)

Aerial view of Epstein's Zorro Ranch in Stanley, New Mexico, forty miles south of Santa Fe. The property includes an airstrip and vintage railcar. (*Drone Base / Reuters*)

Behind white gates and tall hedgerows, Epstein's house at 358 El Brillo Way in Palm Beach, Florida, which went on the market in 2020 for $21.995 million. (*Emily Michot* / Miami Herald / *Tribune News Service* / *Getty Images*)

At a press conference in November 2019, victim Teala Davies looks on as attorney Gloria Allred holds up a photo showing Davies, then seventeen, flying in a helicopter with Epstein over the U.S. Virgin Islands. (*Timothy A. Clary / AFP / Getty Images*)

Aerial view of Epstein's Little St. James Island. According to the attorney general of the U.S. Virgin Islands, Epstein was bringing girls as young as eleven and twelve there as recently as 2018. (*Marco Bello / Reuters*)

The purple cover of the notebook that victim Michelle Licata kept as a teen, showing her wearing braces. "I had blamed myself all these years," she said. (*Emily Michot* / Miami Herald / *Tribune News Service* / Getty Images)

Sarah Kellen with Epstein at Little St. James in this undated photo. She was referred to as Ghislaine Maxwell's "lieutenant." (*The Mega Agency*)

Bill Clinton and Jeffrey Epstein's personal masseuse Chauntae Davies, then twenty-two, during a trip to Africa in 2002. She called the former president "a complete gentleman" but accused Epstein of rape. (*The Mega Agency*)

Jean-Luc Brunel with his model roster in Paris in 2001. He allegedly provided underage girls for Epstein, including sending twelve-year-old triplets from France. Brunel has vehemently denied the accusations. (*MDP-Robert Espalieu / Starface / Polaris*)

Epstein with Professor Alan Dershowitz in 2004. In a 2020 Netflix documentary, Dershowitz dared Virginia Roberts Giuffre to "look in the camera" and accuse him of having sex with her—and she did. (*Rick Friedman / Corbis / Getty Images*)

Former Israeli prime minister Ehud Barak was photographed entering Epstein's Manhattan townhouse in January 2016. Barak claimed he "never met Epstein in the company of women or young girls." (*Jae Donnelly / Probe-Media*)

Harvey Weinstein, Jeffrey Epstein, and Ghislaine Maxwell attend Princess Beatrice's eighteenth birthday costume party at Windsor Castle in 2006. Weinstein reportedly once tried to abuse one of Epstein's "favorite girls." (*The Mega Agency*)

On March 15, 2005, the day Palm Beach police opened their investigation into Epstein, he and Ghislaine Maxwell were seen attending an event in NYC. (*Joe Schildhorn / Patrick McMullan / Getty Images*)

After serving his sentence in Florida, Epstein was photographed with Prince Andrew in Central Park in December 2010. Andrew later claimed he traveled to New York to end their friendship. (*Jae Donnelly / Probe-Media*)

(L–R) Epstein associates Nadia Marcinkova, Michele Tagliani, and Sarah Kellen at a New York City event in 2004. Two years later, Marcinkova and Kellen were named as "potential coconspirators" but received immunity under Epstein's non-prosecution agreement. (*Rob Rich / SocietyAllure*)

At a 2005 event in New York City, Epstein is seen with Adriana Ross, who was also named as a "potential coconspirator." (*Neil Rasmus / Patrick McMullan / Getty Images*)

Virginia Roberts during a photo shoot in Australia in 2011, when she broke her silence to *Mail on Sunday* reporter Sharon Churcher. (*Michael Thomas*)

Haley Robson provided this photo of herself as a teenager. She became a subject of the Palm Beach police investigation for recruiting girls for Epstein. (*Courtesy Haley Robson*)

Epstein, director Woody Allen, and Allen's wife, Soon-Yi Previn, after leaving Epstein's Manhattan home in 2013. Allen was one of the well-known figures who remained friendly with Epstein following his Florida conviction. (*Elder Ordonez / SplashNews*)

(*L–R*) Epstein, Palm Beach businessman Pepe Fanjul, and Leon Black, billionaire chairman of Apollo Global Management, in 2005. Black caught heat for admitting he turned to Epstein for financial guidance. (*Joe Schildhorn / Patrick McMullan / Getty Images*)

Epstein is seen out with an unidentified woman in Manhattan in September 2016—the same month he repeatedly invoked his Fifth Amendment right against self-incrimination during a legal deposition. (*SplashNews*)

Outside the White House on July 12, 2019, President Donald Trump listens as U.S. Labor Secretary Alexander Acosta announces his resignation over his handling of the Epstein case. (*Brendan Smialowski / AFP / Getty Images*)

Epstein's photo for the New York State sex offender registry, taken in March 2017. The following month, he visited MIT; he was still being courted as a donor by its Media Lab director, Joichi Ito, who later resigned over his Epstein ties. (*New York State Sex Offender Registry / AP / Shutterstock*)

Epstein's final mug shot—dated July 8, 2019, the day following his arrest at New Jersey's Teterboro Airport after he'd touched down from Paris in his private jet. (*U.S. Department of Justice*)

Epstein with girlfriend Karyna Shuliak in 2014. She was the last person he is said to have telephoned before his death. (*Billy Farrell / BFA*)

As shown in this photo released by CBS's *60 Minutes*, multiple nooses fashioned from orange bedsheets were found in Epstein's cell after his death. (*Via New York City Office of Chief Medical Examiner*)

Paramedics wheel Epstein—still in his orange jail jumpsuit—into New York Downtown Hospital around 7:30 A.M. on August 10, 2019, after he was found unresponsive in his cell. He was later declared dead at the hospital. (*William Farrington / Polaris*)

Courtroom artist's sketch of Epstein's accusers waiting to make impact statements in the U.S. District Court in Manhattan on August 27, 2019. Judge Richard Berman called the statement opportunity "a measure of respect for the victims." (*Jane Rosenberg*)

Victim "Jane Doe 15," at the office of her attorney, Gloria Allred, in Los Angeles in 2019, said she believed Epstein "was only a small part of an insidious system of privilege that exploits children." (*Robyn Beck / AFP / Getty Images*)

Lawyers David Boies (*L*) and Bradley Edwards (*R*) flank victim Annie Farmer after she confronted Epstein at a 2019 detention hearing at the U.S. District Court in Manhattan. (*Timothy A. Clary / AFP / Getty Images*)

(*L–R*) Victims Sarah Ransome, Virginia Roberts Giuffre, and Marijke Chartouni find support in one another after the August 27, 2019, court hearing. (*Emily Michot / Miami Herald / Tribune News Service / Getty Images*)

Victim Jennifer Araoz outside court. She was brought to Epstein's Manhattan townhouse for the first time at age fourteen. (*Yana Paskova / AFP / Getty Images*)

Victim Teala Davies, also outside court. Epstein abused Davies for two years, beginning at age seventeen. (*Yana Paskova / AFP / Getty Images*)

Four days after Epstein's death, Ghislaine Maxwell was seen in public for the first time in three years—at an In-N-Out Burger in Los Angeles, on August 14, 2019, reading a book about CIA operatives. (*The Mega Agency*)

In this aerial view, dense forest surrounds the 156-acre property where FBI agents took Ghislaine Maxwell into custody on July 2, 2020. Her hideout was a $1 million, four-bedroom mountaintop retreat called Tuckedaway, in Bradford, New Hampshire. (*Drone Base / Reuters*)

This courtroom artist's sketch shows Ghislaine Maxwell on July 14, 2020, at a bail hearing in Manhattan, appearing on a video link from a Brooklyn jail. At some points she was seen wiping her eyes. (*Jane Rosenberg / Reuters*)

The unmarked stone crypt believed to be Epstein's final resting place at the IJ Morris Star of David Cemetery near Loxahatchee, Florida. The tomb to the left of his holds the remains of his parents. Names were removed from both graves to prevent vandalism. (*Jose Lambiet*)

# 23

# ROCK STAR

JEFFREY EPSTEIN WAS ACCUSTOMED TO THE DEFERENTIAL TREATMENT afforded to the wealthy and powerful. On the tarmac at the VIP section of West Palm Beach International Airport, at the dining establishments in Palm Beach, and of course on Little St. James, he was usually greeted with a "Yes, sir, Mr. Epstein," or a "How are you, sir?" from luggage handlers, waiters, and his staff. It was a perk of fortune.

Usually when wealthy men go to prison, these perks are suspended. At the Palm Beach County Criminal Justice Complex, though, nothing was routine about Epstein's stint behind bars.

As Deputy Sheriff Michael Gauger would later comment, "We received Mr. Epstein under conditions that we were not used to, and we did the very best we could under the parameters that we had."[1]

ALMOST IMMEDIATELY FOLLOWING EPSTEIN'S ARRIVAL at the stockade, the problems began. "Jeffrey Epstein was a man who was the master of his own domain, always in control of his world," attorney Spencer Kuvin would comment, and jail was one of the only places in his adult life where he wasn't in control: no vegan dinners, and the thermostat was not set to a perpetual 54-degree chill. There were ways, though, to make his stay more comfortable.

Sheriff's deputies in charge of the jail treated Epstein with kid gloves. "I/M Epstein is a 'first time offender' who will be serving a long sentence at this facility and that is a very rare occurrence," Lieutenant Mark Chamberlain wrote to his bosses at the Palm Beach County Sheriff's Office. "He is poorly versed in jail routine and society and his adjustment to incarceration will most likely be atypical. For the time being, I am authorizing that his cell door be left unlocked and [that] he be given liberal access to the attorney room where a TV will be installed."[2]

Epstein was housed in T-Block, a remote low-security wing of the jail. His lawyers were constantly visiting him, and although he wasn't provided access to the jail's Wi-Fi, he was allowed to use the laptops that his attorneys brought with them. It was a rare set of privileges that few sex offenders could have expected.

Like all inmates of the jail, regardless of their wealth and dependent solely on the severity of their crimes, Epstein was allowed to apply for work release. He filed the permit application and his request was immediately approved. Thus, for the duration of his sentence, Epstein was allowed to spend twelve hours a day, six days a week, working outside the jail at his office at 250 South Australian Avenue in West Palm Beach. He left every morning at 8:00 A.M. and his driver/bodyguard returned him to the jail at 8:00 P.M.

According to an article in *The Palm Beach Post,* Jeffrey Epstein's twelve-hour workday began when his driver, Russian MMA fighter Igor Zinoviev, picked him up at the stockade and drove him to his office, home to the Florida Science Foundation, a nonprofit organization he had conveniently created seven months before accepting the plea bargain.* He ate well, lived well, and carried on with his life.

---

* The Florida Science Foundation never received its nonprofit certification from the Internal Revenue Service, and Epstein conveniently dissolved it forty-five days after he completed his jail sentence.

As journalist Jane Musgrave would comment, "It was as if all he had to do was sleep in a really crappy motel."[3]

An off-duty sheriff's deputy accompanied him to work; he had to wear an ankle monitor at all times. For them, it was a lucrative gig. The deputies were paid on average $42 per hour with a minimum guarantee of three hours worked; supervisors were paid $49 per hour, and Officers in Charge of Special Events received $55 per hour.

Epstein, like other sex offenders, was supposed to attend counseling, but his lawyers told court officials that he didn't have to because he had a private psychiatrist working with him. The judge was skeptical but agreed anyway.

ONE STIPULATION OF THE WORK release—a seemingly obvious one—was that Epstein would not engage in any illegal activity. Most of his time was spent in an office behind closed doors; women staffers were around. There was an approved list of visitors Epstein was permitted to interact with at his office. Deputies kept a log of all the people who came and went; the reports were kept under lock and key in the Sheriff's Office.[4] Old habits die hard, though—even under the watchful eye of the Palm Beach County Sheriff's Office.

Two lawsuits, filed after his death in 2019, alleged that Jeffrey Epstein arranged for two women he had recruited in New York City to be flown to Florida during the period of his sentence. Once the girls were in the Sunshine State, Epstein forced them to perform sexual acts on him.[5] One girl, a dancer identified only as Priscilla Doe, told attorneys filing a civil suit on her behalf that Epstein flew her to Florida during his imprisonment and had sex with her at his mansion while he was wearing an ankle monitor. The other woman, identified as Kaitlyn Doe in court papers, said Epstein promised to help her pay $20,000 for a needed medical procedure in exchange for sex.[6]

Provisions of his work release arrangement allowed Epstein to be at 358 El Brillo Way between the hours of 12:30 P.M. and 2:30 P.M. Toward the end of his first year behind bars, according to internal

Palm Beach County Sheriff's Office emails, sheriff's officials then made the work release even more lenient, approving Epstein to leave his office each day in July 2009 and go back to his mansion.[7] His home was never searched before the off-duty deputy took him inside.


THIRTEEN MONTHS INTO EPSTEIN'S SENTENCE, Jack Goldberger, one of his attorneys, returned to the Palm Beach County State Attorney's Office to ask that his client be released for good behavior. Barry Krischer had left the office in 2008; Krischer's successor, Michael McAuliffe, granted the request. As Chief Deputy Sheriff Michael Gauger would later say of Epstein, "He was cooperative. He was friendly. He created no issues during his incarceration period."[8] Epstein was walked out of jail on July 21, 2009.

Sex offenders are not allowed to live within a thousand feet of a school, park, or other areas where children assemble, but 358 El Brillo Way was close to a mile from the nearest school. Although he'd remain on probation for another twelve months, Jeffrey Epstein's life could continue as if nothing had happened.

In an interview with a journalist shortly after his release, Epstein, sounding tired but relaxed, said that "I'm looking forward to getting my life back."[9]

A new army of attorneys, however, was aiming to make sure that that would never happen.

# PART FIVE

# JUSTICE DELAYED

I'm not a sexual predator, I'm an offender. It's the difference
between a murderer and a person who steals a bagel.
—JEFFREY EPSTEIN[1]

# 24

# SYMPATHY FOR THE DEVIL

"My experience of Jeffrey is of a thoughtful, kind, generous loving man, with a keen sense of humor and a ready smile—a man of principles and values and a man of his word. If he made a promise, he would always follow through. In fact, I never saw him break a promise. He is disciplined in business and conscientious. A man always quick to help someone who is down, or to offer an opportunity to someone to pursue a dream or a goal."

Those eighty-four words, attributed to Ghislaine Maxwell, were one of several glowing testimonials included in a 2007 document that Jeffrey Epstein's lawyer Jack Goldberger forwarded to Palm Beach state attorney Barry Krischer as Epstein's non-prosecution agreement was being hammered out.

Maxwell, however, was physically removed from Epstein's world by this time. She was dating Ted Waitt, the founder of the Gateway computer company. Just like Maxwell's father, Waitt owned a luxury yacht, the *Plan B,* which she and Waitt used for sailing trips. The name seemed a fitting descriptor for Maxwell's new life. Just as Maxwell had sought to transform Epstein's image a decade earlier, she reportedly undertook efforts to make the once ponytailed Waitt more stylish, urging the billionaire to shave his head and wear fashionable sunglasses. Thanks to Maxwell's makeover, Waitt became "a virtual doppelgänger for Jason Statham," according to a report in *The New York Times*.[1]

But moving on from Epstein's inner circle was easier said than done, especially as legal and public scrutiny of Epstein's activities picked up steam. What seemed clear from the warm and fuzzy testimonial, whether she composed it or it was penned by Epstein's lawyer with her name attached, was that Maxwell had no plans to turn against Epstein, for financial and other reasons.

The investigations by the Palm Beach police and the FBI had not broken up Epstein's tight inner circle. His personal assistant, Story Cowles—who has never been accused of wrongdoing—had visited him 130 times while he was technically behind bars. Two of the four "potential coconspirators," Nadia Marcinkova and Sarah Kellen, also made a combined seventy visits to the Palm Beach County Jail, according to records.

In subsequent years, although Epstein's attorneys had secured immunity for Marcinkova, Kellen, Lesley Groff, and Adriana Ross as part of the negotiations for his NPA, those in the old inner circle would distance themselves from him. Marcinkova's lawyer would report that she was "severely traumatized," while Kellen's spokesperson painted her client as a victim who was "extremely vulnerable" when she initially found herself caught in Epstein's web.

For now, though, Epstein's luck appeared to be holding up.

But he still had to get past his probation to be a free man again.

A PROBATION VIOLATION, NO MATTER how small, can mean heading right back to jail. In the Sunshine State, however, career criminals often scoff at the lax probation enforcement. The system is overwhelmed. Florida's prison population since 2015 is the third largest in the United States, with more than 100,000 in state facilities, according to Project 180. In 2020, there were more than 164,000 parolees under the supervision of approximately 4,700 probation and parole officers in the state.

In Epstein's case, violating the terms of his probation would have meant his return to the county jail for another nine months. There were other risks to stepping out of line. Several months before Epstein was released from jail in July 2009, Barack Obama won the presidency in a historic election in 2008, and a few months later, Alex Acosta was replaced as U.S. attorney in the Southern District of Florida by an attorney tapped by the Obama administration, Wifredo Ferrer. If Epstein misbehaved in any way, the Palm Beach Sheriff's Office could have recommended that the non-prosecution agreement be torn up and that Epstein and all his coconspirators be tried in federal court and risk prison time.

There seemed little need, however, for Epstein to violate the probation conditions set by the Palm Beach County Sheriff's Office. Just like the special treatment that had resulted in his "work privileges" during his thirteen-month period of incarceration, Epstein was afforded a slew of special privileges that were mind-bogglingly generous while he was on probation. Officially, he was under house arrest for a year, and all his movements were subject to the approval of his probation officer.[2] He was allowed to go to work. He was allowed to go to the grocery store once a week. He was allowed to get his hair cut once a month. He was allowed to see a personal physician for medical care and a psychiatrist for counseling.

But that wasn't all. Epstein was allowed to travel to New York and any of his other homes and real estate holdings in Manhattan. He was even allowed to travel to Little St. James on his 727.[3] He received permission from Palm Beach County Circuit Court judge Jeffrey Colbath to travel overnight for business or to confer with his attorneys.

While Epstein was barred from traveling on weekends, and all plans to leave the county ostensibly had to be approved by his probation officer with at least a forty-eight-hour heads-up, travel records of

Epstein's movements while on probation show that he traveled just as freely as he did before he was incarcerated.[4] Logs revealed that between January 6, 2010, and April 8, 2010, Epstein traveled to New York City nine times and to Little St. James nine times.[5] All of these trips involved overnight visits, far from the eyes of the Florida Department of Corrections Probation Services.

But Epstein's probation officer wasn't the only one tasked with monitoring his comings and goings.

MIKE FISTEN, A TWENTY-FIVE-YEAR VETERAN of the Miami-Dade Police Department, had spent most of his career as a detective and sergeant working robbery, homicides, and narcotics cases, including an infamous police corruption case that was detailed in the documentary *Cocaine Cowboys*. In 2009, Fisten was hired by Bradley Edwards, an attorney for Virginia Roberts, to assemble evidence against the financier that would later be used in a civil suit against him.

Almost immediately Fisten noticed his target's brazen violations of probation. Fisten was able to document at least two accounts of women, brought from another state at the age of eighteen, being taken to Epstein's office and meeting with him behind closed doors. During these meetings, Fisten reported, Epstein was naked but for his Department of Corrections–supplied GPS ankle monitor.[6]

Staking out 358 El Brillo Way from his parked car, Fisten witnessed Epstein coming and going from his mansion while tucked inside one of his many Cadillac Escalades; all had tinted windows. Fisten followed him to the Miami InterContinental Hotel and even photographed Epstein emerging from the lobby. The results of his detective work were immediately forwarded to the probation office— Fisten was sure that Epstein would be busted for these violations. "Every time I brought the probation office a case, they kept telling me the same thing," Fisten recalled in an interview for the 2020 Netflix *Filthy Rich* documentary. "'What would you like us to do? He's a celebrity.'"[7]

When Edwards initially hired Fisten, neither understood how extensive Epstein's trafficking operation really was. "One after another, three girls turned into four girls, turned into five, six, seven, and so on," Fisten said. "I couldn't help but think this could've been my daughter or your daughter or my next door neighbor's daughter."

Fisten said he was particularly angered with how Epstein's private investigators tried to harass the victims. "They were former Miami cops. He paid an extremely large retainer to them and all they had to do was to follow the girls around and intimidate them," Fisten said. The FBI, he claimed, looked into possible obstruction of justice or witness tampering charges against Epstein, but the charges were never brought.

BY EVERY REASONABLE EXPECTATION, JEFFREY Epstein's network of wealthy and powerful friends should have abandoned him after the Florida conviction. Child molesters are usually scorned by society—even by other kinds of violent criminals. In the wake of his release from jail, however, Epstein was able to slip back into his old routines—not just his abuse of young girls, but also his easy courtship of another group of people: elite figures from across media, politics, and academia. This seemingly overnight rehabilitation of Epstein's image is one of the great mysteries of his adult life.

It was impossible not to know of Epstein's legal entanglements; the headlines traveled far beyond the Palm Beach courthouse and became national news. If Epstein's conviction was a scarlet letter, however, many old acquaintances and new ones chose to overlook it. Almost immediately after his probation began, Epstein's home on Manhattan's Upper East Side resumed its status as a beacon for the rich, the famous, and the powerful.

He no longer had Ghislaine Maxwell, though, to engineer his social life. She had effectively dropped out, and the role of greasing access for Epstein now fell to others. Epstein's longtime financial patron Les Wexner, meanwhile, had followed Maxwell out the door, severing his ties with Epstein in the fall of 2007, some three years after his foundation gave Epstein's foundation more than $10 million, according to *The Wall Street Journal*. But others continued to seek his counsel, his company, and his cash.

In 2010, Epstein met with titans from the technology industry, including Microsoft founder Bill Gates, Tesla founder Elon Musk, Amazon founder Jeff Bezos, and Google cofounder Sergey Brin.[8] According to a report in *The New York Times*, Gates met with Epstein on "numerous" occasions, including three at Epstein's home in Manhattan. "His lifestyle is very different and kind of intriguing although it would not work for me," Mr. Gates would email colleagues in 2011 after meeting Epstein for the first time, just two years after Epstein's release from Florida jail.[9]

Two months out of jail, Epstein attended a party at the home of billionaire industrialist David Koch. Reportedly, Wilbur Ross, Rudy Giuliani, Steve Mnuchin, and Chris Cuomo were also in attendance. Picking up the gossip, the *New York Post*'s "Page Six" asked: "Why would David Koch invite Epstein to this party two months after he was released from prison for soliciting a minor and accused of a multitude of sex crimes involving young girls?"

Epstein hung out with Ross again, this time in the company of Leon Black. The three attended a movie screening in March 2011 in Southampton, England. And a year later, Epstein was still listed as the director of the Barbara and Leon Black Family Foundation despite resigning his post in 2007. (The foundation later called this an error.)

Black, who heads up one of the largest private equity firms in the world, Apollo Global Management, had been friendly with Epstein since the late 1990s. Years later, Black would be scrutinized for a 2011 business deal involving Epstein three years after the Florida conviction. The two men, along with Black's four children, according to *The New York Times*, invested in a company that makes emission control products, Environmental Solutions Worldwide. (In 2019, in an email to Apollo's employees and a conference call to investors, Black maintained that his contact with Epstein was not related to company business and stressed it was for estate planning and philanthropic advice, according to *The New York Times*.)

Barclays CEO James E. Staley, known as Jes to his associates, had been a friend of Epstein's since 1999, when he was running the private banking business of JPMorgan and using Epstein as a contact. Staley visited Epstein at least ten times after he had been arrested. Staley and his wife, Debora, sailed on their boat to Little St. James in April 2015, and Epstein used Staley as a reference when he applied to set up a bank, Southern Country International, in the Virgin Islands, on March 20, 2013.[10]

ACCORDING TO THE OFFICE OF the U.S. Attorney for the Southern District of Florida, Jeffrey Epstein had paid his debt to society after serving his sentence under the VIP conditions of the Palm Beach County Sheriff's Office. But Epstein—and his crew—faced other debt collectors in the form of his many alleged victims, some of whom had by now obtained sophisticated legal representation. Maxwell, too, found herself in the legal crosshairs of civil suits. In September 2009, a process server walked through the packed lobby of the Sheraton Hotel toward Ghislaine Maxwell, who was attending a gathering of the Clinton Global Initiative in New York City. "Maxwell was huddled in a small group talking to other guests," journalist Conchita Sarnoff recalled, "as the server approached her. He called out her name, and with so many people surrounding her, Maxwell was unsuspecting. She confirmed her identity and he served her notice," Sarnoff recounted in her book, *TrafficKing*.[11]

In 2009, in the course of reporting on the lawsuits that had been filed against Epstein, New York *Daily News* columnist George Rush heard that lawyers for Virginia Roberts had served papers on Maxwell and he was looking to do a story. Rush reached out to Maxwell for comment and also contacted a spokesperson for Epstein, Howard Rubenstein.[12] In the course of his research, he came across an affidavit in which Virginia Roberts, now Giuffre, recounted how

Ghislaine Maxwell had procured her for massages and sex. Rush was familiar with Maxwell—they had interacted on New York's social scene, even going out to dinner once with mutual friends. He thought of her as a "charming" person, even a "sparkling conversationalist."

Epstein, who rarely spoke with journalists, agreed to talk to Rush, but he stipulated that, on the advice of his lawyers, the chat—with Rush and a pair of *Daily News* editors—would need to remain off the record. Years later, Rush described the interview as "a self-serving rationale for how [Epstein] had been tormented by the lawyers" and the alleged victims they represented.[13]

In an interview for this book, Rush described how Epstein laid it on thick during the phone call, leaning into "his working-class roots and his Brooklyn accent" in an attempt, seemingly, to develop a rapport with the journalists. Epstein portrayed his victims as "like experienced sex workers" who had worked as strippers for clubs where their age "would have been verified." Epstein also high-lighted the differences among various states when it came to the minimum age of consent. The "statutory aspect to his prosecution was unfair" in Epstein's view, Rush said, because if he had "done the same things in a different state there would be no cause to arrest him. . . . So, he quibbled about whether he had done any-thing wrong and his regret was not so much about having had sex with them—and I think he emphasized several times that there was no penetration—but that he should have been smarter about checking their age. Like it wasn't the act itself that was bad, it was his sloppiness."

Watching Epstein concoct these explanations, Rush was struck by the financier's evident knack for manipulation. Epstein attempted to redirect the focus of the *Daily News* story. Instead of "going after the rich guy," he suggested to the *Daily News* staffers, "a better story . . . would be to go after shady lawyers who were preying on the rich guys," Rush said.[14]

In the interview, Epstein also expressed his concern about Ghis-laine Maxwell. Epstein told Rush that Maxwell had "nothing to do with any of this" and the fact that lawyers had included her in the civil suits was an attempted money grab. "He was adamant about protecting Ghislaine's good name," Rush said. Epstein felt "she shouldn't have to suffer the consequences."[15]

APPEARING AMID GOSSIPY ITEMS ABOUT New York society, with no mention of Epstein having spoken to him, Rush's article of December 19, 2009, went largely unnoticed. The off-the-record spin Jeffrey Epstein gave to the *Daily News* was part of a larger effort to rehabilitate his image. As much as he tried, Epstein was no longer anonymous, or a figure of nominal curiosity who hung around in the background of certain social circles of Manhattan and Palm Beach. He was, according to the U.S. Department of Justice, a sex offender. His crimes were now a matter of public record—and his apparent fondness for young women and girls became a subject of conversation.

Epstein's brand was tarnished, and he appeared eager to do what he could to make the public forget the nasty headlines of his multi-year battle with the authorities in Florida, not to mention the more than twenty civil suits that continued to dog him. In New York City, there is an army of professional publicists happy to collect steep fees in return for pumping out positive press for their clients. Epstein turned to Peggy Siegal, one of the most powerful and energetic publicists in the business.[16]

Siegal once described herself to a *New York Times* reporter as "a Jewish princess from New Jersey who always wanted to be a queen." If Epstein tended to duck away from the paparazzi flashbulbs, Siegal headed directly for them. Both residents of the Upper East Side, she and Epstein were already friends. Following Epstein's release from jail in Florida, the bombastic Siegal did what she could to gloss over the inescapable and incriminating truths about his criminal perversions.

Siegal had great affection for Epstein. "He lives in a different environment," she told *New York* magazine in 2007. "He's of this world. But he creates this different environment. He lives like a pasha. The most magnificent townhouse I've ever been in, and I've been in everything. . . . How did he get himself into [this legal] pickle? That's the mystery of Jeffrey Epstein. He's very mysterious. Not that many people get close to him. Not that many people know him."[17]

In 2010, Siegal invited Epstein to attend the New York premiere of the Oliver Stone film *Wall Street: Money Never Sleeps*. At the parties that followed, Epstein mingled with future Trump administration cabinet members Steve Mnuchin and Wilbur Ross as well as former New York City mayor Rudy Giuliani. In 2011, Siegal threw a lavish dinner party at Epstein's East Seventy-First Street mansion to honor the financier's friend Prince Andrew. This time the guest list included Woody Allen and his wife, Soon-Yi Previn; comedian Chelsea Handler; and journalists Katie Couric, Charlie Rose, and George Stephanopoulos.[18]

Years later, after photos were released of Prince Andrew and Jeffrey Epstein walking together in Central Park, embarrassed guests had to explain themselves to reporters. Siegal soon lost clients.[19]

IF SOME ACQUAINTANCES DISTANCED THEMSELVES from Jeffrey Epstein following his Florida conviction, one dimension of Epstein's life was seemingly little affected. Even after Epstein's 2008 Florida conviction, prominent scientists continued to make social calls to Epstein's mansions. Perhaps a criminal past—especially when it involved a murky non-prosecution agreement—was possible to overlook when there was scientific research to fund and projects to grant. Epstein knew that as long as the checks kept coming, his special friends would provide even a tarnished figure with the armor of legitimacy.

One of the most famous scientists to share Epstein's company was Marvin Minsky, a top cognitive scientist who researched artificial intelligence and self-training algorithms. Minsky, a New York

City native like Epstein, was the recipient of the esteemed Turing Award and the author of several books. He and Epstein shared an accent and, seemingly, many of the same interests.

Virginia Roberts identified Minsky in court documents as one of the men she was ordered by Epstein to massage and pleasure before she was eighteen years old. According to Roberts, Minsky visited the Manhattan mansion and the grounds of Little St. James. Even after Epstein's arrest in Florida, Minsky continued to hold court with Epstein and accept his research grants. In 2012, Minsky even cohosted a scientific conference on Little St. James.[20]

When details of Virginia Roberts's 2016 legal deposition were unsealed by a court three years later, a colleague of Minsky's at MIT sparked controversy when he blamed Roberts for being a willing party. "The word 'assaulting' presumes that he applied force or violence, in some unspecified way, but the article itself says no such thing. Only that they had sex," computer scientist Richard Stallman wrote, referring to an article about Roberts's testimony that she was forced to have sex with Minsky. "The most plausible scenario is that she presented herself to him as entirely willing," Stallman wrote in an email published by *Vice*. Minsky died of a brain hemorrhage in 2016 at the age of eighty-eight.

JOICHI ITO, WHO RAN THE Massachusetts Institute of Technology's famed Computer Science and Artificial Intelligence Laboratory, known simply as MIT's Media Lab, was another figure who maintained contact with Epstein—and his money—following the Florida conviction. Ito, a Japanese entrepreneur and venture capitalist, sat on the boards of *The New York Times* and the MacArthur Foundation.[21] A two-time college dropout, he became wealthy by making early investments in tech companies, including Twitter, Kickstarter, and Flickr.[22]

Ito was a frequent guest at 9 East Seventy-First Street, and Jeffrey Epstein rewarded him with investments, including up to

$1.7 million to advance the Media Lab's research. Epstein also served as a matchmaker between Ito and hedge funds, such as that of Leon Black, the founder of Apollo Global Management.[23]

In 2019, after Epstein's arrest in New York by the FBI and subsequent scrutiny over Epstein's financial ties to MIT and other leading scientific institutions, Ito resigned from the MIT Media Lab.

JOHN BROCKMAN, A LITERARY AGENT who specialized in representing top scientific authors, has been termed by the *New Republic* Jeffrey Epstein's "intellectual enabler." Brockman's agency, founded in 1973, represented figures like Minsky and Ito, among numerous others.[24] Brockman had also founded the Edge Foundation, a nonprofit with the lofty mission "to arrive at the edge of the world's knowledge, seek out the most complex and sophisticated minds, put them in a room together, and have them ask each other the questions they are asking themselves."[25] The organization held several events each year and conducted annual projects, notably "Questions," which collected and published leading thinkers' answers, in brief essay form, to questions like "What is your most dangerous idea?" and "What are you optimistic about?" and "Is the Internet changing the way you think?"

Brockman and the Edge also threw an annual event known as the Billionaires' Dinner, a gathering of what *GQ* termed "row upon row of the world's most successful (and richest) human beings."[26] Epstein—and sometimes members of his staff—attended the lavish affairs; often, Epstein bankrolled them. In 2011 Epstein attended the Billionaires' Dinner in Long Beach, California, that was also attended by Jeff Bezos, Sergey Brin, and Elon Musk.[27]

Reporting that emerged after Epstein's death revealed that between 2001 and 2015, the Edge Foundation received $638,000 from Epstein and various foundations run by the financier.[28] In a 2013 email exchange with journalist Evgeny Morozov, who was a Brockman agency client, Brockman wrote that "Epstein had been extremely generous in funding projects of many of our friends and clients." In the email, Brockman also recounted a visit of his to Epstein's Manhattan townhouse: "[The] last time I visited his house (the largest private residence in New York City), I walked in to find him in a sweatsuit and a British guy in a suit with suspenders, getting foot massages from two young well-dressed Russian women." He continued that at a certain point he realizes "that the recipient of Irina's foot massage was His Royal Highness Prince Andrew, the Duke of York."[29] Curiously, the point of Brockman's message to Morozov was to encourage Morozov to meet Epstein, whom Brockman wrote that he considered "extremely bright and interesting" even if he was "a different kind of animal."

When Epstein, due to legal difficulties, stopped donating money to Brockman's group, the Edge Foundation reportedly ceased the annual Billionaires' Dinner.[30]

In August 2019, a few weeks after Epstein's death, Dr. Kate Darling, a leading expert in robot ethics and a researcher at the MIT Media Lab, wrote a damning opinion piece about the financier's ties to the science community for *The Guardian*. In the piece, titled "Jeffrey Epstein's Influence in the Science World Is a Symptom of Larger Problems," she wrote, "The Epstein web can appear inescapable, and for those entangled in it, there's a temptation to break out and cut all ties with his enablers." She continued, "It was hard not to feel that my whole professional environment had been complicit."

# 25

# NOTORIOUS

FROM 1994 TO 2013, SHARON CHURCHER RAN THE AMERICAN DESK for a mass-circulation British weekly newspaper, *The Mail on Sunday*. A nineteen-year veteran, Churcher had earned her stripes investigating the biggest political, crime, and celebrity stories in New York and beyond, and Jeffrey Epstein fascinated her—and her paper. The Oxford University graduate had a hunch that Epstein's enormous wealth and his connection to the rich and powerful were preventing witnesses from coming forward.

In May 2009, Churcher came across a lawsuit filed against Jeffrey Epstein in a Miami courtroom by a woman identified only by a pseudonym, Jane Doe 102. "In addition to being continually exploited to satisfy Defendant's every sexual whim, Plaintiff was also required to be sexually exploited by Defendant's adult male peers, including royalty, politicians, academicians, businessmen," the court papers stated. The lawsuit was just one of more than two dozen that had been lodged against Epstein between 2008 and 2014 but had gone largely unnoticed by journalists. To quickly extinguish the civil suits, Epstein doled out confidential settlements to more than two dozen victims represented by numerous lawyers. Years later, *The Palm Beach Post* reported that three were settled for a total of $5.5 million.

One Epstein and Maxwell connection that particularly fascinated Churcher was Prince Andrew, and so the inclusion of the word "royalty" in the Jane Doe 102 court document leaped out at her. "The court papers didn't name any 'royals,' but the only royal I knew of who hung out with Epstein was Prince Andrew, the queen's second son," Churcher recalled in an interview for this book. She had broken a series of stories about Andrew's "bad-boy" behavior, which confidants of his ex-wife, Sarah Ferguson, blamed on Epstein and Maxwell. In the court papers, Churcher read that Jane Doe 102 was asserting that she had been recruited into Epstein's web by Maxwell in 1999 at age fifteen. (It's subsequently been established that she was sixteen.) Could the allegations in the lawsuit be related to Churcher's reporting on Andrew's antics? The journalist sought to track down the unnamed accuser.

Churcher's quest to identify Jane Doe 102 began in Palm Beach. According to the lawsuit, Churcher learned that the girl was recruited at Trump's Mar-a-Lago club, where she worked and where her father was a maintenance manager. But the club had employed scores of maintenance workers over the years, some of whom were undocumented and had returned to their home countries in Central America.

Jane Doe 102's lawyers, Robert C. Josefsberg and Katherine W. Ezell, didn't return the reporter's calls, but Churcher kept digging. "A source who knew about the original investigation into Epstein told me that it was going to be extremely difficult to get anyone to talk because the feds had struck this secret non-prosecution deal with Epstein," Churcher said.

To Churcher's source, the debacle of Epstein's NPA was "just a straightforward cover-up." Churcher stated, "My source was outraged by the agreement. It appeared to involve the government arranging for Epstein to pay off more than forty underage victims, including Jane Doe 102."

In January 2011, Churcher discovered Jane Doe 102's maiden name: Virginia Roberts.

IN HER REPORTING, SHARON CHURCHER learned that the settlement Virginia Roberts had signed might not be airtight. "It barred her from disclosing how much Epstein paid her in return for dropping her lawsuit against him," Churcher said. "But it also gave her the right to waive her anonymity and do an interview."

Churcher learned that Roberts had moved to Australia, but she could not immediately determine her married name. Through property records, Churcher tracked down an address for Roberts's high school boyfriend's family. The family had since moved, but a neighbor confirmed that the boyfriend, Tony Figueroa, had dated Roberts. The neighbor recalled Roberts as "a sad, anorexic-looking girl with a drug problem" who had vanished after being "delivered" to Epstein to work as a "prostitute." Churcher heard more rumors from other acquaintances. One said that Roberts had sunk into drug addiction and begun to skip school after being molested by a family friend.

Churcher was able to track down Figueroa in the small town of Flowery Branch, Georgia, and he told the journalist an astonishing story when they met in a coffee shop.

Figueroa revealed that Roberts had tried to straighten out her life by going to rehab. The New York *Daily News* reported the fifteen-year-old, in 1998, was living in the substance abuse treatment facility Growing Together in Lake Worth, Florida.[1] More than a year later, she had begun working for Epstein—"work" that, as Figueroa learned, included participating in threesomes with the financier and Maxwell.

According to Figueroa, he moved into Roberts's apartment in Royal Palm Beach after she began working for Epstein. Figueroa sometimes accompanied Roberts to Epstein's house in Palm Beach, and he, too, benefited from the arrangement, receiving $200 each time he would hang out there. "Jeffrey treated me as a friend,"

Figueroa said. "I never got any weird vibes until [Virginia] told me what was going on."

Gradually Figueroa came to learn more about the nature of Roberts's relationship with Epstein. Once, when he picked her up after Roberts had taken a trip to London on Epstein's jet, she blurted out that she had met Prince Andrew—for what she said was a massage session. Roberts showed Figueroa a photo of herself with the middle-aged royal. By now Figueroa had come to understand that "massage" in Epstein's world meant sex. Figueroa was devastated by his girlfriend's account of the rendezvous with Prince Andrew, which Roberts said was ordered by Maxwell. "I was getting really serious," recalled Figueroa. "I tried to get her to stop the trips with Jeffrey, but she didn't. I think she was scared. I was freakin' eighteen, nineteen."

In September 2002, Figueroa drove Roberts to the airport as she embarked for Thailand, the trip purportedly for a massage training program that Roberts intended as her escape from Epstein. In Thailand, Roberts met her future Australian husband. The billionaire repeatedly phoned him, demanding to know her whereabouts. "He was pretty angry," Figueroa said. "It was kind of like he owned her, she was his belonging."

Later, according to Figueroa, Roberts wrote him a letter and said how sorry she was about what had happened. They never spoke again.

In addition to his account of Roberts's ties to Epstein, Figueroa provided Churcher with a crucial lead on his former girlfriend's current whereabouts: the name of her dad, Sky Roberts. When Churcher called a phone number associated with Sky Roberts, a woman who said she was Virginia's aunt answered. Churcher told the woman that she was trying to reach Virginia because she believed Virginia knew Epstein.

A day later, on February 4, 2011, Virginia Roberts—now Virginia Giuffre—emailed Churcher. "Hope to hear from you soon," she noted. They agreed to a call. "The first word from her lips when I reached her was 'Andrew,'" Churcher recalled later. Giuffre told Churcher she had read about a dinner Epstein had thrown for Prince Andrew in New York a couple of months earlier, in December 2010, and she'd seen the tabloid photos of the pair strolling in Central Park. She was beside herself with rage, she told Churcher. Giuffre told Churcher that when she signed her settlement in the case, federal authorities had indicated that Epstein was going to do hard time.

Virginia gave Churcher an update of her biography. Now twenty-seven, she was a married mother of two sons and a daughter. But she still had nightmares about her years with Epstein and Maxwell and would sometimes wake up in a pool of sweat remembering details of this time. "It was disgusting," she said.

Churcher then flew to Australia to meet with Giuffre. When Giuffre came to the door to greet Churcher at her home near Sydney, Giuffre was gripping in her hands a print of the photo that would soon go around the world. The photograph depicted Andrew, then forty-one, draping his hand around Virginia Roberts's bare waist as they stood on the upstairs landing at Maxwell's London townhouse.

Shortly after Churcher arrived in Sydney, the FBI discovered that *The Mail on Sunday* would soon run Churcher's story about Virginia Roberts. Word reached Churcher that Ann Marie Villafaña, one of the assistant U.S. attorneys from Alex Acosta's office, wanted to talk to her. Churcher called Villafaña from Australia. "She said she'd heard I was talking to Virginia and the FBI would like to fly to Sydney to interview her."

The FBI dispatched two agents to Sydney. Churcher said she escorted Virginia and her husband, Robert Giuffre, to meet with the agents at the U.S. embassy in Canberra. "I wasn't allowed inside but she told me she confirmed the story she'd given me and named the who's who of men to whom she'd been pimped," Churcher said.

Giuffre also handed the original print of the Prince Andrew photograph over to the FBI, along with a twenty-four-page firsthand account she had composed, scribbled in ungrammatical longhand in a notebook.

As mentioned earlier, although Prince Andrew has tried to suggest that the picture was somehow faked, law enforcement has never questioned the photo's veracity.

WHAT CHURCHER AND GIUFFRE DID not know in 2011 was the possibility that Epstein might have secretly cooperated with the FBI at the time his lawyers negotiated the non-prosecution agreement in the Florida case that let him off so easily. This disclosure did not come to light until May 2018, when the FBI released dozens of heavily redacted memos about the case via their website "The Vault." In an article about the documents, *The Palm Beach Post* seized upon a single sentence in a memo written by a bureau agent that read "Epstein has also provided information to the FBI as agreed upon."

A *Palm Beach Post* reporter, Jane Musgrave, sought a reaction to the memo from Bradley Edwards, the attorney who represented many victims and knew the intricacies of the case better than most. Edwards, who represented Virginia Roberts and others when he accused the Justice Department of violating the Crime Victims' Rights Act in 2008, told Musgrave that the "sentence obviously means something, but I, too, am at a loss as to what it really means."

ON FEBRUARY 27, 2011, SHARON Churcher's article on Jeffrey Epstein and Prince Andrew made the front page of *The Mail on Sunday* under the headline ANDREW AND THE SEVENTEEN-YEAR-OLD GIRL AT THE CENTER OF UNDER-AGE SEX CASE THAT HAS SCANDALIZED AMERICA.

Slowly, details of Jeffrey Epstein's abuse and trafficking operation were finding their way into news stories. Roberts's statements to

Churcher regarding the powerful men Epstein allegedly made her have sex with would have consequences for not only them but others caught in Epstein's web, including Alexander Acosta.

In her "Perversion of Justice" series in the *Miami Herald,* journalist Julie K. Brown pointed out that after Roberts's interview was published, "she filed an affidavit in federal court in Miami" and "the ensuing news media firestorm forced Acosta, then dean of the law school at Florida International University, to explain why he declined to prosecute Epstein."[2]

Roberts would later say that her motivation for going public with her story to Churcher was the birth, a year earlier, of her daughter in January 2010.

# 26

---

# CIVIL ACTIONS

WHEN SHE FIRST GOT TOGETHER WITH JEFFREY EPSTEIN, THE TWO were inseparable. But if Ghislaine Maxwell had once dreamed of marriage, by 2015, even her friendship with Epstein was virtually extinguished. In the words of victims' lawyer Bradley Edwards, Maxwell had become "a ghost."

When she was charged by federal authorities in the summer of 2020, a July 10 court filing stated that Maxwell had had "no contact with Epstein for more than a decade." In a report for *The Daily Beast*, Thomas Volscho pointed out that this statement wasn't entirely true. Citing court filings from Virginia Roberts Giuffre's suit against Maxwell in 2015, Volscho noted that Epstein and Maxwell had communicated via email for twenty-one days between January 6, 2015, and January 27, 2015.

Some content from the email exchange was unsealed from court documents on July 30, 2020. In one such correspondence, Epstein wrote to Maxwell: "You have done nothing wrong and I would urge you to start acting like it. Go outside, head high, not as an escaping convict. Go to parties, deal with it." Epstein further pushed her to make a connection with a Swedish diplomat, Lisa Svensson, who like Maxwell was an advocate of ocean-related issues. Epstein wrote, "She said no one on her ocean panel takes this stuff seriously and you would be welcome to the ocean conference." But Maxwell, at the time, couldn't think beyond wanting to distance herself from Epstein and wrote back to him: "I would appreciate it if Shelley would come out and say she was your g'friend—I think she was from end [19]99 to 2002." Epstein replied, "Ok with me."*

There was also other contact between Epstein and Maxwell—of a financial nature. Between 2007 and 2011, more than $20 million from offshore accounts associated with Epstein was transferred to Maxwell, prosecutors said after Maxwell's 2020 arrest, adding that millions were later transferred back to Epstein.

While she may have no longer been at Epstein's side, Maxwell, seemingly oblivious to Epstein's growing criminal and legal problems, did not shy away from opportunities to climb social ladders. On July 31, 2010, she watched Chelsea Clinton walk down the aisle at her wedding to Marc Mezvinsky in Rhinebeck, New York. That fall, she attended Circa's Kick-Off Cocktail Party for the New Yorkers for Children 2010 Fall Gala. Within two years, she was associating herself with the Clinton Global Initiative through her newly formed environmental nonprofit focusing on ocean protection, the TerraMar Project. Virgin Group owner Richard Branson became one of her "founding citizens."

On April 24, 2012, Maxwell was even in attendance at the *Time* 100 Gala for the most influential people in the world. In 2014, she was making the scene at the *Vanity Fair* Oscar party, one of the most exclusive parties in the film world. It was here that she famously

---

* The "Shelley" referenced in the email was later identified as Shelley Anne Lewis, an English-born "spiritual entrepreneur" who had worked at Christie's auction house in New York at age twenty-two, in 1999, when she reportedly met Epstein and began dating him, according to *Mail Online* on August 1, 2020. Flight logs showed she traveled with Epstein alone on his private jets to New York and the Virgin Islands. She was not accused of any wrongdoing.

appeared in a photo standing next to the tuxedoed Tesla CEO Elon Musk, who later claimed, "She photobombed me."

Maxwell seemed to be everywhere. In May 2014, she was posing for photographers at the ETM Children's Benefit Gala at the Manhattan club Capitale. That year, *New York Post* columnist Richard Johnson wrote, "It's hard to top Ghislaine Maxwell in the globe-trotting department" after she returned from a trip to Alaska to watch the Iditarod dogsled race.

But no matter where she went or what party she attended, she couldn't escape her past with Epstein. On September 21, 2015, Virginia Roberts Giuffre sued Maxwell over the latter's "concerted and malicious campaign to discredit [Roberts]." Maxwell's attorneys had called Roberts's underlying allegations "obvious lies." Roberts's suit alleged that Maxwell had made such statements "in close consultation with Epstein."[1]

ONE OF THE FACTORS THAT may have contributed to Maxwell's diminished allegiance to Epstein was his relationship with the Dubin family. Throughout his years of sexual crime—and even during his arrest and incarceration—one friendship he seemingly maintained consistently was with the Dubin Family. Eva Andersson-Dubin, his one-time girlfriend, had remained close to Epstein after her 1994 marriage to Glenn Dubin—a man implicated in explicit acts with Virginia Roberts.[2]

The Dubins were fixtures at Epstein's homes. Their daughter, Celina, was close to Epstein and referred to the family friend as Uncle Jeff. Eva and Glenn wrote impassioned letters attesting to Epstein's stellar character to the Palm Beach County state attorney in the attempt to secure a lenient sentence for the financier. They wrote an email to his probation officer saying they were "100% comfortable" with Epstein spending time with Celina, who was then fourteen, and their two other minor children.[3] There is no evidence that Epstein ever abused Celina, but in 2014, he was quoted as telling associates that if he ever married anyone, it would be her.[4]

She was nineteen at the time. He was sixty-one.


THERE WAS AN EERIE EMPTINESS to Jeffrey Epstein's existence. He could buy anything and anyone, but he couldn't buy love. He had no wife. No children. Other than his staff and a long list of people who came calling with hat in hand, he had few friendships. He was a man of numbers and science, and his world was cold.

Had Epstein married, the gesture—even with nefarious motives—might have helped rehabilitate his image. A conventional marriage would have been a bargain compared to the retainers he paid his publicists; and of course his fortune would have been protected by even the simplest boilerplate prenuptial agreement. But Jeffrey Epstein was incapable of conventional relationships.

In Florida, Epstein's modus operandi had been to lure underprivileged girls with the promise of perpetual payment—a pedophiliac pyramid scheme of sorts in which those who produced new talent early and often could reap enormous rewards. But that tactic had backfired on him, creating a seemingly endless succession of potential plaintiffs. He also no longer had Ghislaine Maxwell or Sarah Kellen at his side to do his bidding. Still, he continued his pursuits.

Dance studios became a new hunting ground, especially in New York City. A twenty-two-year-old ballet dancer named Nadia Vostrikov was introduced to Epstein through a friend. The two spoke over Skype. Epstein was now his own fixer. He no longer had his inner circle of women to make the arrangements.

"When I got online we both used the camera feature, so his image appeared," Vostrikov recalled in an interview for this book. "My first reaction was that I was not expecting to see an older man. I think that was surprising. I didn't know that it would be a man, and I didn't really ask, either. But I was surprised when I saw that. My first instinct just generally was it's not ideal. I think, just a natural flag probably went up to be like, 'Oh, okay, let's see what's going on before we make any decisions.'"[5] In a bizarre attempt to endear himself to the young dancer, Epstein told her, "Just so you know, my last name is Epstein. Look me up. I've been in the news." She remembered his saying, "I'm a registered sex offender."[6]

Vostrikov was wary of the louche old man who wanted her to travel to the Virgin Islands on his private plane. He offered her the chance to be a ballet instructor, but she suspected an ulterior motive and turned Epstein down. Vostrikov later reflected that his approach to her was right out of the same script he had used in many contexts with many women and girls: "He had his exact script because he had gotten in trouble before. He found a way to still do what he was doing within the confines of the dance world."[7]

## 27

# UNDERGROUND NEWS

Civil litigation against Jeffrey Epstein had begun in 2008. Virginia Roberts, as Jane Doe 102, took legal action a year later and others soon followed. There was no shortage of victims seeking to make the financier pay for his crimes in civil courts, in light of what many viewed as the absence of justice in the criminal courts. There were plenty of attorneys in Florida and New York eager to take a shot at him.

Epstein might have avoided a lifetime in federal prison for operating a global trafficking operation for underage girls, but even his best efforts at hiding in plain sight couldn't prevent the process servers from finding him in connection with these civil suits. There was little that Epstein could do to protect himself from appearing at depositions, under oath, while attorneys for his victims interrogated him.

The depositions were hell for Epstein; they were embarrassing. He was asked questions about countless aspects of his life—one that had been lived far from public view. He was even asked about his genitals by West Palm Beach lawyer Spencer Kuvin, representing three victims, in 2009: "Is it true, sir, that you have what's been described as an egg-shaped penis?" Kuvin continued: "Sir, according to the police department's probable cause affidavit, one witness described your penis as oval-shaped and claimed when it was erect it was thick towards the bottom but was thin and small towards the head portion and called it egg-shaped," adding, "Those are not my words, I apologize."

Epstein got up and walked out of the deposition. Kuvin said a psychologist he hired to profile Epstein determined that what he had on his hands was a narcissist whose self-image meant more to him than anything else.

In all his depositions, Epstein's attorneys contested virtually every question as argumentative. Still, the questions challenged his sense of control, and control was Epstein's suit of armor. Although his attorneys did their best to protect him from ridicule and self-incrimination, the sessions were videotaped, preserved for eternity. It was truly ironic that this tactic Epstein used against so many victims was now being used against him.

ONE SUCH SIT-DOWN OCCURRED ON January 25, 2012. Bradley Edwards, attorney for Courtney Wild, Jane Doe 1 in the suit filed against the government, victimized at age fifteen while still in braces, prepared questions—specific queries meant to solidify the claims of the girls, some of them now adult women, who were accusing the financier of harming them.

In the videotaped depositions, Epstein appeared calm and composed. He sat at the head of the table—the center of attention, as always—his hair brushed back in debonair fashion. His arms were folded for much of the back-and-forth. Small pink-framed reading glasses were perched on his nose. His appearance, his demeanor, seemed to be an act—the same sort of disarming approach to adversaries that he had used his entire life to get a teaching job, and then to survive being found out about having lied on his résumé at Bear Stearns.[1] But hard-nosed attorneys who were set on unmasking a monster were not the head of human resources at an elite prep school or a trading firm on Wall Street. This was trench warfare under oath, and the stakes were enormous.

During one deposition, which appears in the Netflix documentary *Filthy Rich*, Epstein was asked if he was bisexual. He balked at the question.[2]

"How long have you been attracted to underage minor females?" asked Edwards, who over a decade would represent fifty-six alleged victims.

"Harassing, argumentative," Epstein's lawyers barked back.

"Were you sexually molested as a child?" Edwards asked Epstein.

"Are you kidding? I assert my Fifth, Sixth, and Fourteenth Amendment rights."

In one case alone, Epstein faced seven depositions from May 1, 2009, to April 14, 2010. The legal fees for all these cases were astounding, not to mention the cost of the settlements themselves. Epstein may have paid more than $20 million to his victims in thirty-nine known out-of-court settlements, based on research done for this book. Just three victims were paid a total of $5.5 million. But many others received sums ranging from only $40,000 and $50,000 each.

Money could buy one's way out of a lot of grief. But small legal victories—and delaying tactics—could not protect Jeffrey Epstein from the impending storms that were looming over his horizon.

THE LAST FEW YEARS OF Epstein's life were an unending cascade of legal cases and unfavorable media attention. Remarkably, as Epstein grappled with the fallout of his numerous civil cases, his pursuit of girls seemingly did not abate.

In March 2016, Richard Johnson, the *New York Post*'s famed society and gossip correspondent, wrote a piece for the paper's "Page Six" column that centered on a specific type of female visitor to

Epstein's mansion—young Russian women. The article was head-lined JEFFREY EPSTEIN'S EAST SIDE MANSION HOUSES RUSSIAN PLAYMATES.[3]

The article stated that Epstein was "not letting his conviction for soliciting prostitution from a teenager interfere with his lifestyle." Rather than "having his assistants troll local high schools, the billion-aire money manager—and registered sex offender—is importing his playmates from Russia," Johnson declared. "A recent visitor tells me Epstein has a house full of young beauties at his East Seventy-First Street mansion. 'Half of them are from the former Soviet Union and the other half are a mix of Americans and Europeans.'"[4] The *Post* piece indicated that the women appeared to be at least seventeen years old, the age of consent in New York State.[5]

The article also mentioned one person who allegedly helped pro-cure these "beauties": Peter Listerman. Peter Grigoryevich Lister-man owned a modeling agency that was known to connect Russian oligarchs with young and beautiful women. Born in Ukraine, Lister-man monetized his access to models, actresses, and young beauties from rural towns in the former Soviet Union who dreamed of a better life in Vladimir Putin's kleptocracy. Listerman was a powerful figure protected by the state-run security services and hired guns who pro-tected his movements. He was a well-known character in Odessa and a frequent guest on Russian television.

But Listerman's clients weren't just Russians. He liked to brag that he connected some of the most famous and powerful people in the world with beautiful young women. "My Hollywood clients and oligarchs are sick of emancipated women, who resemble robots," he was quoted as saying to a Russian tabloid. "Everybody is sick of these evil women, they want gentle and romantic!"[6] Listerman recoiled at being called a pimp, however. He preferred to be known simply as a matchmaker. Still, Listerman's visits to 9 East Seventy-First Street raised eyebrows.

Another visit to Epstein's Manhattan mansion that sparked

curiosity and wonder was a January 2016 visit by former Israeli prime minister Ehud Barak.

Photographers from the *Daily Mail* photographed Barak, wearing a heavy winter coat and a Russian fur hat, as he entered and—hours later—exited Epstein's Manhattan home.[7]

Epstein, who never welcomed publicity, was seeing his guarded and once controlled life play out in real time in the media. Three years before the *Miami Herald* published their series on the government's failure to bring justice in the Florida prosecution, a Palm Beach neighbor of Epstein's brought out a book that examined what had occurred in the Florida case. The author was James Patterson, who happened to be the world's top-selling novelist. With the help of investigative reporters John Connolly and Tim Malloy, Patterson took on his fellow Palm Beach resident in *Filthy Rich,* which was published in 2016. In a 2020 interview with *Rolling Stone,* Patterson reflected about what drew him in to the case: "It seemed just impossible that this could happen," he stated. "The more I dug into it, the more insane it seemed."

Compared to Patterson's other titles, the book was a modest bestseller. Even after the attention that publication of the book drew, Patterson marveled that his target was still getting a pass. Epstein was still "on the loose in New York."

IN ADDITION TO THE LAWSUITS and unwanted media attention, another headache was on the horizon for Jeffrey Epstein. His former friend and houseguest Donald Trump was running for president and would soon occupy the world's media fascination virtually twenty-four hours a day.

On June 16, 2015, Donald J. Trump descended the gold-plated escalator of Trump Tower, his flagship Manhattan landmark, to announce his candidacy. Trump and Epstein were no longer friends. A mysterious falling-out had occurred years earlier at Mar-a-Lago over events that troubled one of the two men to the point where a once close friendship had cooled, seemingly forever. It isn't clear whether it was Epstein's or Trump's behavior that caused the rift, though Trump has claimed that he ended the social association.

But Trump's claim to have taken the initiative in breaking off the friendship was disputed by one of the financier's closest confidants. According to this person's account, they were told by Epstein in 2016, "If people knew what I know about Trump and Clinton, they'd cancel the election." Epstein told the person that "he stopped hanging out with Trump" for a specific reason. Before their falling out, Epstein claimed to this person that Trump had visited his office about financial matters. Epstein also recounted a story about one conversation he had with Trump. "Jeffrey asked [Trump], 'How come you sleep with so many women when you are married?' And Trump said, 'Because it's so wrong,'" according to this person's account.[8]

IN A MATTER OF MONTHS in the Republican primary campaign, Trump bulldozed his way through a small army of Republican hopefuls—all seasoned politicians—to dominate the electorate and, most important, the global news cycle.

Trump's candidacy was a curse for Epstein. It didn't take long for photos of the two men to emerge. There was video footage as well. One snippet showed Trump laughing as a motionless Epstein cracked a smile at a Mar-a-Lago event. There is an infamous photo taken of the two men at the event, a party for a celebrity tennis tournament at Mar-a-Lago on February 12, 2000. The photo shows Trump and his Slovenian-born then girlfriend and future third wife, Melania Knauss, Jeffrey Epstein, and Ghislaine Maxwell; Prince Andrew is also in the photograph.

The Trump candidacy survived Epstein. It survived the *Access Hollywood* tape on which Trump boasts about "grabbing" women "by the pussy." It survived his lifetime of womanizing. On November 8, 2016, Donald J. Trump lost the popular vote but managed to squeak by with enough Electoral College votes to become the forty-fifth president of the United States.

The Trump presidency coincided with the emergence of the

powerful #MeToo movement protesting the systemic and historical sexual abuse that women had endured from powerful men. The tactics of intimidation used by harassers and abusers in positions of power for years were starting to falter.

The #MeToo movement's first target was Hollywood mogul Harvey Weinstein, the president and CEO of Miramax Films. Weinstein, like Epstein, was a serial predator. Rather than preying on underage girls from broken homes, though, Weinstein targeted Hollywood hopefuls, including Rosanna Arquette, Eva Green, Daryl Hannah, Salma Hayek, Rose McGowan, and others.

As the #MeToo movement produced more and more evidence of wrongdoing on the part of powerful men, the social connections among accused predators were unmissable. Photographs emerged showing Weinstein, Epstein, and Maxwell together at the eighteenth birthday party for Princess Beatrice, Prince Andrew's oldest daughter. The event, widely covered by the press and paparazzi, was held in 2006 at Windsor Castle. Weinstein was dressed in a classic white tie and tails. Epstein wore a U.S. Navy dress white uniform with captain insignia; the Trident badge of the U.S. Navy SEALs adorned his left chest above a series of store-bought medals. Ghislaine Maxwell wore a mask.[9]

There was no more shielding the monsters who sexually preyed upon women—and girls—without fear of repercussion or retribution. The atmosphere of the #MeToo movement shattered the tactics of silence and intimidation that men like Weinstein and Epstein had relied on for so long. Threatening a victim with personal and professional vengeance simply did not work any longer. As the movement gathered steam, newsrooms across the county began devoting more and more resources to reporting accusations of sexual impropriety. For Epstein, who had managed to evade real justice for so long, the clock was ticking louder and faster.

TRUMP'S ASCENDANCY WORRIED EPSTEIN FOR another reason. Less than a month after being sworn into office, President Trump nominated Alex Acosta, the former U.S. attorney who had overseen the federal investigation of Epstein in his Florida case, to the position of secretary of labor. For Trump, Acosta looked like a win-win. Acosta was Hispanic in an overwhelmingly white cabinet and an upward mover in Florida's Republican Party to boot. Trump had taken quite a bit of heat from his opponents over a wide array of anti-Hispanic messaging—from "They are rapists and murderers" in his candidacy announcement speech to his determination to build an anti-immigration wall along the U.S. border with Mexico—and he thought that Acosta's pick would quiet his critics.

Any man or woman nominated for a cabinet post becomes the subject of intense scrutiny. Government investigators probe deep into a nominee's personal background, past occupations, and financial history. The objective is to vet political appointees so that by the time they sit down for confirmation by the U.S. Senate, they are above scandal. Government agents from a dozen law enforcement agencies sifted through Acosta's history. They found nothing that they felt could endanger the confirmation or, more important, embarrass the president. On April 28, 2017, Acosta was easily confirmed by the Senate.

The major investigative outlets, *The New York Times* and *The Washington Post* and others, take a close look at these appointees as well. Reporters look for something headline-worthy—some skeleton in a closet that might challenge the perception of a candidate put forward by the administration. In some cases, there are simply no aspersions to be cast. But Trump's pick of Acosta set off alarms for those who understood his role in the 2007 Epstein non-prosecution agreement. By selecting Acosta as labor secretary, Donald Trump inadvertently placed a blinding spotlight on the past crimes of a former close friend and associate—one that could be an embarrassment to the office of the president.

Julie K. Brown, an investigative journalist for the *Miami Herald*, ran with the story.

Brown, a Temple University alumna, was known for her fastidious

work, and she was relentless in pursuit of the truth of how a pedophile and sex trafficker could have received such incomprehensibly
favorable consideration from a U.S. attorney. Brown spent over a
year researching a series of articles that would be collectively published in late 2018 under the title of "Perversion of Justice." Brown
interviewed hundreds of people connected to the case. She found
more than eighty victims whose suffering had been brushed aside.

Rather than look at the salacious aspects of Jeffrey Epstein's
crimes, Brown and video journalist Emily Michot chose to focus
on the prosecution of the case and how law enforcement—and, in
particular, Acosta's office—may have failed the victims by orches-
trating a highly suspect arrangement with a figure of wealth and
prominence.[10]

Brown's exposé revived the case with the U.S. Attorney's Office
for the Southern District of New York, one of the most powerful
regional commands in the entire Department of Justice. The #MeToo
movement sparked interest in sexual assault and harassment cases
that were mishandled. Brown's reports in the *Miami Herald* turned
what had been largely contained as a Florida story in the media into
a national outrage.

Brown received numerous accolades for her groundbreaking
reporting—and some notable flak. One person who was unhappy
about her work was Alan Dershowitz. The Epstein friend and
attorney—who had become a vocal defender of Donald Trump during the special counsel investigation by Robert Mueller into the president's ties with Russia—contacted the panel deciding the Pulitzer
Prize and urged them not to reward Brown with what he referred to
as "fake news and shoddy journalism."[11]

# 28

# MIDNIGHT IN PARIS

THERE ARE NINETY-THREE U.S. ATTORNEY'S OFFICES THROUGHOUT the United States—one for each federal judicial district. The Southern District of New York, the SDNY, is one of the largest in the entire Department of Justice—and considered the most prominent. Although it is under the jurisdiction of the Department of Justice, the SDNY is known as a highly independent—almost autonomous— office. It is sometimes called the "Sovereign District of New York," and it has a reputation for prosecuting high-profile cases regardless of the political fallout. As a result, the office handled cases that could not be handled by other jurisdictions.

There was no Attorney Thin Blue Line in which the appointed U.S. attorneys circled the wagons to protect one another. The office required political ambition and ruthlessness. If a U.S. attorney could steal a case from another jurisdiction and score hard-earned headlines even at another's expense, it was done zealously. The case of *People v. Jeffrey E. Epstein* was one such instance.

• • •

As 2018 CAME TO AN end, Julie K. Brown's series in the *Miami Herald* on Jeffrey Epstein became a significant topic of chatter in legal circles in Washington, D.C., and New York. Epstein's name became a notorious symbol of how the filthy rich were able not only to skirt justice but also to continue their criminal ways while thumbing their noses at the justice system. The #MeToo movement, though, placed men like Epstein inside the crosshairs of public disgust and anger. Alex Acosta's deal with Jeffrey Epstein became another scandal for the Trump presidency that was growing into a call for action. Brown's reporting had changed the norm. Thanks to her series, the federal judiciary was pressured into reviewing the NPA between Jeffrey Epstein's dream team of lawyers and Alex Acosta. As David Boies, who represented seven victims, told *The Washington Post* in 2019, "There is a good chance that if Acosta had not gotten appointed, Epstein would still be free."

On February 21, 2019, Judge Kenneth A. Marra, of the Federal District Court in West Palm Beach, Florida, announced that Alex Acosta had violated the Crime Victims' Rights Act when he concealed a plea agreement from Epstein's victims. Judge Marra came short of overturning the original NPA or issuing an order resolving the case. Instead, he gave federal prosecutors two weeks to confer with Epstein's victims and their attorneys and come up with an accord that satisfied all sides.

The outcry over the ruling was deafening. In the eyes of many, it didn't go far enough. Under pressure, the Justice Department further announced that it was opening a new probe into the case. Dozens of members of Congress—both Republicans and Democrats— demanded that the plea deal from 2007 be reexamined.[1] "The fact that federal prosecutors appear to have crafted a secret, sweetheart deal for this child rapist should enrage moms and dads everywhere," Senator Ben Sasse, the Republican chairman of the Senate Judiciary Oversight Subcommittee, wrote to Inspector General Michael Horowitz at the Justice Department. "The fact that this monster received such a pathetically soft sentence is a travesty that should outrage us all," he added.[2]

Epstein might have moved in the same circles as men born with silver spoons in their mouths, but he was a middle-class kid with inherent street smarts. The public furor over his plea deal should have made the hairs on the back of his neck stand up. He could have regrouped, put his house in order, and planned his great escape. There were dozens of countries that had no extradition treaty with the United States where a man of Epstein's fortune could have lived an extraordinary life of comfort and decadence. But perhaps Epstein believed that he was still above the law.

Epstein traveled extensively as the Department of Justice reopened his case. It was as if he didn't have a worry in the world. But behind the scenes, the more than capable Manhattan U.S. attorney Geoffrey Berman of the Southern District of New York knew otherwise.

Because Epstein had committed crimes at his Manhattan residence, Berman's office would assume control of the case. While the eventual charges would also involve his sex trafficking in Palm Beach, the old non-prosecution agreement spelled out that no further prosecution could take place "in this District"—meaning in the Southern District of Florida.

Geoffrey Berman finally had heat and ammunition.

JEFFREY EPSTEIN'S HOME IN PARIS flew under the radar compared to the financier's other lavish lairs. A former handyman known only as Gabriel told a reporter that Epstein bought the apartment in the early 2000s for just under eight million euros; it was decorated by his friend Alberto Pinto, a famous interior decorator, who died in 2012.[3]

The apartment was located on Avenue Foch in the very fashionable 16th arrondissement, near the city's embassy row.[4] The palatial flat had guest and servant accommodations and also included a gym and a massage room. The grand residence was secluded, far from prying eyes. Epstein moved in and out of his Paris home secretly. It was a safe haven. The French are masters at minding their own business.

There was a laissez-faire acceptance of the odd and eccentric in Paris that Epstein adored. The noted French writer Gabriel Matzneff, for example, continued to win literary awards and accolades while never hiding the fact that he regularly engaged in sex with girls—and boys—in their teens and younger. He wrote countless books on the subject, including one titled *Les moins de seize ans* (*The Under Sixteens*), and he promoted his work on French television.[5] The legal age of consent in France is fifteen, and Matzneff has never been arrested for his crimes or suffered professionally for his indulgences.[6] The Oscar-winning director Roman Polanski, who fled the United States on statutory rape allegations, also found a welcoming refuge in France.

The staff who maintained Epstein's Paris address described him as kind. "He was polite, well-educated, and [a] generous" man, Gabriel the handyman recalled. "He was part of the family." Epstein gave his Parisian employees birthday gifts including trips to New York and tickets to Broadway shows, and even helped out with costly medical emergencies.

Epstein's staff noticed that he spent most of his time alone on his computer. He was highly secretive. Discretion was a job requirement, though, and there were always women around Epstein's Parisian flat, Gabriel recalled. "Epstein entertained young women at his apartment but kept these girls away from business or social activities. And [he] made them eat in the kitchen."[7] Epstein also made it a point to keep the identities of these young women a secret.

Gabriel told Radio France that the young women were paid by Epstein for their company. "He was regularly surrounded by young women, who stayed a few hours or a few days."[8] Some also traveled with Epstein for jet-skiing and other amusements in the Caribbean.[9]

Being in Paris put Epstein together with his longtime friend

Jean-Luc Brunel. Another notable visitor to the apartment was Steve Bannon, the former adviser to President Donald Trump, who visited Epstein in Paris in the fall of 2018; Bannon's spokesperson later denied that he ever stayed at the Epstein home, insisting that he "systematically" stayed at the Hotel Bristol during his trips to Paris.[10] Other guests of Epstein at his Parisian home reportedly included Bill and Melinda Gates, Prince Andrew, and former Israeli prime minister Ehud Barak.

There is some evidence that scrutiny from the U.S. Department of Justice was starting to get to Epstein, though. He purchased a sedan that was bullet- and blast-resistant and retained the services of an armed bodyguard. Epstein was still seeking ways to bolster his public image. He was in touch with R. Couri Hay, a New York society publicist with a reputation for creating—and in some cases restoring—reputations among the plutocrat class.[11] "I don't want 'Billionaire pervert' to be the first line of my obituary," Hay said Epstein had told him.

The publicist blueprinted an aggressive plan to soften and then rehabilitate Epstein's soiled image. This included sex addiction rehabilitation, the intervention of a rabbi, and signing most of his wealth over to good causes, including charities supported by such über-wealth icons as Warren Buffett and Bill Gates.[12]

EPSTEIN WAS NOT THE ONLY one who was now feeling the heat.

On June 5, 2019, Ghislaine Maxwell and Prince Andrew met in London.[13] Perhaps the Duke of York received advance word of the impending legal avalanche as the new U.S. federal investigation steamrolled ahead. Were the longtime friends meeting to get their stories straight? The public scrutiny of Prince Andrew's friendship with Epstein—and what he might have done with some of Epstein's underage victims—was an embarrassment for Buckingham Palace. In 2015, attorneys Paul G. Cassell and Bradley J. Edwards wrote to

Andrew requesting that he submit to an interview under oath concerning events that took place around the time he was with Virginia Roberts.

With the Epstein probe reopened, and with intense scrutiny on the royal, there was a lot for Maxwell and Prince Andrew to talk about. Five months later, Andrew would appear in the now infamous BBC interview in which he acknowledged meeting Ghislaine Maxwell at Buckingham Palace but denied that the two discussed Epstein.

Maxwell was being seen less and less in public, and before the year was over, she had dissolved her environmental nonprofit, the TerraMar Project. But she had taken on another wealthy suitor. Her relationship with Ted Waitt had ended, and Maxwell was now reportedly seeing a man named Scott Borgerson, whom she had known since they met at a 2013 conference in Iceland. Borgerson, then forty-three, was the handsome and bearded CEO of CargoMetrics Technologies. He had been both a commander and a navigator in the U.S. Coast Guard and had been a member of the Council on Foreign Relations.

Maxwell was rumored to have lived for a time with Borgerson in his $3 million, five-bedroom home thirty miles north of Boston in the tiny village of Manchester-by-the-Sea, Massachusetts. (In August 2019, Borgerson denied she had lived there and said the two were not romantically linked.)

It may have been a last-ditch attempt by Maxwell to have a conventional life.

# PART SIX

# SECRETS TO THE GRAVE

I don't want "Billionaire pervert"
to be the first line of my obituary.
—JEFFREY EPSTEIN
to publicist R. Couri Hay in 2016[1]

# 29

# THE STING

On the afternoon of July 6, 2019, a force of NYPD officers and FBI agents were, appropriately enough, in a holding pattern at Teterboro Airport in New Jersey. A small air terminal just twelve miles from Manhattan, Teterboro is popular among celebrities, CEOs, and others with the means to fly private.

The high that Saturday was a sweltering 88 degrees. Skies were overcast and the humidity made the tarmac feel even hotter. A few of the federal agents and New York City detectives were wearing suits and ties; others perspired in their navy blue windbreakers, known as raid jackets, stamped with the yellow letters FBI. As the airport's grounds crew looked on, the small army of law enforcement—close to fifty in all—assembled near "Hangar One," an area adjacent to a U.S. Customs and Border Protection office. They were awaiting the arrival of Jeffrey Epstein.[1]

The arrest team had been poised for this moment ever since word came down hours earlier that Epstein had boarded his Gulfstream G550, tail number N212JE, in Paris.[*2] Four days earlier,

---

* The Federal Aviation Administration allows plane owners the opportunity to

United States Southern District magistrate judge Barbara Moses had signed a sealed arrest warrant for Epstein.[3]

The operation at Teterboro would be the denouement of a carefully calibrated, confidential effort that Geoffrey Berman, the U.S. attorney in the district, and his team of prosecutors had begun some six months earlier. Reporter Julie K. Brown's 2018 "Perversion of Justice" series in the *Miami Herald* had rekindled interest in Epstein and the simmering controversy over whether he had been let off lightly in the Florida case. The subsequent investigation involved federal agents and detectives assigned to the FBI-NYPD Child Exploitation and Human Trafficking Task Force, a multiagency unit operating under the aegis of Berman. The investigation had resulted in a thirteen-page sealed indictment with new charges that carried a possible sentence of forty-five years behind bars.

The problem, however, was that Epstein wasn't in the country. He was in France. Law enforcement tracked the movements of his private jet. They knew their best chance for a clean apprehension would be right after he touched down in the United States. Trying to arrest someone like Epstein in one of his palatial homes presented challenges and dangers that the FBI and NYPD were keen to avoid.

Epstein had taken off from Paris four other times that year. His last flight, in April, took him from the French capital to Rabat, Morocco, for a nine-hour visit.[4] Flights to and from Teterboro were routine for him—like taking a car service. He expected to be back in his mansion within an hour or so of N212JE's crossing into American airspace over Maine.

The arrest team waited.

· · ·

---

select their own "N numbers," so Epstein's was equivalent to a vanity license plate, as it carried a dual reference to the 212 area code for his Manhattan address and his initials.

IT WAS PERHAPS FITTING THAT Epstein was to be taken into custody at an airport carved out of a former swamp. Teterboro had been an essential point of transit for Epstein for nearly twenty years. According to statements made in criminal and civil court filings since 2008, it was from Teterboro that Epstein deployed aircraft that delivered dozens of young women to and from his Manhattan mansion, his ranch in New Mexico, and his hideaways in the Caribbean.

Epstein's fleet at various times included a Cessna, a Gulfstream jet, and a Boeing 727. His aircraft recorded at least 730 flights to and from Teterboro between 1995 and 2013.[5] David Rodgers, who was among at least six pilots employed by Epstein at various times, recorded 322 flights between Teterboro and Palm Beach, the site of Epstein's waterfront mansion; he also flew Epstein's planes another 112 times between Teterboro and the U.S. Virgin Islands.[6] Flight logs released a day prior to Epstein's death showed that two women, Epstein assistants Sarah Kellen and Nadia Marcinkova, identified in the NPA as potential coconspirators, had taken eighty-two and forty-eight trips, respectively, to and from Teterboro.[7]

The G550, which could reach speeds of nearly 600 miles per hour, was the newest addition to Epstein's fleet—a replacement for his older Boeing 727, the aircraft the media had dubbed the Lolita Express.[8] Epstein had modified the G550 with seating for twenty-nine passengers and an interior that sported such accoutrements as carpet-padded doors and a large circular bed.[9] Jim Dowd, a former substitute pilot for Epstein, told *Vanity Fair* that in addition to the "big round bed with mirrors on the walls," the aircraft's tacky touches included zebra skins and leopard-print pillows.[10]

The G550 was a sleek and powerful luxury commuter jet, the most successful in Gulfstream's history. The price tag was a whopping $61.5 million in 2018, though Epstein's plane, which was officially registered to an Epstein holding company in the Virgin Islands called Plan D LLC, appears to have been purchased in March 2008 for far less, according to FAA and other records.

At 5:20 P.M., Epstein's Gulfstream made its final approach to

Teterboro. Did Epstein glance through one of the aircraft windows and scan across the Hudson to get the breathtaking view of Manhattan baked in golden sunlight as afternoon turned to evening? He had made similar trips dozens of times. He knew what to expect. His car would be waiting outside Customs.

THE POLICE OFFICERS AND FEDERAL agents who made up the arrest force at Teterboro had arrested hundreds of violent felons among them—only seasoned officers and agents with impeccable service records were handpicked for task force work. But the Epstein operation and its secrecy made some nervous. Epstein was rich and had ties to powerful figures in New York media. A source close to the investigation said lawmen feared that someone would give the financier a heads-up. More than twenty-eight hundred journalists hold press passes issued by the NYPD Office of Public Information, known as DCPI. Epstein's impending arrest was potentially a career-making scoop for a resourceful reporter with sources in law enforcement. If a journalist were to find out, the arrest team worried, could Epstein himself be tipped off that his landing in Teterboro was a trap?

"[Federal officials] were afraid if Epstein learned about the planned arrest in flight, he would turn into Roman Polanski and order his pilot to make a detour, to a place from where he could not be extradited," said Lieutenant Gene Whyte of the NYPD, a DCPI official who had assisted federal agencies in the past with the transportation of infamous "high risk" prisoners, including terrorists linked to the 9/11 attacks and Joaquín Guzmán Loera, the notorious narcotics trafficker known as El Chapo.[11]

Lieutenant Whyte, who assisted in the Epstein operation, insisted that the law enforcement higher-ups involved in the plan to arrest Epstein maintain absolute secrecy to keep any details from being leaked to the press.[12] The element of surprise was everything. "[We] didn't want to spook him because they were going to arrest him as soon as he landed and before his pilot could restart the engine," Lieutenant Whyte recalled.

The precautions turned out to be unnecessary. As Epstein's aircraft taxied to a stop on the tarmac, it was met by sedans and SUVs with lights and sirens blaring. NYPD detectives and FBI agents swarmed the aircraft. They wore their blue windbreaker raid jackets; their sidearms were out. Epstein offered no resistance as he was placed in cuffs. It was 5:30 P.M.

No one else on the plane was taken into custody. (Some media reports indicated that thirty-year-old Karyna Shuliak—a Belarusian émigré and dentist who was one of Epstein's latest romantic interests and a woman with whom he had grown closer of late—had been vacationing with Epstein at his Paris apartment and that she had been on his jet when Epstein was arrested. Law enforcement sources familiar with Epstein's apprehension, however, dispute this, insisting Shuliak was not on the arriving flight.)

After clearing U.S. Customs, Epstein was turned over to the custody of the U.S. Marshals Service and driven some ten miles south, to the Metropolitan Correctional Center, in Lower Manhattan, near Wall Street, a federal jail known as the MCC, where prisoners charged with federal crimes are detained while awaiting arraignment or trial.

Even with their lights and sirens cutting a path through the gridlock, the traffic heading to New York City on the George Washington Bridge was a nightmare. But the NYPD and federal agents had gotten their man.


AT 7:53 P.M., *The Daily Beast* first blasted out news of Epstein's arrest, attributing the bust to "three law enforcement sources." The report, by Pervaiz Shallwani, Kate Briquelet, and Harry Siegel, was simply headlined JEFFREY EPSTEIN ARRESTED FOR SEX TRAFFICKING OF MINORS. A subhead stamped in red said LONG TIME COMING.

Hours after Epstein was taken into custody, task force members executed a search warrant at Epstein's 21,000-square-foot, seven-story Manhattan townhouse at 9 East Seventy-First Street. They broke through the front door with a handheld battering ram and searched every crevice of the building, finding, among other things, a chessboard with custom figurines clad in underwear; a photorealistic mural of a prison scene complete with depictions of Epstein, correctional officers, barbed wire, and a guard station; photos of Crown Prince Mohammed bin Salman, Woody Allen, and Bill Clinton (signed); a life-sized female doll hanging from a chandelier; a small room arranged to look like a beach scene; and a massage table with sex toys.

Inside a locked safe, investigators also found a trove of hundreds of photos of semiclothed or nude females. The New York Post cover splashed HIS SAFE OF EVIL. Task Force members also recovered an expired Austrian passport—one that had been used by Epstein, but under a different name, indicating he resided in Saudi Arabia—along with $70,000 and forty-eight loose diamond stones, ranging in size from approximately 1 to 2.38 carats, as well as a large diamond ring.[13] The stash of cash and gems was what one law enforcement official described as his "cut-and-run" funds—fluid currency and tradable assets he might suddenly need if he had to leave town on short notice.

Authorities also removed computers and other electronics. (Epstein accuser Maria Farmer told CBS This Morning that she had previously seen in his Manhattan home extensive surveillance devices, including pinhole cameras.)

Six days after Epstein's arrest at Teterboro, Alex Acosta, under pressure, submitted his resignation as the U.S. labor secretary.[14]

# 30

## FAVOR BANK

THE METROPOLITAN CORRECTIONAL CENTER, OR MCC, IS A rust-colored twelve-story fortress located on Park Row, in Lower Manhattan, across the street from One Police Plaza, the headquarters of the NYPD. It also sits across the street from both the offices of the United States Attorney for the Southern District, the agency that brought the prosecution against Jeffrey Epstein, and the new federal courthouse, where Epstein's future would be decided.

The MCC has been called Little Gitmo thanks to its role in housing terrorists such as Khalid Sheikh Mohammed, the mastermind of the September 11 terrorist attacks, and Ramzi Ahmed Yousef, who coordinated the 1993 bombing of the World Trade Center. Other famous prisoners held at one time in the MCC included El Chapo, mobsters John Gotti and Sammy "The Bull" Gravano, and Bernie Madoff.

The MCC was built in 1975 and designed to hold 480 inmates. Overcrowding at the MCC was endemic, though, and by the time Epstein was ushered into federal custody, the facility held more than 760 prisoners. The facility, chilly in winter and oppressively warm in summer, is infamous for its unsanitary and dispiriting conditions, including cell glass that obscures natural sunlight, rodent infesta-tion, and floors covered with cockroaches.[1]

Conditions at the MCC were so deplorable that in 2011, Amnesty International wrote to Attorney General Eric H. Holder, Jr., express-ing concern that the facility amounted to cruel and inhumane treatment.[2]

JEFFREY EPSTEIN HAD GROWN UP in modest surroundings, but he had never experienced conditions like those in the MCC. For a man who had long since grown accustomed to a pampered life, landing in the MCC was a rude awakening, far harsher than anything he'd experi-enced twelve years earlier in the county lockup in Florida. At the MCC there would be no massages or a daytime work release in which to enjoy meals from his personal chef.

As Inmate No. 76318-054 exchanged his custom-tailored sports-wear for an orange jumpsuit, another factor of his new reality would seem daunting. Epstein was six feet tall and weighed only 185 pounds.[3] He was trim and fit for a guy in his mid-sixties. But there was no mistaking him for a tough guy. He wasn't a man who had been hardened growing up inside the system, and prisoners were not kind to sexual predators. Throughout his life Epstein had been able to spot the soft underbelly of any exigency that presented itself, no matter how bleak it might seem, and find a means to exploit it. There was no one to exploit inside the MCC, though. Murderers, drug deal-ers, and cybercriminals had little use for what Epstein could offer. Instead, the financier attempted to feather his precipitous fall by tapping into the favor bank he had built up among the power brokers outside the prison walls.

ROBERT BOYCE HAD RETIRED FROM his job as the NYPD's chief of detectives in April 2018 after a thirty-five-year career with the de-partment. Even though Boyce was no longer the department's top detective, his gregarious nature and close relationships with top brass within New York's law enforcement community made him an inviting go-between for someone hoping to assist the beleaguered financier without so much as leaving a fingerprint.

Unlike some in New York's corridors of powers, Boyce had become a popular figure without projecting a bombastic or grandiose persona. The Chief of D's, as the chief of detectives is known, is one of the most important positions in the NYPD hierarchy, and Boyce was eminently comfortable in his own skin. He had been the department's mouthpiece, explaining NYPD efforts to solve some of the city's most desperate moments. Mayor Bill de Blasio turned to him to field reporters' toughest queries at a City Hall news conference in March 2015 when a gas explosion destroyed three buildings in the East Village. And it was Boyce who spearheaded the high-profile six-month investigation into the August 2016 slaying of Karina Vetrano, a thirty-year-old aspiring writer who was attacked, sexually assaulted, and killed while jogging in Howard Beach, Queens.

Not only did the chief of detectives have to inspire subordinates to bring closure to the most complex criminal investigations in the city, but the role also required adept political skills. That meant maintaining close relations with the city's top philanthropic swells—including with the Police Foundation, a politically powerful charity that finances NYPD pet projects not funded by taxpayers. The foundation was established in 1971 by a private group headed by real estate magnate Lewis Rudin, and since its inception, it has been credited with distributing more than $120 million in NYPD grants.[4] A significant portion of those funds were generated at an annual fall gala at which Manhattan's moneyed class eagerly bumped shoulders with *real* policemen and policewomen for a couple of hours.

THE POLICE FOUNDATION—FOUNDED FOLLOWING THE recommendations produced by the Knapp Commission, a police corruption inquiry that shook the NYPD to its core in the 1970s—has always been subject to the whims and desires of both police commissioners and its influential donors, and this tension has frequently resulted in controversy and public scrutiny.[5]

In an interview for this book, Boyce revealed how in the days following Epstein's July 2019 arrest, a handful of Police Foundation benefactors—those he termed "one-percenters"—embarked on what amounted to a stealth lobbying campaign on Epstein's behalf meant to ease his discomfort while behind bars. Despite the common knowledge that Epstein was a convicted sex offender, these "sweet people" believed the favor bank was open for business, and each caller importuning him sought to make a withdrawal on Epstein's behalf.[6]

Boyce said he received such calls from at least three different people trying to assist Epstein while he remained incarcerated in the MCC. None of these callers seemed aware that others were making identical entreaties on Epstein's behalf, leading Boyce to conclude they were likely acting independently of one another but at the behest of Epstein or a common surrogate. "They were upper-crust elites who met [Epstein] over cocktails and thought he was charming. He won them over," Boyce explained.[7]

The foundation members making calls on Epstein's behalf had each, at one time, been generous benefactors of the Police Foundation—one contributed as much as $50,000. "You know, they're calling not to say, 'Hello, Bob,' but rather, 'We're concerned about a friend of ours who is imprisoned,'" Boyce explained. "They wanted to buy him things, certain comforts while he was in his jail cell, like a pillow or toiletries," Boyce said. The callers gave Boyce the impression that each was prepared to cut a personal check on Epstein's behalf on the spot.[8]

Boyce was not inclined to help. By the time the callers reached the former chief of detectives, word had reached him through another former law enforcement official about the nature of the cache of lurid photographs that had been seized from Epstein's townhouse. The trove of photos numbered in the hundreds, and the subjects were suspected victims of Epstein's predations. One detail from the official's account of the photographs was particularly chilling, Boyce recalled in an interview with reporter Philip Messing for this book: "'They're really young and a lot of them have braces,'" Boyce said the law enforcement official told him.

Boyce diplomatically discouraged the callers' misguided impulses. "I told them, 'Look, just walk away. This is a bad guy. He is much worse than you can ever know. Don't walk. Run!'"

"They immediately said, 'Thank you very much, chief,' and hung up."

As THE FIRST RAYS OF light broke through the slotted openings on the ninth floor at the MCC on July 8, 2019, Jeffrey Epstein had already spent two nights in federal custody. He was due to appear in Manhattan Federal Court for his arraignment later that day—his first hearing in connection with the new indictment—but before he would have his time to face a judge, Geoffrey Berman, then the United States attorney for the Southern District, took the opportunity to present in a press conference the accusations being brought.

"Today, we announce the unsealing of sex trafficking charges against Jeffrey Epstein," he told a roomful of reporters. "Epstein is alleged to have abused dozens of victims at his mansion in New York and his estate in Palm Beach, Florida." Berman went on to lay out the shocking scope of the allegations against Epstein: that the victims, all underage girls, were recruited by Epstein or his employees under the pretext of providing him paid massage, and that the massages generally became "increasingly sexual and would typically include one or more sex acts," and that Epstein paid some of the victims to recruit additional girls who were also abused, creating "an ever-expanding web of new victims."

Berman, who eleven months later would be dismissed from his position at the urging of President Donald Trump, stressed two particularly egregious points: how Epstein's illegal activities had persisted for such a long time and how they violated the most basic norms of decency within a civilized society. These victims had been as young as fourteen at the time of the alleged abuse. Berman said that Epstein was well aware that many of his victims were minors and that, not surprisingly, many of the underage girls Epstein allegedly victimized were particularly vulnerable to exploitation. "The alleged behavior shocks the conscience."[9]

As Berman, joined by Assistant Director William Sweeney of the FBI, stated the case before the court of public opinion, Jeffrey Epstein was ushered to a holding cell at 500 Pearl Street ahead of his arraignment.[10] In the courtroom, he appeared disheveled in a navy blue jumpsuit and jail-issued orange shoes.[11] He stared silently ahead while seated between two of his lawyers, Martin Weinberg and Marc Fernich.[12] A not guilty plea was entered before U.S. magistrate judge Henry Pitman to the two charges he faced, sex trafficking and sex trafficking conspiracy.

A third defense lawyer present, Reid Weingarten, told the magistrate that Epstein had led a "law-abiding life" since 2008. He implied that the new indictment was little more than a case of sour grapes and buyer's remorse by the government, as the Justice Department had been left badly embarrassed by having willfully signed off on an incomprehensibly generous deal in the Florida case nearly a dozen years before. "This indictment is essentially a do-over, this is old stuff, this is ancient stuff," Weingarten said.[13]

At the press conference, Geoffrey Berman underscored the government's view that the new charges were not barred by the Florida non-prosecution agreement. "The Southern District of New York . . . is not a signatory on that agreement," stated Berman. Epstein's lawyers pushed a diametrically contrary assessment, however, claiming that the new case was legally unsupportable as a matter of law because the September 2007 NPA in Florida had effectively indemnified their client from being brought up on the remarkably similar charges detailed in the new indictment.[14] To permit the new case to go forward, Epstein's attorneys insisted, would violate the constitutional ban against double jeopardy, that is, attempts to criminally try a defendant twice for the same crime.

Epstein's attorneys fixated on a passage in the NPA noting that the accord that had been reached "seeks to resolve globally his state and federal criminal liability"—a passage they believed made the new charges moot. Federal prosecutor Alexander Rossmiller countered that Epstein had not been chastened by his earlier brush with the law, which made him a continued risk to young girls everywhere. "This is not an individual who has left his past behind," Rossmiller said.

Epstein's attorneys also submitted a request that the jailed financier be allowed to await trial under house arrest in his Manhattan mansion. Rossmiller objected that Epstein's phenomenal wealth and ready access to private transportation made him a major flight risk. "He is a man of nearly infinite means," Rossmiller argued. Prosecutors also noted that Epstein had made $350,000 in payments to potential witnesses against him, a discovery that came through records obtained from an unspecified financial institution.[15]

These payments, the government suggested, had been made shortly after the *Miami Herald* began publishing its series of damning articles about Epstein in late 2018 that refocused attention on the allegations against him—and on the scant punishment resulting from the Florida case.

Judge Pitman set the case over to resume deliberations on July 15. Jeffrey Epstein was returned to the MCC.


JEFFREY EPSTEIN FACED THE DAUNTING prospect of enduring pretrial detention at the MCC for what promised to be at least six more grueling months. Epstein's lawyers fought to have him released on what amounted to house arrest, whereby he would post his $56 million Manhattan mansion—the crown jewel of his real estate portfolio that boasted a front sidewalk specially engineered to melt falling snow—to guarantee that he wouldn't flee. His lawyers were also proposing that Epstein would wear a monitoring device and pay for an around-the-clock security force to monitor his whereabouts and, more astonishing, that he would pledge his fortune of at least $559 million as collateral.[16]

Judge Richard M. Berman would have none of it. The bond package proffered by defense attorneys was "irretrievably inadequate," he argued. Two of Epstein's accusers—Annie Farmer and Courtney Wild—provided the court with moving testimony concerning fears for their safety if the financier were released.[17]

On July 18, Judge Berman presented a thirty-three-page decision concluding that Epstein was simply too dangerous and too likely to flee for him to be released.[18]

# 31

# JAILHOUSE CONFESSIONS

THE FIRST NIGHT BEHIND BARS IS A TEST OF SURVIVAL INSIDE A SYSTEM that shows no mercy toward weakness. Anyone who has ever been incarcerated knows the horror of the moment the lights are extinguished for the first time and a cellblock tier fills with unknown noises.

At the MCC, an initiative called the Inmate Companion Program has been established to assist at-risk prisoners—especially newcomers to the system—who might be overwhelmed by the experience of incarceration. Prisoners wishing to serve as counselors were given a four-hour course and paid forty cents an hour for their work.

Michael "Miles" Tisdale was the inmate who ran the companion program. The thirty-three-year-old was inside for selling oxycodone to an undercover Drug Enforcement Administration agent. Tisdale pleaded guilty and served approximately fifteen months; he was then freed on parole but was returned to the MCC in February 2019 for violating the terms of his release. Soon after Jeffrey Epstein arrived at the MCC, Tisdale assigned one of his counselors, inmate William "Dollar Bill" Mersey, to serve as Epstein's companion.[1]

Mersey, a former cabbie, was a colorful longtime resident of Manhattan's East Village. Now a gaunt-looking sixty-nine-year-old, Mersey was processed into the MCC on January 3, 2019, and was serving the last few months of the one-year-and-a-day sentence he had received after pleading guilty to federal tax fraud charges. Mersey had run a website, Dollar Bill's Psycho Roundup, that advertised the services of women in the sex trade industry and also peddled his book, *A Kid in the Candy Store: My Life in the Escort Business,* for three dollars a copy.

At the MCC, Mersey's first job was in the kitchen, but he had also become one of Tisdale's counselors. Both he and Tisdale would become close to Epstein during his five weeks behind bars.

Epstein's first night inside the MCC was spent in what's referred to as the general population. Ninety percent of the MCC population was in "Gen Pop," including most pretrial prisoners, who tend to be more agitated and potentially more dangerous than those who have been sentenced and are awaiting a prison transfer, or those due for imminent release.

The tier Epstein was first sent to—7N—included gang members of MS-13 and various Bloods factions. It was a holding home for murderers, narcotraffickers, and other violent criminals, and jail-house assaults—either to settle a score or for hire—were common.

In an interview for this book, inmate Tisdale remembered one altercation that occurred around the time of Epstein's incarceration in early July 2019. Tisdale was working in the library, where he often assisted inmates researching their legal cases. Such efforts, he recalled, often included helping them use the computer's DVD players so they could view videos tied to their pending cases. Early one afternoon, a group of inmates affiliated with the MS-13 gang had gathered around a single computer and were watching a video. The 7N inmates grew boisterous, laughing and seeming to congratulate one another as they pointed at the screen. Seemingly curious, another group of inmates affiliated with the Bloods, who had been seated nearby, pulled up their chairs. "I'm looking at what's going on and thinking, 'They're probably looking at porn,'" Tisdale recalled. "I go over and look at the computer and see a bunch of these guys that are sitting there stabbing a guy in the neck and one of them is yelling, 'That's us! That's us!'" On the video, five or six men could be seen stabbing another man to death, Tisdale said.[2]

ON EPSTEIN'S SECOND DAY BEHIND bars, the Bureau of Prisons administrators transferred Epstein from 7N to the ninth floor south, or 9S, and the Special Housing Unit, or SHU (pronounced "shoe"). It was also known in MCC vernacular as the Hole.

Inmates assigned to the SHU can include those who are at risk due to their notoriety, including cooperating witnesses, former cops, and pedophiles, all of whom are targets for retribution, as well as unruly inmates sent there as punishment for disciplinary infractions.

Epstein's accommodations in the SHU wing were dreary. A SHU cell is typically about fifty square feet and contains a toilet and bunk beds, as the cramped living quarters are ordinarily shared with a cellmate, or "bunkie." Beds have thin and uncomfortable mattresses, with upper berths that are uncomfortably close to the cell's ceiling.

In the SHU, prisoners are confined to their cells for much of the day and evening. They have limited opportunities to make phone calls and are permitted to shower only three times a week. Evenings on the cellblock were "very noisy," one inmate recalled. Many SHU inmates are housed there for disciplinary infractions, meaning they are prone to loud and disruptive behavior, particularly when everyone else is hoping to go to sleep.[3]

The MCC was a hard place to keep secrets. The nature of Epstein's crimes became known inside the building. Rather than harming Epstein physically, several young prisoners in the unit initially sought to intimidate and extort him, according to Tisdale. "He was 'run out,'"

Tisdale explained, meaning Epstein was ostracized from other prisoners in the housing unit. Tisdale said he heard about this effort initially from one of the guards and later from Epstein himself. "[Other inmates] tried to extort him . . . they tried to control him by selling him commissary items (like snacks, sodas, and certain meals) for way above what they're supposed to be sold for," Tisdale said.

According to inmate accounts, Epstein did use commissary sales in an effort to secure his safety within the jail. Soon after Epstein entered the MCC on the evening of July 6, a rumor spread among the staff and inmates that he was looking to ensure his safety by adding money to the commissary accounts of several prisoners. The money would allow recipients to buy various snacks, personal toiletries, and extra meals, William Mersey explained. A guard, Mersey said, would later confirm to Mersey that Epstein had ordered the transactions.

In conversations with Mersey under the auspices of the inmate companion program, Epstein voiced concerns about the prospect of what awaited him, not just in the MCC but in a federal penitentiary, should he be convicted. In particular, Epstein expressed to Mersey, who is white, the fear that he would be targeted by black inmates (Epstein did not raise these specific fears with Tisdale, who is black). As Mersey understood it, Epstein's worries about his safety were related to his experiences and feelings about race. "He mentioned he'd been bullied at school in Coney Island by black kids—not by Italians, not by the Irish, but by black kids," Mersey recalled.

In one conversation, Mersey recalled Epstein asking, "Do I need a big *shvar*?" (*Shvar,* or *shvartze,* is a pejorative Yiddish term for a black person.) Mersey said he tried to admonish Epstein about his insecurity, advising him to look fellow prisoners in the eye and stand his ground. Epstein's consternation over this topic grew so acute, Mersey said, that he continued to raise the question of hiring an intimidating inmate who might be willing to protect him.

Epstein lawyer David Schoen would later deride media reports that Epstein had agreed to put money on the commissary accounts of fellow inmates out of fear for his safety, insisting he had personally counseled Epstein against doing that very thing, warning him that to succumb to such overtures would only make him a bigger target.

WITHIN A FEW DAYS OF being assigned to the SHU, Epstein was put on "suicide watch," which meant he was moved to an even grimmer environment. The suicide watch area consists of four-cell units on the second floor of the jail that provide some of the most restrictive housing in the facility. Inmates assigned to suicide watch are not permitted to leave their cells. Beds are without sheets; clothing is more minimal to prevent self-harming behaviors; lights are never turned off; and inmates are supposed to be under 24/7 watch by both prison guards and staff, with each detail about their behavior, whether awake or asleep, recorded in a logbook every fifteen minutes.[4] But the MCC was in fact in such a chaotic state of operations, according to a report in *The New York Times*, that other inmates, not Bureau of Prisons employees, were pressed into service to help keep some inmates from killing themselves.[5]

Tisdale remembered seeing Epstein in the unit, citing the distinctive jailhouse mufti worn by inmates on suicide watch—a gown with Velcro straps—as proof. Tisdale and William Mersey would both assert that Epstein was moved to suicide watch soon after he became an inmate on July 6.[6]

"They would not move him from the SHU to suicide watch unless he indicated to a prison psychologist or someone that he felt a desire to kill himself," Mersey insisted. "You don't go there unless you express intent to 'hang up,'" prison parlance for a desire to take one's own life.

The revelation of this previously unreported first instance of Epstein's being placed on suicide watch raises new questions about prison officials' efforts to safeguard their high-profile inmate. (A representative for the Bureau of Prisons declined to comment on the allegation.)

After several days spent on suicide watch, Epstein was transferred back to the SHU, where all seemed okay until the morning of July 23.[7]

Five days after his request to be remanded to house arrest was denied by a federal judge on July 18, Epstein was found on the floor of his cell, semiconscious in the fetal position, with marks on his neck.[8] Epstein's cellmate, Nicholas Tartaglione, a muscle-bound former police officer from a New York suburb accused of a drug-related quadruple homicide, summoned guards by yelling.[9] Tartaglione was in SHU as punishment after being caught with a contraband cellphone.[10] Tartaglione told guards that he had discovered Epstein in the process of harming himself, with a bedsheet tied around his neck.[11]

A jail supervisor, following protocol, dialed 911. Epstein was transported to nearby NewYork–Presbyterian Lower Manhattan Hospital, where he was revived, discharged, and sent back to the MCC.

The incident was immediately leaked to the press, and at 9:48 P.M. on July 24, Radar Online was first up with a breathless post, quoting a source that Epstein was "blue in the face" and "sprawled out on the floor." The following morning, at 8:00 A.M. on July 25, the Associated Press moved the story, attributing it to "a person familiar with the matter."

In response to inquiries, Justice Department officials acknowledged that following the incident, Epstein was placed on suicide watch. He remained there for twenty-four hours before being transferred to "psychological observation" on the same hospital wing floor, which is less restrictive than suicide watch but still required monitoring twenty-four hours a day, federal officials said. On July 30, seven days after the mysterious incident, he was transferred back to the SHU.

Tartaglione told guards that he had noticed that Epstein had a bedsheet around his neck and appeared to be trying to kill himself, but Epstein later denied that, claiming instead that he had been attacked—an allegation that Tartaglione vehemently denied.[12]

Tisdale was one of the first inmates to see Epstein after the incident. "What happened up there?" Tisdale recalled asking Epstein. "All he did is make a strangling motion to himself with his hands around his neck and I said, 'Someone else tried to strangle you?' And he gave me a little nod."

To William Mersey, Epstein offered a different explanation. "He told me, 'I woke in the middle of the night to get a glass of water and that's the last thing I remember,'" Mersey said, adding that he found Epstein's account dubious.

According to David Schoen, one of Epstein's lawyers, Epstein told MCC officials he'd simply blacked out and wasn't aware of how he had ended up in distress on his cell floor—an account that matched Mersey's.

"He told the MCC he couldn't remember what happened," Schoen said in an interview for this book. When pressed for his own belief as to whether Epstein had tried to harm himself or had been attacked, Schoen said, "I don't think it was a suicide attempt or an attempt by someone else to kill him. My conclusion [is that] it was something he agreed to go along with."[13]

Tartaglione denied any complicity in the incident. His lawyer, Bruce Barket, told NBC News that "any suggestion that Mr. Tartaglione assaulted anyone is a complete fabrication." Barket said he was subsequently sent an email from jail officials stating that Tartaglione had been criminally cleared of any wrongdoing in connection with the incident.[14] In a brief phone interview for this book, Barket insisted that not only had his client *not* tried to kill Epstein, but he had promptly notified jailhouse authorities.[15]

Bureau of Prisons administrators at the MCC inexplicably failed to preserve video footage of the area around Epstein's jail cell that might have offered proof about what transpired in Epstein's cell on the morning of July 23.[16] Prosecutors later offered the vague explanation of "technical errors" for this oversight. Tartaglione's attorney,

Bruce Barket, had sought a copy of the video to present as proof that his client had tried to save Epstein's life.[17]

Jeffrey Epstein went back to the SHU only six days after his purported suicide attempt.[18]

EPSTEIN WASN'T THE FIRST "CELEBRITY" inmate that William Mersey had dealt with at the MCC. In June 2019, a month before Epstein arrived at the jail, Mersey met Paul Manafort, the longtime Republican Party campaign consultant and lawyer who had chaired the Trump presidential campaign in the summer of 2016. Manafort was later indicted on eighteen charges related to financial crimes, including tax evasion, bank fraud, and money laundering. Whereas Epstein would project a degree of nervousness about potential threats to his safety while behind bars, Manafort, who was more than four years older than Epstein, projected a degree of hardcore grit that was surprising, Mersey recalled.

During their first meeting, Mersey assured Epstein that he meant no harm. "I said, 'Listen, I'm here on a tax fraud charge. I'm set. I don't need any of your money,'" Mersey told him. After Mersey explained the ins and outs of his business advertising escorts, Epstein perked up, Mersey said. "He had a healthy interest in the escort business," Mersey recalled, noting that Epstein talked with him about the topic for at least ninety minutes, asking him a series of detailed questions about how the business worked.

Mersey could lay legitimate claim to be the inmate at the MCC who became closest to Epstein. Mersey spent some thirty hours chatting with Epstein, mostly in the early evenings, usually as Epstein sat sidesaddle on the toilet in his cell while Mersey remained just beyond the cell's entrance.

The chats, as per the design of the program, were intended to cheer up prisoners by avoiding discussions about their pending cases. "We were told, 'Keep 'em upbeat. Don't talk about yourself and don't talk about what they may have done,'" Mersey reflected. Epstein was stoic about his predicament, although he did on one occasion express his displeasure about being given the wrong laxative by jail personnel. "He looked at the bottle he'd been given, and he said, 'I told them don't give me Docusate, but they gave me Docusate,'" Mersey remembered.

Mersey once said he asked Epstein about Donald Trump. "Epstein liked the question. It aroused his interest," Mersey said. Talk of Trump brought back agreeable memories to the financier and he began telling Mersey stories. "One time, we're flying in my private plane and I was with this French girl," Epstein said, according to Mersey's account. "And Trump said to me, 'Why don't we land in Atlantic City and I can show your friend my casino?' I told Trump, I'm not landing in Atlantic City, all you have is white trash down there. The girl I was with, because she was French, asked me, 'What does "white trash" mean?' Donald Trump told her, 'That would be me without money.'"

Talking about the good old days changed Epstein's somber mood. "He went on, unsolicited, about Bill Clinton," Mersey remembered. Epstein volunteered how Clinton's days as a Lothario were a thing of the past. "He told me, 'He can't do anything like that now because he's had a couple of heart surgeries.'"

When Epstein would grow weary of the near-nightly chats with Mersey, he said, he'd announce, "Okay, Bill, I'm going to go to sleep now," before throwing a sock across his eyes to block the light. He was usually asleep within minutes.

There was comfort in having a friend inside the lockup, even for a pronounced introvert like Epstein. The financier grew comfortable enough with Mersey that he inquired if he might consider being his cellmate. Prison rules prohibited such an arrangement, though— Mersey was due to be released in a few months and Epstein was a pretrial detainee.

THOUGH MERSEY WAS TECHNICALLY EPSTEIN'S assigned companion, Tisdale, who ran the overall program, also spent significant time with

Epstein, and at a certain point he moved to take over the companion duties—out of curiosity. "Billy went down there and met him for the first time. He comes up the next day, 'I had this great conversation with Epstein.' He gave me the whole 411," he said. After the well-publicized July 23 incident in which Epstein purportedly tried to kill himself, Tisdale said he opted to essentially rescind Mersey's assignment. "I told Billy, '*I'm* the guy who gets to meet him,'" Tisdale recalled with a laugh.

Tisdale said he had numerous "companion" sessions with Epstein, spending at least twenty hours with him from late July through August 5, 2019, when Tisdale completed his sentence and was released from the MCC. Tisdale remembered heading down to the prison's second floor to await Epstein's arrival the first time they met. In the first of what became five or six such meetings, which usually went from about seven to eleven o'clock at night, the two inmates began opening up to each other. Epstein spoke to Tisdale about his family's modest background, and "how he made his money, through finance and investments and those type of things." Tisdale told Epstein that the latter could "ask anything" and Epstein "immediately reciprocated," seeking Tisdale's input on the safety of his jail housing unit.

At one point, Tisdale recalled, he showed Epstein a book on currency trading, and the former financier's face "lit up" and he proceeded to spend a "good thirty to forty-five minutes explaining the basics of currency trading" to Tisdale.

Tisdale recalled that Epstein's explanation involved sexually graphic imagery: "He said to me, 'My advice to you is to pick one currency and to focus on that currency, just like there's a lot of pussy out there. You don't want to mess with all of them, you want *that* pussy—the pussy that speaks to you. You know how that pussy acts, how her mood will be next month and maybe in two months—that's the same way to look at currency. Keep your eye on that one currency, as that's the currency for you.'"

At a subsequent session the following evening, Tisdale recalled, Epstein responded in the same crude manner. "He had asked me to ask him questions, so one of the lame questions I asked was, 'How did you become so good with money? How did you become so good with budgeting?' He replied, 'Miles, you have to have a goal. You have to have a goal that you're putting the money to, whether it's a car, whether it's a house, whatever it may be.'"

"Well, what's *your* motivation? Is it a house? What keeps *you* going?" Tisdale had asked. "He said, 'Miles, I'll tell you . . . one thing: pussy.' I'll never forget him saying that."

Tisdale remembered that at one of their early meetings, Epstein made a specific reference to his alleged crimes. "He said to me, 'Miles, you know, I don't know what you've heard, but they are talking about these girls being underage, but they're fifteen, sixteen, seventeen, and eighteen years old—not eight or nine years old!'"

For the most part, Tisdale recalled, Epstein remained focused on his safety, not only in jail but potentially in federal prison should he be convicted. He grilled Tisdale about how to navigate his environment so he might stay alive. "He was asking me how the various other prison locations are set up. 'Are they like this?' I said, 'I don't have that much experience, but when you go to a prison, there is more movement, there are more programs, more things to do. You have *more* freedom.' It seemed to mildly pacify him," Tisdale said.

INCARCERATION WAS ALL ABOUT PASSING time—from one hour to another and one day to the next. Most of Epstein's day behind bars was spent with his attorneys. Meetings with attorneys were held on the second floor, in Spartan conference rooms that afforded little comfort but a small semblance of confidentiality. Epstein would regularly vanish for up to twelve hours a day to a second-floor conference room to consult with his lawyers, seemingly eager to stay away from the cellblock for as long as possible.

It was a costly routine. The top lawyers employed by Epstein reportedly billed their services at more than $1,000 an hour; the less prominent ones received half that.[19] By one estimate, Epstein was burning through as much as $200,000 a week for the privilege of chatting with his lawyers.

There were so many attorneys present at these meetings that sometimes there weren't enough chairs, according to one of the lawyers present. David Schoen said four or more lawyers would be seated near Epstein at a second-floor conference table at any given time, while a couple other defense attorneys were reduced to standing outside the conference room. The scene resembled a veritable game legal musical chairs. During these long meetings, the legal team raided the commissary for snacks and beverages.

Epstein's many counselors would certainly be billing a lot of hours. "The one thing about having money," Epstein told Mersey, "was that everybody wanted a piece."

# 32

## LAST RITES

On July 31, 2019, Jeffrey Epstein was ushered back into a federal courtroom to learn when his criminal trial would begin. In front of a packed courtroom, Assistant United States Attorney Alison Moe requested that a June 2020 trial date be set, noting a public interest in bringing this case to trial as swiftly as possible. Martin Weinberg, one of Epstein's lawyers, countered by insisting that the defense team would not be ready before Labor Day 2020, explaining that prosecutors had delayed bringing charges for alleged crimes that had occurred almost twenty years earlier.

Just a week had passed since Epstein had been found semiconscious in his cell. Unlike his previous court appearances, at which he seemed animated while interacting with his attorneys, on this occasion, Epstein sat "passively," with his hands folded in front of his face through much of the twenty-minute proceeding.[1] The blue prison jumpsuit drooped over his frame. Occasionally, Epstein gazed at courtroom artists and reporters seated in a jury box.

Judge Richard M. Berman, who said he anticipated a six-to-eight-week trial, set a tentative start date of June 8, 2020, acknowledging that it might be necessary to push the trial's start further back at the defense's request. Berman also ordered written arguments on the defense's motion to dismiss the case because it amounted to double jeopardy to be filed by September 13, with oral arguments in October.[2]

FEDERAL PROSECUTORS RARELY BROUGHT CASES to trial unless the expected outcome was highly favorable. In calendar year 2018, there were nearly 80,000 defendants in federal criminal cases, but of the total, 8 percent had their cases dismissed and an astounding 90 percent pleaded guilty to one or more of the offenses.[3] Only 2 percent opted to go to trial before a judge or jury, and of that scant number who opted to put their fate in jurors' hands, a tiny fraction—only 320 individuals out of 79,704 cases—went to trial and won an acquittal, according to the Administrative Office of the U.S. Courts. In 2018, the Department of Justice reported a 93 percent conviction rate, according to official government statistics.[4]

The timing of Epstein's arrest did not bode well for him. A year earlier, in May 2018, film mogul Harvey Weinstein was charged by the Manhattan District Attorney's Office with rape, criminal sex act, sex abuse, and sexual misconduct in cases involving two separate women.[5] Two months later, Weinstein was indicted on an additional charge of predatory sexual assault for forcing a woman to perform oral sex on him in 2006.[6] Weinstein's case had ignited the global #MeToo movement. It was impossible to think of the crimes of the one man without raising those of the other.

Epstein and Weinstein had much in common. Both were Jewish men who had grown up in modest circumstances in the outer boroughs of New York City (Weinstein was from Flushing, Queens). Weinstein was ten months older. Each had a sole sibling, a brother who was two years younger and with whom each had a somewhat contentious relationship. Each displayed a palpable sharp-elbowed drive and had become maniacally focused on attaining success at all costs, be it finance for Epstein, or Hollywood for Weinstein.

The men had at one time been friends. Bradley Edwards, a lawyer representing some of Epstein's accusers, recounted in his book *Relentless Pursuit* that Weinstein was allegedly at Epstein's Paris apartment receiving a massage from one of Epstein's girls when he aggressively attempted to turn the interaction into a sexual encounter. "The girl rejected his advances. As the story goes, Harvey then verbally abused her for rejecting him," Edwards wrote. Years later, Epstein confirmed the account to Edwards, referring to Harvey as "a pig."[7]

DAVID SCHOEN, A POWERFUL ATLANTA-BASED attorney, had met Epstein in 2008 when the financier was preparing to serve his sentence in the Palm Beach County Jail. The two had kept in touch over the years, with Epstein occasionally calling on Schoen for advice. In the summer of 2019, Epstein once again turned to Schoen. "The word was that from him and his inner circle, he trusted me," Schoen later told a reporter.[8]

The two met at the MCC on August 1 for close to five hours. Epstein expressed concern that his legal team had grown too large and become unwieldy. He wanted Schoen to take charge. "He had asked me to quarterback the whole case. I agreed but told him I'd have to meet with his lawyers, because they didn't know who I was," Schoen said.[9]

As Schoen came onto the scene, Epstein was facing more than one legal challenge. One was to keep him from rotting inside a federal penitentiary for forty-five years. The other was to keep some of his vast fortune. On July 29, Epstein's attorneys had filed court papers seeking to thwart progress in a civil lawsuit brought in Florida eleven years earlier by two victims. The litigants—identified only as Jane Doe 1 and Jane Doe 2—were challenging Epstein's NPA deal. Epstein's lawyers requested another month to file a reply, claiming that it would be difficult for Epstein to review paperwork while locked up; the victims' attorneys countered that Epstein's lawyers certainly seemed able to "file legal pleadings rapidly . . . when it serves his purposes."

The subsequent five-hour meeting between Schoen and Epstein gave an optimistic charge to Epstein's demeanor, Schoen would later recall. The defense continued to hinge their case on the earlier non-prosecution deal that had been reached with federal prosecutors, one that had been greenlighted by top Justice Department officials and that they contended would make the new charges tantamount to double jeopardy.

Throughout the session, the financier did not show the slightest hint—either by what he said or how he acted—that he was harboring thoughts of harming himself.

Their chat was briefly interrupted for a few minutes when a jail psychiatrist cited her need to interview Epstein as part of a mandated "suicide protocol." The request, Schoen said, was something he and Epstein briefly joked about.

Six days after the meeting, Schoen received a call from another member of the defense team who had just visited Epstein and who told him the imprisoned suspect was still cheerful about his prospects and looking forward to having Schoen orchestrate his defense. "On Tuesday [August 6], someone who had visited him called me up and said, 'Boy, does this guy love you!'" Schoen recalled in an interview for this book. "Everything was very 'future-looking.'"[10]

ON AUGUST 8, JEFFREY EPSTEIN signed a document titled "Last Will and Testament of Jeffrey Epstein."[11] As complicated an event as it was to prepare and sign this will, it allowed him some control, and perhaps even some peace, with his freedom uncertain.

The twenty-one-page document bequeathed his assets to the "1953 Trust," so called for the year Epstein was born, and was filed in St. Thomas. His holdings listed in the will closely resembled the inventory list Epstein's lawyers had submitted the previous month in Manhattan Federal Court as part of his failed bid to post his fortune for bail, with two additions: a list of "Aviation Assets, Automobiles, and Boats," a collection worth $18,551,700, and his offbeat art collection, renowned for its odd sexual theme, that was described as "fine arts, antiques, collectibles, valuables" and whose value the document noted was "TBD," pending an appraisal.

Two Brooklyn lawyers were listed as witnessing the document's signing; one of them was Mariel A. Colón Miró, a twenty-six-year-old attorney who had recently represented drug kingpin Joaquín "El Chapo" Guzmán.[12] Epstein assigned two longtime associates— lawyer Darren Indyke and businessman Richard Kahn—to serve as executors. Epstein allocated $250,000 for their services and "reasonable" expenses. A third man, Boris Nikolic, was listed as an alternate.

There were no details on the trust's beneficiaries. Court papers state that Epstein's only potential heir was his brother, Mark Epstein.

According to the new will, Jeffrey Epstein was worth $577,672,654, or about $18 million more than he had previously stated in court papers when futilely trying to obtain bail on federal sex trafficking charges. There was $56,347.22 in cash, another $14,304,679 in fixed income investments, a whopping $112,679,138 in equity, and $194,986,301 in what was described as hedge fund and private equity investments.

The Upper East Side mansion was valued at $55,931,000, considerably less than the $77 million figure reported in various press accounts.* He listed each of his real estate properties—except for two apartments he owned on fashionable Avenue Foch, in Paris, worth a total of $8.6 million—in the names of Virgin Islands corporations named for streets from the Sea Gate neighborhood of his youth:

---

* In July 2020, two of Epstein's homes were put on the market for a combined total of about $110 million—according to the properties' listing agents. The Upper East Side seven-story townhouse, described as a "once in a life-time opportunity to own the largest single-family home in New York City," was listed at $88 million; the waterfront property in Palm Beach was given a price tag of $21.9 million.

his East Seventy-First Street home was owned by Maple Inc., named after the avenue on which his family's home in Sea Gate had been located; Zorro Ranch in Stanley, New Mexico (worth $17,246,208), was owned by Cypress Inc.; the property at 358 El Brillo Way in Palm Beach ($12,380,209) was owned by Laurel Inc.; the Great St. James property ($22,498,600) was owned by Poplar Inc.; and the Little St. James property ($68,874,223) was owned by Nautilus Inc.[13]

ON THE MORNING OF FRIDAY, August 9, Jeffrey Epstein and his lawyers received news that dampened their optimism. A Manhattan federal appeals court ruled that roughly two thousand pages of documents, filed in connection with a previously settled defamation lawsuit by Epstein victim Virginia Roberts Giuffre against Epstein's former close associate Ghislaine Maxwell, should be made public.[14] The cache of documents, including photos, amounted to a sickening array of details that more than thirty media organizations had filed suit to obtain. The released data served to pulverize the shattered remnants of Epstein's reputation.

Among the information released was the September 2016 deposition in which Epstein repeatedly invoked his Fifth Amendment right against self-incrimination in refusing to answer questions like whether it was "standard operating procedure for [Ghislaine] Maxwell to bring underage girls up to your room for you to sexually abuse."[15] In another released document, Giuffre stated that Maxwell directed her to have sex with former Senate majority leader George Mitchell, a Maine Democrat, former New Mexico governor Bill Richardson, and other prominent people.[16] (Both men would issue statements denying the allegations.)

The federal appeals court decision was a blow to Epstein's chance to avoid dying behind bars. The avalanche of information—two caches of still sealed documents—contained any number of future embarrassments about his disturbing past that were likely to be made public once vetted by a federal judge.

ON THE DAY THAT THE newest raft of revelations was being made public in a massive document dump, Jeffrey Epstein, not known for being sentimental, arranged to make a phone call, one that proved to be his last. The call was to Karyna Shuliak, the thirty-year-old émigré from Belarus who some media accounts mistakenly claimed had been traveling with him when Epstein was arrested July 6 at Teterboro Airport after his jet touched down from Paris.[17] After Epstein's arrest, Shuliak, who had been with Epstein in Paris, left France for Belarus, where she was staying with relatives, according to a confidential source in an interview for this book.[18]

Epstein and Shuliak had known each other since at least January 2015, when she was seen emerging from his East Seventy-First Street mansion with other people from his inner circle.[19] Shuliak, a dentist registered to practice in both Florida and California, listed her home address as St. Thomas, U.S. Virgin Islands (where she is also licensed to practice dentistry).[20] In October 2013, Shuliak entered into a marriage with Jennifer Kalin, a close and trusted friend of Epstein's. The two women divorced in July 2019, the same month Epstein was arrested upon his return from Paris. The marriage between the two women, sources familiar with the arrangement said, resembled other same-sex sham marriages Epstein had set up to keep certain foreign women he favored—usually from Eastern European countries—in the United States beyond when their visas permitted.[21]

It remains unclear what prompted Epstein to reach out to Shuliak while she was still in Belarus, nor whether he had been in regular contact with her during the nearly five weeks he'd been imprisoned at the MCC following his July arrest.

One source requesting anonymity said it would have made perfect sense for Epstein to reach out to her, as the pair had grown increasingly close in the weeks leading up to Epstein's arrest the previous month. "She loved Jeffrey, and I am given to believe that he loved her," the source added.

Shuliak's lawyer, Maurice H. Sercarz, declined to provide details about his client, other than to acknowledge that she and Epstein had a special bond. "I will say that Karyna occupied a very important space in his life. She is the woman who occupied the most significant position in his life at the end," Sercarz said in an interview for this book.[22] Sercarz described Epstein as "a master at compartmentalizing his life" and asserted that when Epstein concluded his call with Shuliak on August 9, "she had no idea that he was acutely distressed."

If there were significant changes to Epstein's mental outlook, William Mersey—his inmate companion and de facto suicide counselor—missed them, too. Mersey did notice one small modification in Epstein's behavior in the days before Epstein died: "The only thing I noticed is he was eating his meals on the floor. He would just say, 'It's easier this way.' I didn't see anything to suggest, 'Oh, he's spiraling down,'" Mersey recounted.

One other key development occurred on August 9: Epstein's cellmate transferred out, with no immediate replacement.

Epstein had his cell to himself.

# 33

# NIGHT MOVES

THE AUGUST HEAT WAS PARTICULARLY OPPRESSIVE IN NEW YORK CITY on the night of August 9. Temperatures broke 90 degrees, with high humidity. Lower Manhattan, where tall buildings blocked any hope of a breeze, suffered more than the outer boroughs, and the air inside the MCC was particularly stifling.

Jeffrey Epstein spent most of that afternoon conferring with attorneys. As the final hints of daylight filtered through the slatted openings of the fortress-like facility, thirty-one-year-old MCC guard Tova Noel was summoned to return Epstein to his cell. Prison authorities later reported the exact time of the move as 7:49 P.M., and said it had been recorded on video.[1]

In what would have been the last meal served to Epstein, a database from the Federal Bureau of Prisons shows the dinner that night was likely baked ziti or a tofu pasta alternative.[2] By ten, Epstein and the other inmates were locked in their cells for the night.

MCC OFFICIALS CLAIMED THAT WHEN they moved Epstein back to the SHU on July 30, one of the steps they undertook to guard against suicide attempts was to assign him the cell closest to the correctional officers' desk.[3]

Noel was working a double shift in the SHU that night. Her regular shift was from 4:00 P.M. to midnight, but that night she would work an additional shift on overtime, from midnight to 8:00 A.M. Fellow guard Michael Thomas was also assigned to the midnight shift.

Overnight shifts were notorious for "cooping," the law enforcement term for sleeping on the job. According to jail policy, Noel and Thomas were required to make rounds every half hour and count the prisoners. However, according to an official indictment, Noel and Thomas were seated at the correctional officers' desk in the SHU common area approximately fifteen feet from Epstein's cell and did not in fact leave that post at any time to conduct the required rounds.

The locked doors to Epstein's cell in the SHU could only be opened remotely by an officer in the jail's control center. A second locked door was one to which only correctional officers assigned to the high-security housing unit had the key.[4] But it mattered little. The indictment, citing surveillance footage, said that for approximately two hours Noel and Thomas sat at their desk without moving. They appeared to have been asleep. At some point during the night, the guards used the Internet to shop for furniture and motorcycles.

Other than an overnight supervisor who made a brief visit to their station at 4:00 A.M. and a correctional officer who walked by at 6:00 A.M., nobody else entered the SHU during this time. According to the prison's official account of the night's events, no correctional officer conducted any count or check between 10:30 P.M. and daylight the next day.

There were surveillance cameras in the general vicinity of Epstein's cell, but not in the cell itself.

SHORTLY AFTER 6:00 A.M. ON Saturday, August 10, 2019, Tova Noel and Michael Thomas were still the only guards in the SHU when they received a delivery of breakfast carts. At approximately 6:30

A.M., prison staff began taking breakfast to prisoners around the cell-block. As a prison employee made the rounds of Epstein's block, the employee discovered Epstein hanging from his bed and unresponsive. A noose made of orange bedsheets was around his neck; the other end of the bedding was attached to the lower level of the iron frame of a bunk bed.

An emergency alarm was sounded. According to a report later issued by the jail, "a supervisor who had just started his shift responded to the alarm as Noel approached the door to the SHU to open the door for [the supervisor]. Noel told [the supervisor] that 'Epstein hung himself.'"

Guards cut the ligatures from Epstein's neck, releasing his body. Some subsequent reports have alleged that cutting the ligature from a prisoner—particularly someone who might have been dead for a long time—was a violation of protocol, as to have done so would have drastically altered a potential crime scene. However, according to Robert Hood, a retired Bureau of Prisons warden who served as the warden at ADX Florence, the so-called Supermax prison facility in Florence, Colorado, it would have been standard for BOP guards to have "called and cut"—that is, removed the prisoner from his hanging position, called for backup, and cut any ligature around a prisoner's throat, in an immediate bid to save an inmate's life.[5]

THE MINUTES THAT FOLLOWED THE discovery of Epstein's body were chaotic—the kind of confusion that makes it easy to imagine possible efforts to cover up mistakes.

According to a transcript obtained through a Freedom of Information Act (FOIA) request filed with the New York City Fire Department, the first call from a jail official to 911 requesting emergency medical attention for Epstein came at 6:37 A.M., approximately four minutes after Epstein was first found by guards lying on the floor of his cell.[6]

Less than one minute later, the NYPD reported what was called an "aided case"—someone in need of medical attention—who was an "unknown male and unknown condition," according to the FDNY transcript. At 06:38:35—a minute and a half after the first 911 call was made—two Emergency Medical Service technicians from the FDNY were dispatched to the prison.

At 06:40:40—three and a half minutes after a prison official first called 911 for help—an operator stated that there was a "POSS ARREST AT LOC," according to the FDNY transcript. Frank Dwyer, the chief spokesman for the FDNY, citing the continued sensitivity of the case, declined to detail, in lay terms, the real-time conversations that took place among the 911 operator, the FDNY dispatcher, jail officials, and Emergency Service Squad personnel who were responding to the scene.[7] Peter Gleason, a criminal defense attorney who is a retired veteran of both the NYPD and FDNY, said the reference to a "POSS ARREST AT LOC" was an indication the jail was requesting an ambulance in connection with a possible *criminal* arrest rather than any suggestion that a *cardiac* arrest had occurred. Had the reference been to a cardiac arrest, he insisted, the transcript would have stated as much.[8]

Police and fire radio transmissions in New York City are routinely monitored by news desks and freelance photographers poised to chase breaking news—and Gleason suspects that an MCC official suggested a criminal arrest had occurred at the jail to hide any hint that help was being requested for Epstein. Any request for an ambulance at the MCC for an inmate being *arrested* was unlikely to arouse a reporter's interest. By comparison, Gleason contended, a report on an FDNY radio band stating that an ambulance was needed at the MCC for a *suspected suicide*—or a *potential homicide*—would have set off alarm bells. By suggesting to the 911 operator that a possible *criminal* arrest had occurred—when none was known to have taken place—the call may have served to buy prison officials time during the chaotic situation unfolding at the facility. "It was a classic diversion tactic by [jail officials] to prevent a bevy of photographers and journalists from showing up at the scene," said Gleason.

Gleason's contention that an MCC official may have intention-ally sought to mislead a 911 operator by stating that a *criminal* arrest might have taken place is buttressed by another FDNY document released pursuant to the Freedom of Information Act request. That document, titled "Incident History Report," reveals that at 06:40:40, a call was made for a specific "Incident Type," which is followed by a single word, in block letters: "ARREST." The document does not say "CARDIAC ARREST."

The call to 911 was curious for another reason. At the same moment during the 911 call reflected in the FDNY transcript— 06:40:40—when the emergency operator mentions that a prison official spoke about a "possible arrest"—the 911 operator further-more notes that there was no information on the stricken patient while cryptically adding "BUT MED REQUESTED DEFIB." That last state-ment, Gleason and others contend, appears to be a notification to arriving emergency medical personnel to be sure to bring a defibril-lator to the scene, suggesting that medical personal at the jail did not have a working defibrillator on the premises. (The Federal Bureau of Prisons declined to respond to phone and email inquiries about Epstein's time at the MCC.)

The retired BOP senior administrator Robert Hood acknowl-edged that "it does appear that a defibrillator was requested" when he was presented with a copy of the FDNY transcript of the 911 call. Hood cautioned that it was difficult to draw definitive conclusions from a single FDNY document, but he said a functioning defibrilla-tor is standard equipment inside each of the BOP's 122 institutions. Additionally, BOP supervisors are required to regularly train staffers on how to use defibrillators in the event of emergencies in which a prisoner or BOP employee appears not to be breathing. Any failure to have a functioning defibrillator available at the MCC would have constituted a serious breach of protocol, Hood said.

At 06:40:48—just eight seconds after the request for a defibrilla-tor was made—the FDNY noted that an ambulance had been dispatched to the prison, according to an FDNY document released as part of the FOIA request. Fourteen seconds later, the FDNY noted that "triage" efforts at the MCC had ended. Three first responders—two EMS paramedics and an EMS lieutenant—arrived five seconds later.

In total, four paramedics, three EMTs, and one EMS lieutenant responded to the emergency call. They were instructed to deploy to the rear of the jail, where they were told via radio communication that they'd be met by BOP personnel.

THE EMTs ATTEMPTED TO REVIVE Epstein, including intubating him in the cell for at least seven minutes. Their efforts were unsuccessful, and he was rushed to NewYork–Presbyterian Lower Manhattan Hospital on William Street, only six-tenths of a mile from the MCC. A Brooklyn news photographer, William Farrington, somehow managed to be on the scene as paramedics wheeled the gurney bearing Epstein's lifeless body into the hospital. His exclusive photo would be splashed on the cover of the *New York Post*'s Sunday edition with the headline "SUICIDE" SCANDAL.

Emergency room personnel began further efforts to revive Epstein at 07:16:22. Less than two and a half minutes later, at 07:19:45, the transcript shows a single word in block letters: NOTIFY, the indication that emergency room workers believed Epstein was dead at that time and the notification process was to begin. The death certificate officially lists the time of Jeffrey Epstein's passing as 7:36 A.M. on August 10.

At 8:16 that Saturday morning, *BuzzFeed News* later reported, the far-right message board 4chan had carried an anonymous post reading DONT ASK ME HOW I KNOW, BUT EPSTEIN DIED AN HOUR AGO FROM HANGING, CARDIAC ARREST. SCREENCAP THIS.

At 08:24:39, the FDNY transcript marked the case CLOSED.

## 34

## SIDESHOW

MARK EPSTEIN WAS AT HOME EARLY IN THE MORNING OF AUGUST 10 when the telephone rang. The caller informed the sixty-four-year-old real estate investor that his older sibling had died. "When I first heard this, I was having breakfast and I said [to myself], 'Okay, my brother committed suicide,'" Mark Epstein told journalist Philip Messing in a brief interview for this book. "Then I started questioning it," Mark Epstein continued, "and I said, 'Wait a second, this doesn't look like a suicide. This looks more like a homicide than a suicide.'"[1]

He wasn't the only one who would leap to such conclusions.

IT DIDN'T TAKE LONG AFTER his brother's sudden death broke wide via a tweet from ABC News reporter Aaron Katersky at 8:54 A.M. ET, and NBC News interrupted network programming with a "Special Report," for the questions to begin.

Ninety minutes later, Epstein's death provoked a terse statement from the United States Department of Justice: "On Saturday,

August 10, 2019, at approximately 6:30 A.M., inmate Jeffrey Edward Epstein was found unresponsive in his cell. . . . Mr. Epstein was transported by EMS to a local hospital for treatment of life-threatening injuries and subsequently pronounced dead by hospital staff. The FBI is investigating the incident."[2] From the beginning, government officials presented Epstein's death as a likely suicide. Bolstering Bureau of Prisons conclusions, authorities pointed out that two locked doors were not breached. The first, to the unit, could only be opened from the jail's control center, and the second could only be opened by correctional officers assigned to the high-security unit.

Over the following hours, piecemeal details would emerge concerning the circumstances of Epstein's death. Three of Epstein's lawyers—Reid Weingarten, Marty Weinberg, and Michael Miller—soon issued a joint statement expressing their sorrow and demanding a full probe of the circumstances of their client's passing.[3]

Jena-Lisa Jones, one of Jeffrey Epstein's victims, said, "I am extremely mad and hurt thinking he once again thought he was above us and took the easy way out."[4]

ATTORNEY GENERAL WILLIAM BARR ATTEMPTED to get out in front of the burgeoning scandal—one that seemed to transfix not only much of America but much of the world, too. "We are now learning of serious irregularities at this facility that are deeply concerning and demand a thorough investigation," Barr said during remarks at a law enforcement conference in New Orleans.[5] Barr said he was "appalled" and "angry" at what had taken place, insisted that the Justice Department would "get to the bottom" of what happened and vowed accountability for those who aided Epstein's criminal schemes involving young girls.[6]

On August 13, three days after Epstein's death, Barr placed correctional officers Tova Noel and Michael Thomas on administrative leave.

Both were on duty—at least on paper—on the night when Epstein was allegedly left dying while he was unattended.*

Barr also reassigned MCC warden Lamine N'Diaye to an administrative position, replacing him with James Petrucci, formerly the warden of the federal prison in Otisville, New York.[7] Barr even jettisoned Hugh Hurwitz, the acting director of the Bureau of Prisons.[8] Epstein's death was the second huge black eye for the BOP in less than a year. Nine months earlier, on October 30, 2018, racketeer and serial murderer James "Whitey" Bulger—eighty-nine years old, frail, and confined to a wheelchair—was brutally killed inside a federal lockup in Hazelton, West Virginia, just hours after being transferred there from another facility.[9] Like Epstein, prison officials knew Bulger was an at-risk prisoner who needed close monitoring.

BARR'S PUBLIC FULMINATIONS OVER HIS subordinates' missteps were fueled, at least in part, by his knowledge that Epstein had been put on suicide watch following his July 23 attempt on his own life. He must have known that Epstein had spent twenty-four hours on suicide watch following that incident and then six subsequent days in "psychological observation" before being transferred back to the Special Housing Unit where he was found dead—or dying—eleven days later.[10]

There was, however, one nuance of Epstein's status at the MCC that Barr almost certainly did *not* know: the credible claims that Epstein had been placed on suicide watch *before* the highly publicized July 23 incident, as noted previously by Epstein's former inmate counselors William Mersey and Miles Tisdale. Each man contends

---

* MCC guard Tova Noel and her partner Michael Thomas were subsequently indicted for having failed to check on Epstein, and covering up such failures, during Epstein's last night alive. According to the indictment, Thomas told a supervisor minutes after he and Noel found Epstein unresponsive, "I messed up." Noel said: "We did not complete the 3:00 A.M. nor 5:00 A.M. rounds." Thomas then said: "She's not to blame, we didn't do any rounds."

Epstein was sent to suicide watch on this first occasion, rather than to psychological observation.[11] If their accounts are correct, the future decision to transfer him out of suicide watch following the July 23 suicide bid becomes even more troubling.

While Epstein was admitted to the prison on July 6, the government would later contend he was not placed in the SHU until July 10. Where was Epstein housed during those first four nights he was inside the MCC, from July 6 through July 10? It is conceivable he was placed in the general population during that time, although Tisdale explicitly refuted this. He insists that Epstein was placed in the general population only on the first night he was in the MCC. Was Epstein placed on suicide watch during the successive three nights?

Mersey and Tisdale both noted that while BOP officials make a distinction between suicide watch and psychological observation, as a practical matter, they were largely indistinguishable. "You're under the same scrutiny whether you're in suicide watch or psychological observation," Mersey insisted. The big difference between the two, Mersey recalled, is that suicide watch inmates are issued more limited clothing—booties instead of shoes with laces, for example—and mattresses without bedsheets. "Whether you're under suicide or psych watch [psychological observation], you still have one inmate watching you twenty-four hours a day, taking notes on everything you do," Mersey said. "The difference for the inmate companions who do the watching is that you put your notes in a different-colored book depending upon the designation. You used a red book for psychological observation, and yellow [books] were for suicide watch," he recounted.[12]

A BOP spokesman declined to address Mersey's and Tisdale's accusations. If their claims are correct, it would mean that BOP personnel allowed Epstein, a troubled inmate, to be shifted from the impregnable area of suicide watch, where his safety was inviolate, to less secure housing in the SHU, where his safety could not be guaranteed, on two separate occasions.

Robert Hood, who not only helped formulate training for the

entire agency but at one time headed the bureau's internal affairs unit and ran the country's most notorious prison, the "Supermax," said it made no sense for Epstein to have been placed on suicide watch on July 23 and not kept in that status indefinitely. "Epstein entered the BOP as a high-profile offender with many 'at risk' conditions. He should have been placed on suicide watch early during his incarceration and remained on that program well after his suicide attempt on July 23, 2019. Placement of cameras or ongoing staff observations should have occurred."[13] Hood continued, "[After he was] found in a semiconscious condition in a suicide attempt you would *never* take him off suicide watch. Period!"

Too much had gone wrong that night for the official account not to undergo serious scrutiny. It was hard for the public to imagine that such ineptitude and neglect would be accorded to such a high-profile prisoner.

Although the surveillance cameras provide a partial video account of what took place that fateful night, an inmate who worked with William Mersey in the MCC kitchen told him that sometime between the night of August 9 and the morning of August 10, he had heard the sound of bedsheets being ripped apart coming from Epstein's cell. The inmate said that "nobody came into the tier all night." The implication of this account adds credence to the BOP conclusion that Epstein prepared the means necessary to take his own life. The inmate's claim could not be independently verified, and Mersey is unaware whether any BOP staff or other official ever interviewed the inmate whose cell was adjacent to Epstein's.

# 35

## POSTMORTEM

WHEN PRISON OFFICIALS SEARCHED EPSTEIN'S CELL, THEY FOUND A cryptic note, described as written in blue pen on five horizontal lines of yellow paper common to a lined legal pad.[1] It was not, in the classic sense, a "suicide note," although some have interpreted it as such.

The note is comprised of four terse sentences: "[— —] *kept me in a locked shower stall for 1 hour. Noel sent me burnt food. Giant bugs crawling over my hands. NO FUN!!*"

Later, this ambiguous note—seeming to refer more to complaints Epstein had with recent treatment in the jail than to any existential angst—would further suspicions that foul play and not suicide had been responsible for his hanging.

THE DEATH OF JEFFREY EPSTEIN created a media frenzy. Was he murdered on the orders of the powerful men he once partied with to secure his silence, or did he simply take the easy way out? In New York, suspicious deaths—regardless of the deceased's financial, social, or judicial status—must undergo an autopsy; all deaths must have a cause recorded in order for a death certificate to be issued and for the body of the deceased to be released to a funeral home.

The New York City Office of Chief Medical Examiner conducted an autopsy of Jeffrey Epstein on Sunday, August 11—the day after his death. The file was marked Medical Examiner Case No. M19019432.

The autopsy was carried out by Dr. Kristin G. Roman, a board-certified forensic pathologist and one of approximately thirty deputy medical examiners employed by the New York City Chief Medical Examiner's office, headed by Dr. Barbara Sampson. Although Sampson did not conduct the procedure herself, as would have been common in such a high-profile instance, she did visit the jail cell where Epstein was found and take photographs of the scene there. A forensic pathologist named Dr. Michael Baden observed the autopsy as part of an agreement worked out between the City of New York and lawyers for Mark Epstein. Baden had become something of a celebrity medical examiner, providing expert testimony and review in notorious homicide trials such as O. J. Simpson's and Phil Spector's. At times, the pathologist had also faced media scrutiny. In a 2019 piece raising questions about Baden's role in the Epstein case, a *New York* magazine writer cited Baden for "unforced errors" and other indiscretions in some high-profile cases.[2]

Dr. Roman's preliminary finding was that the cause of death was "pending further study"—and that was the information entered on a preliminary death certificate issued Sunday, August 11, 2019. "Pending" was a bureaucratic way of saying that the death was not obviously a suicide, not obviously a homicide, and not obviously accidental. If Dr. Roman was leaning toward one particular conclusion or another, the document did not indicate it. The initial ruling meant that Roman had concluded that her office needed more time before she could render a final opinion as to how Epstein had died.

Did she hope to examine the jail cell where Epstein had been found, or did she want to review more closely the photographic evidence of the death scene? Was she awaiting the results of toxicological tests or to review DNA tests that might or might not have been conducted on the bedsheets or ligature found in his jail cell? Did she hope to interview one or more of the many officials who were at the death scene or at the hospital where Epstein was taken, or to analyze the testimony of first-responder witnesses or MCC officials who were yet to be interviewed by the medical examiner's civilian investigators, or even FBI agents? It is entirely unclear, although these were the procedures in such high-profile cases.

On August 16, the medical examiner's office issued a revised ruling: Jeffrey Epstein's demise was "suicidal death by hanging."[3] In a prepared statement, Chief Medical Examiner Dr. Sampson noted that the suicide determination came "after careful review of all investigative information, including complete autopsy findings." She declined to say whether any DNA analysis had been conducted on the orange bedsheets found in the cell, at least one of which had been fashioned into a noose.

The question as to whether there had been any DNA testing on the bedsheet is a matter of considerable forensic interest because if DNA evidence *was* found—and if it was determined to belong not to Epstein, but rather to an unidentified party—that would undercut the finding of suicide. In response to this specific inquiry, a spokeswoman offered this statement: "As a general rule, our office does not release confidential medical information, including the medical examiner's reports, in any cases we investigate. We simply release cause and manner of death."

In the weeks that followed, several of Epstein's lawyers and Baden, the family's pathologist who had observed the autopsy, grew increasingly outspoken in their lack of confidence in the Office of Chief Medical Examiner's determination and began to assert their belief that it was more likely Epstein was the victim of a homicide. Jeffrey Epstein's death became the fodder of media curiosity and social media ridicule. Each day that passed without a credible and definitive explanation added fuel to the raging conspiracy-theory fires.

THIS CONCERN WAS AIRED PUBLICLY during a hearing before Southern District Court judge Richard Berman on August 27, 2019. Reid Weingarten, a lawyer representing Epstein's brother, Mark, stated that there were compelling medical reasons to suggest the death arose from a homicidal assault rather than a suicide.[4]

Martin Weinberg, another lawyer at the hearing, cited "the timing of Mr. Epstein's demise" as a key reason why it was difficult to believe Epstein had killed himself. "It [Epstein's death] was on August 10," Weinberg charged. "On August 12, a bail-pending-appeal motion was being filed in the Second Circuit. [So] the timing for a pretrial detainee to commit suicide on August 10, when his bail-pending-appeal motion is being filed on August 12, strikes us as implausible."[5]

Weinberg also introduced Dr. Baden's analysis of the available medical evidence, which suggested that Epstein had almost certainly been dead for at least forty-five minutes when he was found lying in his cell and that the decision by BOP employees to permit his corpse to be taken to a local hospital by Emergency Medical Service was irregular, if not suspicious.

Judge Berman was perplexed, and seemingly somewhat angered, by the revelation. "Excuse me. He was moved?" he interjected.

Martin Weinberg immediately shot back, "Instead of having the cell in the condition it was found, if he had been dead for forty-five minutes or two hours or four hours, there were efforts to move him and therefore make it more difficult to reconstruct whether or not he died of suicide or some other cause."

Dr. Baden, appearing on the Fox News morning show *Fox & Friends* on October 30, 2019, claimed that Epstein experienced several injuries—including broken bones in his neck—that "are extremely unusual in suicidal hangings and could occur much more commonly in homicidal strangulation." He continued, "I think that the evidence points to homicide rather than suicide."[6]

The question persisted of what exactly had changed between when Dr. Roman presented her initial findings and when she concluded that Epstein's death was a suicide.

Aja Worthy-Davis, a spokeswoman for Dr. Sampson, declined to say, insisting medical records are confidential. "All I can tell you is what Dr. Roman determined in this case. It was her autopsy, and this was her determination," she said in a brief interview for this book.[7]

There is one contention that might explain the medical examiner's about-face in just five days. During his research for this book, reporter Philip Messing learned that requests were allegedly made by Dr. Sampson to Dr. Roman urging her to close the case swiftly. A New York journalist, who asked not to be identified, interviewed two sources in the medical examiner's office and each source stated they independently heard Dr. Sampson, in separate conversations, exhort Dr. Roman in the days immediately after Epstein's death to reach a conclusion before Dr. Sampson was to go on a planned vacation. "Dr. Sampson told the pathologist, 'You've got to get this done before I go on vacation.'"[8] Worthy-Davis declined to respond to this specific allegation. She also repeatedly declined to confirm whether Dr. Sampson went on vacation in the immediate aftermath of the August 16 finding by Dr. Roman that Epstein's death had been a suicide.


FOR DR. MICHAEL BADEN, THE forensic pathologist hired by Mark Epstein to observe the autopsy of his brother, one major contention about the results concerned undisputed medical evidence that showed there had been multiple fractures to Epstein's neck—specifically, fractures of the left and the right thyroid cartilage and the left hyoid bone, a fragile U-shaped, wishbone-like structure in the throat at the rear of the jaw behind the tongue, near the Adam's apple. "They are much more common in homicides than in suicides," he said, referring to the significance of a broken hyoid bone.

In an interview for this book, Dr. Baden noted an array of factors separate from Epstein's neck cartilage fractures or broken hyoid bone.[9] Dr. Baden said Epstein showed signs of petechial hemorrhaging in the conjunctiva (the white part of his eyes). Such injuries are distinguished by tiny pinpoint red marks that often suggest a victim has died of strangulation. While Dr. Baden acknowledged that suicidal hangings will sometimes result in petechial hemorrhages, he insisted it is far more common to see them in the eyes of victims who were strangled.

Baden also points to the fact that the noose from the jail sheet does not appear to match the location of the neck injury. Dr. Baden agreed with an assessment that the sheet, in an official photograph, essentially seemed "pristine," without any sign of blood, even though the wound on Epstein's neck appeared to be raw and furrowed. To Baden, "these particular sheets . . . don't appear to match the ligature mark from the neck." He claimed that the noose material appeared to have been "too wide to cause that type of narrower furrow around [Epstein's] neck" as depicted in the postmortem photo. Dr. Baden said that the available medical evidence further suggested the location of the mark left by the noose or ligature on Epstein's neck was inconsistent with a suicidal hanging. In Epstein's case, he said, the ligature mark appeared to have been located "lower down in the middle of the neck, which is more typical of strangulation" than suicide.

Baden also insisted that the medical examiner's office—or the FBI—should "have taken swabs" from Epstein's neck wound and "should have found DNA on the noose." "They should have taken DNA off the whole sheet," he added. It is unclear whether there was any DNA match between the wound on Epstein's neck and the noose—and it remains unknown whether a DNA test of any sort was conducted before the determination by the medical examiner that Epstein's death was a suicide.

Another factor was lividity, Baden said. Ordinarily, when a person dies, the blood pools in the area closest to the ground as a result of gravity, creating bluish-purple skin discoloration known as lividity. Lividity can be helpful to detectives and pathologists in their efforts to establish the circumstances of a person's death, such as the time a decedent passed on, or whether a victim's body may have been moved from where the victim had been killed to another location.

In Epstein's case, Dr. Baden noted, he had probably been dead for at least two hours, but during the autopsy, and in subsequent autopsy photos provided to him, lividity was visible only on his back, which was indicative of his being kept on his back when his body was stored in the morgue overnight. "I saw no lividity in the legs. Given that he was dead for at least two hours, he should have some lividity on the front and back that should have developed, [but in] the photographs, there was absolutely no lividity on the lower legs," Dr. Baden contended. He continued to point out that lividity in his legs ought to have been expected, given that he presumably died by hanging.

Dr. Baden did not cite any medical evidence suggesting that the autopsy revealed defensive wounds to his fingers or arms that might readily support a conclusion of homicidal assault. Baden's preliminary conclusion—that the available forensic evidence suggested Epstein had more likely been the victim of a homicide than a suicide—was based upon the available medical evidence, and he admitted that further information could cause him to revisit his medical opinion. "My opinions are all dependent upon future information from the scene," he insisted. By March 2020, almost seven months after Epstein's death, Justice Department prosecutors had still "refused to release any infirmary or medical history records" to Dr. Baden or to Mark Epstein, claiming the government could not yet do so because of the planned criminal trial of the two MCC correctional officers indicted for criminal misconduct.

Dr. Baden's findings have been supported by other top experts.

Vernon Geberth, a retired NYPD detective lieutenant and consultant, considered one of the most preeminent homicide experts in the world, said that based upon what has been made public, Dr. Baden's preliminary determination is not only credible but eminently supportable. "I seriously doubt that it was suicide. I respect Baden as a forensic pathologist. [The evidence] is certainly indicative of manual strangulation," said Geberth, whose book *Practical Homicide Investigations: Tactics, Procedures and Forensic Techniques* is widely used by law enforcement in the United States and around the world. "People who hang don't normally break their hyoid bone," he insisted, referring to the fractured bone at the base of Epstein's jaw that Dr. Baden cited as being suggestive of homicide.

Geberth added, "[Dr. Roman] did her autopsy, but she didn't have control of the crime scene. Who from the crime scene appeared at the autopsy? What federal agent, what correctional officer, or other federal official who was present at the death scene was there to tell her about the death scene? She's working blind because she's deprived of crime scene information. After the body has been moved and people have gone through the scene, God knows what you have."[10]

JEFFREY EPSTEIN'S DEATH WAS A black eye for both the BOP and the Department of Justice. The government was determined to find someone guilty for the incompetence and negligence that allowed one of the country's most notorious prisoners to die while in custody. A criminal investigation was launched; at least twenty MCC staff members were subpoenaed in the probe.[11] Federal prosecutors offered a plea deal to Epstein's guards, but both Noel and Thomas decided to have their day in court.[12]

On November 19, 2019, the SDNY indicted Noel and Thomas on one count of conspiring to defraud the United States by "impairing, obstructing, and defeating the lawful functions of the MCC"—an offense that carries a maximum sentence of five years in prison. Noel was also charged with five counts and Thomas with three counts of "making false records," offenses that carry a potential five-year sentence for each count.

Robert Hood has contended that the two prison guards who were indicted for failing to look in upon Epstein as required—and for allegedly trying to cover up their misconduct—likely deserved to lose their jobs, but he questioned whether they should have been criminally charged and suggested they were being scapegoated to obscure agency staffing shortages and other supervisory lapses.

The decision to indict the two guards on criminal charges stands in stark contrast to the refusal of the Justice Department to charge any BOP supervisor for what might be argued was criminal negligence in failing to provide a cellmate to an inmate who had demonstrated suicidal tendencies at least once, perhaps twice, if the claims of Mersey and Tisdale are to be believed.[13]

But Robert Hood had a different take. "From what I know, Epstein committed suicide—with an abundance of help from the federal Bureau of Prisons," he said in an email to journalist Philip Messing. "The agency may not have had the intention or the knowledge of wrongdoing that constitutes part of a crime, but it held the smoking gun of gross negligence. No riots will occur in the streets to protest Epstein's death. Most will be glad he is no longer alive. Investigative reports will classify his death as just another inmate's suicide and be placed in a file cabinet. The 'just us' system will continue to move forward without a blemish until the next spider appears."

THREE DAYS AFTER IT WAS announced that MCC guards Noel and Thomas had been arrested, Attorney General Barr gave an interview to the Associated Press in which he again sought to tamp down the wild conspiracy theories circulating. Barr admitted he had initially had his suspicions about Epstein's death in one of the most secure jails in America but had come to conclude that Epstein's suicide was the result of "a perfect storm of screw-ups."[14]

Epstein's former social wingman President Trump, quick on his Twitter trigger, was eager to push theories of his own. Just hours after Epstein was found dead or dying in his jail cell, Trump implied that the Clintons were behind it all.[15] President Trump retweeted a post from comedian Terrence Williams that had linked the Clintons to the death. According to Williams, a Trump supporter, Epstein "had information on Bill Clinton and now he's dead," his tweet said; the tweet accompanied a two-minute video posted by Williams that noted "for some odd reason, people that have information on the Clintons end up dead."

New York City mayor Bill de Blasio jumped on the conspiracy theory bandwagon as well. "It's just too convenient," de Blasio told *The New York Times*. "It's too many pieces happening simultaneously that don't fit." The mayor noted that Epstein "had information potentially related to some of the wealthiest and most powerful people in the country," which he deduced was a likely motive for foul play meant to silence him.[16]

The "Epstein didn't kill himself" meme raged everywhere. One victim, Jane Doe 15, wore a bracelet with that inscription at a press conference. The statement appeared in TikTok videos and on Instagram. Ricky Gervais threw it into his monologue at the Golden Globe Awards. Arizona Republican Paul Gosar endorsed it on Twitter. A guest on a Fox News show pushed it as a PSA.

Conspiracy theories morphed off one false claim that a news photo of Epstein on a gurney the morning he was found unresponsive was a "body double," claiming discrepancies with his ears compared to a fifteen-year-old photo. Other speculative opinions on his death went viral pegged to the hashtags #ClintonBodyCount and #TrumpBodyCount.

By January 2020, a Rasmussen Reports national telephone and online survey showed 52 percent believed Epstein had been murdered to prevent him from testifying against powerful people with whom he'd been associated. Only 21 percent of those polled thought he'd committed suicide. Twenty-seven percent were undecided.[17]

# PART SEVEN

# A NEVER-ENDING STORY

You have done nothing wrong
and I would urge you to start acting like it.
Go outside, head high. Not as an escaping convict.
—JEFFREY EPSTEIN email to
Ghislaine Maxwell on January 25, 2015;
unsealed by court, July 30, 2020

# 36

## CHEATING JUSTICE

A BRIEF FUNERAL WAS HELD FOR JEFFREY EPSTEIN JUST TEN BLOCKS from his Upper East Side mansion three days after he was declared dead. The ceremony at the Frank E. Campbell funeral chapel on Manhattan's Madison Avenue just off Eighty-First Street was low-key and private. Mark Epstein took care of all the arrangements, and other than a rabbi and a few undisclosed guests, none of the men or women in the inner circle of Jeffrey Epstein's universe attended, including Ghislaine Maxwell. Interestingly, the name of the funeral home was redacted from Epstein's death certificate, but not the address.

Epstein's body was flown to Loxahatchee, Florida, in Palm Beach County, and entombed in a mausoleum at IJ Morris Star of David Cemetery of the Palm Beaches. The cemetery, like many aspects of life near the island where Epstein lived and preyed on young women, was priced for the rich and famous; a hole in the ground cost as much as $250,000.[1] Journalists hounded Mark Epstein for information on his brother's burial. "It's nobody's fucking business. It's a private family matter," Epstein's younger brother replied angrily to one media request.[2]

The entombment was carried out with the cloak-and-dagger of a spy mission. Epstein's body was transported in secret, though the hearse was escorted to the cemetery by squad cars from the Palm Beach County Sheriff's Office. Although Jewish law forbids burying the dead on the Sabbath, the ceremony took place on a Saturday, when there would be no crowds of mourners present and, most important, no witnesses who might talk to the press. Epstein was placed next to his parents, Seymour and Pauline, but to prevent vandalism of the monument, the names had been removed from all the family's gravestones days earlier.[3]

It was, perhaps, a fitting end for a man who shunned publicity and thrived on secrets.

ALTHOUGH IT SPARED TAXPAYERS THE cost of a judicial process that likely would have dragged on through years of appeals, Epstein's demise meant federal prosecutors never had the chance to cross-examine him under oath. The technical details of how his sex trafficking enterprise operated, who was involved, and what evidence his surveillance apparatus captured—including the trove of material seized from 9 East Seventy-First Street on the day of his arrest—would not be revealed in a criminal trial. For Epstein's victims, it would delay, and possibly deny them forever, any sense of closure.

Epstein's death, however, would not mean the end of the flurry of civil suits; civil action was now being directed against Epstein's estate. Lawyers' phones were ringing off the hook. Attorney Lisa Bloom wrote on Twitter after filing suits on behalf of two new victims: "We are talking to five other victims currently and vetting their claims."

And there was the possibility of further criminal action against alleged accomplices. In the wake of Epstein's death, Attorney General William Barr declared that "any coconspirators should not rest easy." The FBI, meanwhile, using speedboats and helicopters, had swarmed Epstein's property in the Virgin Islands two days after his death, hauling off computers and other potential evidence.

On St. Thomas, the new attorney general for the Virgin Islands, Denise N. George, who had taken office in April 2019, launched an investigation into Epstein's actions there, which would lead to a civil forfeiture lawsuit against Epstein's $600 million estate in January 2020. On May 29, 2020, George announced her office had reached a tentative agreement with Epstein's estate to establish a restitution program for the victims.

In another development, on July 7, 2020, Deutsche Bank was slapped with a $150 million fine in New York State regulatory penalties for its financial dealings with Epstein, which began in 2013. The *New York Post* reported that the German bank "should have raised red flags in light of Epstein's sex-offender past—including payments to his alleged accomplices, Russian models and other women from Eastern Europe."

In New York, the late financier's shell-shocked only survivor was trying to wade through what had become a scandal of international proportion. In a brief interview for this book, Mark Epstein said he had one mission with regard to what had occurred with his brother: to find out what had really happened in the Manhattan Correctional Center. "My only job is to find out the circumstances of my brother's death," Mark Epstein said. "This is not about me at all—I don't want the notoriety," he added, before hanging up.

JEFFREY EPSTEIN MAY HAVE BECOME the face of privileged evil, but he didn't act alone. He had enablers. Did they breathe a sigh of relief when the news broke that he was dead? The hope was that interest—both media and criminal—would die along with him. Everyone who was part of Jeffrey Epstein's web of perversion did everything in their power to distance themselves from his memory.

Les Wexner, the Ohio businessman who became Epstein's most important financial patron, went to great lengths to sanitize his legacy. In his role as Wexner's "money manager," Wexner gave Epstein vast influence over his financial affairs, including giving him power of attorney in 1991 and making Epstein a trustee of the Wexner Foundation. Wexner had effectively given Epstein the East Seventy-First Street mansion in Manhattan and allowed Epstein to borrow money and even to sign Wexner's tax returns. Epstein even used his connection with the L Brands founder to masquerade as a Victoria's Secret talent scout in order to procure young women. In the wake of Epstein's death, new scrutiny fell on the now eighty-one-year-old Wexner and why he had granted Epstein such sweeping authority.

By now, Wexner was no longer involved with the day-to-day operation of his company. For a retail empire like L Brands, public image was crucial. The combination of Wexner's association with Epstein and the #MeToo movement was radioactive.[4]

Wexner, who reportedly severed all ties to Jeffrey Epstein in 2007, didn't address why he had given control of such valuable assets to such an unsavory character. Instead, Wexner portrayed himself as another victim of Epstein's. In a statement he made to the Wexford Foundation about his ties to Epstein, Wexner claimed that Epstein "had misappropriated vast sums of money" from him, calling it "a tremendous shock, even though it pales in comparison to the unthinkable allegations against him now." *New York* magazine asked a simple question: "If Epstein stole millions of dollars from Wexner, why didn't he call the cops?"[5] Wexner said he was embarrassed, "like so many others," to have been "deceived."[6]

In December 2019, the Wexner Foundation released the results of a long-awaited internal audit by an independent reviewer to investigate its ties with Epstein. The foundation, which supports an array of Jewish causes and was a passion of Wexner's, claimed that Epstein had had no meaningful involvement with the foundation, even though he was a trustee for fifteen years.[7]

In May 2020, Wexner stepped down as CEO of L Brands after the company sold controlling ownership of Victoria's Secret, its flagship brand, to a New York private equity firm.[8]

. . .

Jean-Luc Brunel, the modeling impresario who has been accused of supplying teenage girls to Epstein, also seemed intent on minimizing his connections to the dead financier. According to a new report, the modeling agent was last seen on July 5, the day before Epstein's arrest, at the members-only Paris Country Club. After the news of Epstein's arrest broke, Brunel vanished. Some reports later placed him in Brazil.

Two months after Epstein's death, Brunel was "quietly selling off" his modeling business, according to a report in *The Daily Beast*. The seventy-four-year-old reportedly had begun his MC2 agency in 2005 with $1 million provided by Epstein. In 2015, Brunel, who has denied any connection to Epstein's trafficking of girls, sued Epstein in Florida, stating in court papers: "MC2 was worth millions of dollars; now, due to the illegal actions of Epstein, MC2 is almost worthless."[9]

Before Epstein's death, Innocence en Danger, a Paris-based organization advocating against child abuse, had published an open letter urging French prosecutors to open a probe into the Epstein case, saying that many of Epstein's victims had French nationality.[10] In the days following Epstein's demise, Innocence en Danger received statements from ten witnesses, people who were either a victim of abuse or had witnessed it. Homayra Sellier, the group's founder, said, "The man who is named by every victim I have heard of, or I have spoken to, is this man, Jean-Luc Brunel." As far as Sellier knew, however, French investigators had never sought to interview Brunel.[11]

If the House of Windsor hoped that Jeffrey Epstein would take his secrets and the controversy to the grave with him, the opposite proved to be the case. Epstein's death returned the unflattering spotlight to Prince Andrew. The Duke of York vehemently denied all of the allegations made against him by Virginia Roberts. "His sweat was like it was raining everywhere," Roberts said in her own BBC interview, regarding her alleged encounter with the prince when she was seventeen.[12]

Prince Andrew's ill-advised BBC interview did not go as planned. His body language looked extremely uncomfortable. In an attempt to counter Roberts's claim of excessive sweating, the prince claimed to have a "peculiar medical condition" as a result of "an overdose of adrenaline in the Falklands War" that made it "almost impossible" for him to sweat.[13] His dubious defense, which only tended to confirm Roberts's account, became the fodder for scorn and ridicule.

In the months that followed Epstein's death, prosecutors went public in turning up the heat on Prince Andrew. On January 27, Geoffrey Berman, the U.S. attorney for the Southern District of New York, told reporters that U.S. authorities contacted Andrew's attorneys to request an interview but that the prince had provided "zero cooperation."[14] Six months later, in early June 2020, they were back at it—sidestepping Buckingham Palace and going directly to the British Home Office, citing a mutual legal assistance treaty to compel his testimony. But Prince Andrew's lawyers claimed the Duke of York had offered his assistance as a witness to the Department of Justice on at least three occasions.[15]

Andrew's legal dream team even attempted to go on the offensive. Solicitors from Blackfords, a top-tier London-based law firm representing the Duke of York, reached out to American lobbyist Robert Stryk.[16] Stryk is a Republican with ties to the Trump administration. His firm, Sonoran Policy Group, which worked pro bono for the Trump campaign in the 2016 election, had a reputation for taking on clients that many in the Beltway found toxic; his known clients include Saudi crown prince Mohammed bin Salman and rogue Venezuelan president Nicolás Maduro. Perhaps Prince Andrew was considered too hot to handle, even for someone like Stryk. Talks between Blackfords and Stryk reportedly fizzled.[17]

Epstein's death did not end Prince Andrew's woes; it merely placed him in an unenviable purgatory. It is virtually impossible to imagine that the British government will turn Prince Andrew over to the United States for questioning or prosecution. It is even more unlikely that British authorities will prosecute a member of the royal family for statutory rape.

Shortly after sitting down with the BBC, Prince Andrew announced he had asked the queen for permission to step back from royal duties for the "foreseeable future."[18]

Some eight months later, in July 2020, the Duke of York would come under renewed scrutiny upon the release of unsealed court documents from a previously settled defamation case involving Virginia Giuffre and Ghislaine Maxwell. While Giuffre's sexual allegations against Prince Andrew and others were reiterated publicly, a troubling new aspect of his involvement in the Epstein saga emerged. Media outlets, including the *New York Post* and *Newsweek,* noted that the legal papers revealed Prince Andrew had allegedly lobbied prosecutors back in 2007 to help Epstein receive a more "favorable" plea deal before his sweetheart non-prosecution agreement was inked with Alex Acosta and the Department of Justice. The disclosure was made in a separate 2015 lawsuit involving two Epstein accusers, Jane Doe 1 and Jane Doe 2, who requested the release of documents to show "Epstein's lobbying efforts to persuade the government to give him a more favorable plea arrangement and/or non-prosecution agreement, including the efforts on his behalf by Prince Andrew." The lobbying disclosure brought another strong denial from Andrew's side: "The allegation is a straightforward untruth. No ifs, no buts."

EPSTEIN'S DEATH ALSO STUNNED THE family-like inner circle of "potential coconspirators" who had been granted immunity as a result of his 2008 non-prosecution agreement.

Adriana Ross was one of four women granted immunity. In a civil lawsuit two years later, she repeatedly invoked her right against self-incrimination. A week after Epstein's death, the *Daily Mail* tracked down the former Polish model at a Catholic church close to her

Miami home. She refused to answer a battery of questions, broke down in tears, and fled with a male companion into a waiting SUV.

Another of the four women, Sarah Kellen, had changed her name to Sarah Kensington, dyed her hair brown, moved to Hawaii, and married the NASCAR driver Brian Vickers.

Nadia Marcinkova, meanwhile, began using the name Nadia Marcinko. The Slovakian-born model also attempted to dissociate herself from Epstein. She became a pilot, flight instructor, and CEO of an aviation website called Aviloop. She reportedly left one thread unsevered: Business records showed she was running her business out of a Manhattan apartment complex tied to Epstein and his brother, Mark.

The fourth alleged Epstein accomplice, Lesley Groff, now fifty-three, actively set out to clear her name. In court papers, she said she was falsely "besmirched" and that allegations of her involvement in any unsavory or illegal activities were "egregiously false." When she worked as one of Epstein's executive assistants, she was on call 24/7 and paid $200,000. When she became pregnant at the age of thirty-eight, Epstein bought her a Mercedes Benz E320 and paid for a full-time nanny. In 2005, he told *The New York Times* in a feature on executive assistants, "There is no way I could lose Lesley to mother-hood." He added his assistants were "an extension of my brain. Their intuition is something that I don't have."

Then there was Ghislaine Maxwell. Named in fresh civil suits and being looked at with renewed interest by prosecutors in the wake of Epstein's death, Maxwell was being hunted by victims' lawyers, federal investigators, and the media. By November 2019, one British tabloid, *The Sun,* was offering a £10,000 reward for information on her whereabouts. According to one Maxwell family friend, Maxwell had come to believe that Epstein was murdered, "just like her father almost thirty years before."

All eyes were now fixed on Ghislaine Maxwell—wherever she was. She had gone from socialite to social pariah. The damage to her reputation was pretty well complete, but she still had her freedom.

# 37

## "TUCKEDAWAY"

THE DAY BEFORE JEFFREY EPSTEIN'S BODY WAS ENTOMBED NEXT TO those of his parents, Ghislaine Maxwell was photographed in Los Angeles. She wasn't seen exiting the office of a high-priced attorney or caught at a public gala by paparazzi. Instead, a photo emerged of Maxwell sitting alone, beneath an umbrella, having a burger, fries, and a milkshake at an In-N-Out Burger.[1] Her hair was short. If she was wearing any makeup, it was subtle. The whole world was looking for Maxwell, but she was hiding in plain sight, reading a paperback copy of *The Book of Honor: The Secret Lives and Deaths of CIA Operatives* by Ted Gup as she wiped ketchup from her chin.

The photo became a mystery in and of itself. Was it staged? Was it photoshopped? "At the very least, it probably was the only time that Ghislaine was ever at a burger joint," a family friend said. "It was hardly her cup of tea."

One report indicated that the photograph might have been arranged by one of Maxwell's lawyers, Leah Saffian. The photo's metadata was linked to a media company owned by Saffian and the dog next to Maxwell's feet in the photo appeared to be the lawyer's dog.[2] "It was done to take the heat off the search for her and also drop a hint with the spy book that Epstein's 'suicide' was hardly what it seemed," a source said.

At the time, one of the great mysteries in the Epstein saga was why Maxwell had never been charged with any crimes. From the time of her arrival in New York until Epstein's incarceration in Florida in 2008, Ghislaine Maxwell had been by many accounts an active participant—or even a proactive lieutenant—in the financier's international child sex trafficking ring. She had been implicated by dozens of victims as an accomplice to abuse and even a perpetrator of it in suits filed against her by Virginia Roberts Giuffre, Sarah Ransome, Maria Farmer, Annie Farmer, Jennifer Araoz, and women known under the pseudonyms Priscilla Doe and Jane Doe.

In 2015, Giuffre sued Maxwell for defamation of character after Maxwell claimed in statements that Giuffre lied about being sexually abused at the hands of Epstein. In May 2017, the suit was settled with Maxwell reportedly paying Giuffre "millions" in damages. The Ransome suit was also settled on undisclosed terms. Other lawsuits were still pending at the time of this book's publication.

MAXWELL WENT TO GREAT LENGTHS to cover her tracks and hide her whereabouts after Epstein's arrest and death. She changed her telephone numbers and used pseudonyms, reportedly registering a cellphone number under the name G Max.[3]

Maxwell's attorneys refused to take calls from the legal representatives of some of her victims, as well as from the press.[4] In February 2020, Manhattan judge Debra Freeman took the remarkable step of serving Maxwell with a lawsuit via email because her location could not be determined.

After she was photographed in Los Angeles, there were rumors that Maxwell was hiding on the beach in Brazil, or perhaps in a luxurious apartment in the French capital—two locations that could complicate extradition back to the United States.[5] Other rumors had Maxwell living with a new boyfriend, the tech millionaire Scott

Borgerson, holed up in his mansion in Manchester-by-the-Sea, Massachusetts. Borgerson denied his relationship to Maxwell and any allegations that she was hiding at his residence.[6]

As HARD AS SHE TRIED to hide, however, Ghislaine Maxwell could not escape the shadow of Jeffrey Epstein in the year following his death. She was embroiled in at least a half dozen lawsuits. Some of the legal entanglements were of her own making. Maxwell was vilified in the press in March 2020 when she sued Epstein's estate in the U.S. Virgin Islands, seeking to recoup legal fees to defend herself. The court papers further said Maxwell managed Epstein's properties in New York, Florida, New Mexico, the U.S. Virgin Islands, and Paris "during their relationship, and that Epstein had 'repeatedly' promised Maxwell that he would support her financially." The lawsuit said she was seeking reimbursement for security costs because she "receives regular threats to her life and safety."

In response to the lawsuit, Virginia Roberts Giuffre wrote on Twitter: "Memo to GM—How dare you play the victim card when you victimised me and countless others. . . . I hope the judge ruling over this laughs you out of court and into jail."[7]

Three months later, in June 2020, Maxwell's lawyers and Epstein's estate filed a joint motion to stay the legal proceedings.

The following month, prosecutors would reveal that between 2007 and 2011, more than $20 million from bank accounts associated with Epstein was transferred to bank accounts associated with Maxwell and later transferred back to Epstein.[8]

DESPITE THE REPORTS THAT PLACED her in more exotic international locations, Maxwell was actually in New England in the first half of 2020. In late 2019, she had purchased a property in the tiny town of Bradford in the "Live Free or Die" state of New Hampshire. Located thirty miles from Concord, New Hampshire, the sleepy town of

1,650 people had a post office, a convenience store, and a pizza shop—but little else. The town's website showed kids playing ice hockey on a frozen lake. For a socialite who was once a regular at New York and London's fanciest events, it was quite a departure.

Maxwell had purchased the house for cash—the deal for the secluded 156-acre property with a mountaintop mansion, listed at $1.07 million, was made through a limited liability corporation (LLC), which allowed the buyer's identity to be shielded, according to prosecutors.[9] A real estate website advertising the property called it "a stunning custom-designed Timber Frame home" that would be "an amazing retreat for the nature lover who also wants total privacy."[10] A boulder at the entrance of the property is carved with the word "Tuckedaway."

Public records showed the property owner as Granite Realty LLC, listed at an address in Boston—the same address as a law firm, Nutter, McClennen, and Fish, that had registered Ellmax LLC in Florida, the name of Maxwell's defunct Florida company.[11] *The Sun* in London reported that the deal to acquire the four-bedroom, four-bathroom, 4,356-square-foot property may have also involved Scott Borgerson.[12]

The broker who sold the property told *The Daily Beast* that she had never met Maxwell and dealt only with a British man, who she assumed to be the husband, who attended the house inspection. He claimed he had just sold his tech company and wanted a residence in the United States. In an interview with *The Daily Beast,* the broker said one unusual question posed stuck in her mind: "She wanted to know what the flight patterns were over the house, which was very strange."[13] It was also later disclosed that a real estate agent told the FBI that Maxwell posed as a journalist named Janet Marshall. The man with her called himself "Scott Marshall" and claimed he was retired from the British military and was writing a book.

The property had tranquil views of Mount Sunapee. But Ghislaine was uneasy. Friends said she knew authorities would be closing in on her. She even prepared a mobile phone by wrapping it in foil in case she had to flee approaching lawmen and go into hiding. Her efforts, of course, were foolish—tinfoil does not shield a phone from the prying ears of the FBI.[14]

According to *Vanity Fair,* Maxwell's pared-down existence had her wearing casual clothes, working out with a punching bag, and cooking for herself. Her meals, inspired by her French mother, were said to include leek soup, boeuf bourguignonne, and red cabbage. Nights were spent lifting weights or stretching in front of the television. She also was said to be reading biographies, including one of Winston Churchill by British prime minister Boris Johnson.[15]

Maxwell wasn't alone in the house. She had a live-in housekeeper, and there was a third person in the house—a man that a neighbor, Richard Morris, identified in an interview for this book as "Martin." The man, Morris said, drove a black Chevy pickup with Massachusetts plates. "I see him come and go all the time," said Morris. "Taking the trash, doing the groceries. I saw nobody else." Morris said he never laid eyes on Maxwell, however.[16]

Prosecutors would later reveal that Maxwell's brother had hired former members of the British military as private security at the compound. A guard who worked at the compound told FBI agents that he was given a credit card in the name of the LLC to make purchases for Maxwell. The guard also told investigators that Maxwell never set foot off the property.[17] Instead, Maxwell's days at the compound were mostly occupied by conversations with her team of lawyers. "This is her universe. Defending all of these [civil] cases is a full-time job," a friend told *Vanity Fair.*[18]

A July 2020 article by Josh Boswell in the *Daily Mail* revealed another possible activity of Maxwell. According to the report, a month prior to her arrest, Maxwell hired two fake news purveyors and Washington "laughingstocks"—Jacob Wohl and Jack Burkman—to smear acting U.S. attorney Geoffrey Berman in order to get him fired so that any possible legal action against the British heiress would be delayed or canceled. Maxwell, the report claimed, paid the men $25,000 for their efforts.

Did Maxwell know that while she was hiding out, the FBI, working with prosecutors in Berman's Southern District, had quietly built a criminal case against her? What Maxwell almost certainly did not realize was that the FBI had closely tracked her movements. After learning of her relocation to the property on East Washington Road in Bradford, prosecutors came up with a plan to take her into custody. "Prosecutors believed they had enough to make a case and a window developed to apprehend her," a law enforcement source said in an interview for this book.

According to the source, there was fear among investigators that Maxwell "would get antsy and decide to leave the country for a safe house elsewhere," most likely Paris. "They didn't want to have to deal with extradition. This was clean—as to her being in the U.S., and she was *gettable*."[19]

There were roadblocks, however. Because of the COVID-19 pandemic, there was a delay in interviewing a victim in London who was crucial to the prosecution, according to one report.[20] Another unexpected wrinkle was the abrupt firing of Berman at the behest of Trump and U.S. attorney general William Barr on June 20, 2020. Barr initially claimed that Berman, who was also overseeing cases involving the president and his associates, was resigning—but Berman stuck his ground and contradicted that before Trump finally had him removed.

Berman knew the Epstein case better than anyone. He was the one who brought the indictment against Epstein before the financier died in the MCC, and Berman was instrumental in moving along the investigation of Epstein's associates. "Berman didn't want the ball to be dropped. His last act was wanting to see Ghislaine brought to justice," said a law enforcement source with knowledge of the case. Audrey Strauss, who had been Berman's top deputy, was made acting U.S. attorney in the wake of Berman's sudden departure. "It was a little bit chaotic, but Strauss expertly picked up the ball and followed through with moving on Maxwell's apprehension," the source commended.[21]

According to the law enforcement source, "a secretive 'go order'" was activated in the days leading up to the Fourth of July weekend after a federal grand jury in New York handed down an indictment. The SDNY formed a task force that encompassed members from six agencies, including the FBI, the NYPD, the U.S. Marshals Service, and local law enforcement in New Hampshire.

Ghislaine Maxwell spent her last night of freedom in "Tuckedaway" on Wednesday, July 1, 2020.[22]

# 38

## A MOST WANTED WOMAN

THE SUN ROSE OVER BRADFORD, NEW HAMPSHIRE, AT 5:12 ON THE morning of Thursday, July 2, 2020.

Mornings were Norman Rockwell quiet in Bradford, apart from the chirping of birds and the occasional barking dog. So the prop plane flying above the sleepy town just after dawn did not go unnoticed. The sound of the low-flying aircraft startled Bradford resident Richard Morris, a neighbor of Ghislaine Maxwell's on East Washington Road whose property is opposite her driveway. "At five thirty A.M., maybe six o'clock, there was a single-engine plane buzzing above, which was odd at that hour of the morning," Morris said in an interview for this book. "Then a second small plane. They were unmarked. They were circling." Later, Morris realized the planes were likely surveilling the property ahead of Maxwell's arrest.[1]

An hour later, a fifteen-vehicle convoy made its way toward Maxwell's house through neatly paved blacktop roads surrounded by sprawling landscapes and pristinely maintained homes. At the foot of the half-mile driveway leading to the house, a member of the arrest team used a bolt cutter to break a lock on a metal gate. Twenty-four armed FBI agents and other police officers, some with the New

Hampshire State Police Gang Task Force, descended on the property. According to the *New York Post,* when the FBI, accompanied by local cops, "rang the bell at the end of Maxwell's quarter-mile driveway," a housekeeper answered.[2] Through a window, agents observed Maxwell dash to another room in the house, quickly shutting the door behind her, prosecutors later wrote. Maxwell "eventually came out and surrendered, immediately asking for her lawyer."[3]

It all happened in a matter of minutes. One of the arresting officers later described the scene to the *Daily Mail.* "Maxwell was up and dressed in the living room, wearing sweatpants and a top. Strangely she didn't seem to have much reaction," the officer said. "It was like it wasn't registering with her. She was turned around very quickly and cuffed."[4]

WHAT WAS IN GHISLAINE MAXWELL's mind as law enforcement officers showed up at her door to make the arrest? As one officer commented, "She had to think at that instant whether or not she was going to give herself up or attempt another way out of this." After all, Maxwell was no stranger to a violent death—her father and two former boyfriends had both met early ends. But Maxwell surrendered without resisting. She was read her rights almost a year to the day after Jeffrey Epstein's arrest at Teterboro Airport.

A few hours after her arrest, Maxwell appeared in front of a magistrate in New Hampshire, who ordered her detained before being sent to New York for further proceedings. Maxwell appeared via video for her first court appearance and answered about a dozen procedural questions from the judge. Her answers were soft-spoken and polite. Maxwell did not enter a plea; she was due to answer the charges when she was formally arraigned in Manhattan.

Maxwell spent her first night behind bars in the Merrimack County Jail in Boscawen, New Hampshire. The facility, built in 2005, was only a twenty-minute drive from her hideout. For a woman born into extreme privilege, the cell was the humblest accommodation of her life.

• • •

WILLIAM F. SWEENEY, JR., THE assistant director in charge of the
FBI's New York field office, hastily called a press conference to discuss Maxwell's arrest that same day. Audrey Strauss, the acting U.S.
attorney, unsealed the eighteen-page indictment charging Maxwell
with six counts, including conspiracy to entice minors to travel to
engage in illegal sex acts. The charges carried a possible thirty-five-
year prison sentence. Strauss called the case the "prequel" to the
case that the SDNY had brought against Epstein before his death.

The indictment listed three minor victims allegedly recruited by
Maxwell from 1994 to 1997, including one who was fourteen. Maxwell also faced two counts of perjury for making false statements in
a 2016 deposition in the civil suit brought against her by Virginia
Roberts Giuffre.[5] According to the indictment, the victims were
"groomed and/or abused at multiple locations," including Epstein's
properties in New York, Florida, and New Mexico and at Maxwell's
home in London.

The Department of Justice's ten-page detention memo called
Maxwell an "extreme flight risk," adding that she had three
passports—American, British, and French—and that there were
more than fifteen bank accounts linked to Maxwell since 2016, totaling more than $20 million.[6] Prosecutors said she had taken at least
fifteen international flights over the past three years, including desti-
nations in the United Kingdom, Japan, and Qatar, and was continuing to move hundreds of thousands of dollars among her accounts up
through the month of Epstein's arrest.

After the Fourth of July weekend, Maxwell was transferred by
the U.S. Marshals Service into the Metropolitan Detention Center,
a grimy federal prison in Brooklyn that had been troubled with power
outages and, at the time, the coronavirus outbreak. To keep her from
harming herself and to prevent any attempt on her life, she was
moved among cells, issued paper clothing, and forced to sleep on
bare mattresses. She was also kept under video surveillance. A source

said, "The last thing [officials] wanted was [to put] her in the MCC," where Epstein's death had occurred under a cloud of mystery. "[Attorney General William] Barr didn't want any more F-ups."[7]

At the bail hearing on July 14, 2020, Maxwell, wearing a dark-colored top, appeared remotely via a video link from the Brooklyn lockup. She answered the judge politely, wiped her eyes at times, and pleaded not guilty to the charges. Mark S. Cohen, one of Maxwell's attorneys, told the court at one point, "She's not the monster that's been portrayed by the media and the government." Her lawyers asked the judge to release Maxwell into home confinement on a $5 million bond. "Ghislaine Maxwell is not Jeffrey Epstein," her lawyers stated in a court filing. Prosecutors argued that Maxwell had resisted arrest and "there should be no question that the defendant is skilled at living in hiding."[8] They introduced a victim, Annie Farmer, to bolster their contention that Maxwell should be denied bail. Farmer told the court Maxwell was "a sexual predator who groomed and abused me and countless other children and young women."

In the end, Judge Alison J. Nathan of Federal District Court in Manhattan denied bail, saying, "Ms. Maxwell poses a substantial actual risk of flight." The judge scheduled the trial to begin on July 12, 2021.[9] Maxwell dropped her head at the news that she would have to remain behind bars for a full year before trial.

During the video conference, one bombshell emerged—that Maxwell was secretly married. Assistant U.S. Attorney Alison Moe divulged the news when accusing Maxwell of hiding her wealth. "The defendant also makes no mention whatsoever of the financial circumstances or assets of her spouse, whose identity she declined to provide to Pretrial Services."

The rumored though unconfirmed spouse was Scott Borgerson, whom Maxwell had allegedly moved in with in 2016. Borgerson did not immediately comment but his family was reportedly said to be "traumatized" over the possible secret nuptials.[10]

• • •

GHISLAINE MAXWELL'S ARREST SPARKED ANOTHER round of frenzied media speculation. Would she cooperate with prosecutors and strike a deal, perhaps in exchange for disclosing criminal sexual—and financial—activities of the men who had seemingly been caught in Epstein's web? Some commenters pointed to the fact that the Southern District had assigned her case to the Public Corruption Unit rather than the office's Violent and Organized Crime Unit.[11]

Lawyers representing the many victims of this tragic episode of justice delayed statements praising the arrest. "Today is a powerful message to all Epstein accomplices that justice will prevail," said Virginia Roberts Giuffre's attorney, Sigrid McCawley. Giuffre said, after hearing the news, "Tears of joy were streaming down my face."[12]

"She is just as evil as Jeffrey Epstein," one victim told Fox News in the wake of Maxwell's arrest. "She is a rapist." The unidentified woman had filed suit against Epstein after his death, joining in a lawsuit of six women. The victim claimed Maxwell allegedly raped her as many as thirty times starting when she was only fourteen.[13]

"I had assumed Ghislaine Maxwell would somehow get away," Haley Robson, whom Palm Beach police had once targeted for recruiting other teen girls for Epstein, told the author after Maxwell's arrest.


THERE WAS, HOWEVER, A SOLITARY voice offering Ghislaine Maxwell a public expression of support. Former Epstein lawyer Alan Dershowitz wrote an essay defending Maxwell for *The Spectator*. "Like every other arrested person, she must be presumed innocent," he wrote, adding, "Keep an open mind about Maxwell."[14]

Nearly a year after Epstein's death, Alan Dershowitz was still fighting to legally clear his name. In 2019, the Harvard Law professor emeritus had sued Virginia Roberts Giuffre for defamation, denying yet again her claims that he was one of the men Epstein had made her have sex with when she was a minor. In depositions, and to anyone who would listen, Dershowitz explained that the women who said they had been sexually abused by him when they were underage were pawns in a larger criminal extortion plot to pressure Leslie Wexner into forking over $1 billion to avoid being accused of sexual misconduct.[15]

In June 2020, in a court filing by Dershowitz's lawyers refuting Giuffre's claims, it was revealed that former Israeli prime minister Ehud Barak was one of the men accused of having sex with Giuffre. That accusation had previously been sealed by the court. Barak responded to the disclosure in Israel's *Israel Hayom* newspaper, saying, "I don't comment on imaginary rumors or false affidavits."

On July 1, 2020, another turn in the ongoing drama played out in the Manhattan courtroom of U.S. district judge Loretta Preska, who ruled on a request by Dershowitz to gain access to a trove of confidential documents—allegedly identifying Epstein's closest associates—that Giuffre's side had obtained and that he believed would help his case. Preska ruled that Giuffre's lawyers had improperly obtained the documents and ordered that the files "be destroyed."

After the judge's ruling, Dershowitz told *Newsweek,* "I oppose the destruction of evidence that may contain smoking gun proof that my false accuser made up her story."[16] Without referencing the *Mail on Sunday* by name for publishing Giuffre's bombshell report in 2011, Dershowitz pointed out that Giuffre "was paid $160,000" for her "made up" story. A week earlier, Dershowitz had announced that he was suing Netflix over its Epstein documentary *Filthy Rich* for including Giuffre's claims that Epstein had trafficked her to the famed attorney and Harvard professor. Dershowitz went on the offensive again, telling Israel's Channel 12, "It's a total lie. I never met her, I never saw her, I never heard of her," adding that his travel records "prove conclusively that I could never have been with her." Dershowitz lambasted Netflix for presenting Giuffre "as a credible witness without allowing the viewers to see her history and her record of lying, and the fact that she admitted that she never met me."[17]

In the documentary, Dershowitz was interviewed and challenged

Giuffre to "look in the camera" and accuse him of having sex with her. In a video clip, she seemingly accepted his dare and said: "I was with Alan Dershowitz multiple times—at least six that I can remember."

SHORTLY BEFORE THIS BOOK WENT to press, Judge Preska announced on July 23, 2020, in a new court ruling, that she was planning to unseal more documents from the Maxwell and Giuffre defamation case. "In the context of this case, especially its allegations of sex trafficking of young girls," Preska ruled, "the court finds any minor embarrassment or annoyance resulting from Ms. Maxwell's mostly non-testimony . . . is far outweighed by the presumption of public access."[18]

The unsealed documents were released seven days later—late on the night of July 30, 2020—and they placed a renewed spotlight on several Epstein acquaintances. Bill Clinton was once again mentioned for allegedly visiting Epstein's island; there was no accusation that Clinton himself engaged in any sexual misconduct. But the papers reiterated claims by Giuffre of sexual dalliances involving Prince Andrew and others. The documents also disclosed sexual accusations by Giuffre against Maxwell. In one unsealed deposition, Giuffre was asked if she was aware of any "distinguishing physical feature" about Maxwell and gave a detailed response about Maxwell's breasts and the color of her body hair.

Maxwell, meanwhile, was able to halt, at least temporarily, the release of more potentially damaging documents. The 2nd Circuit Court of Appeals granted Maxwell's lawyers a stay, keeping those documents from the public until at least September 22, 2020. On August 1, 2020, Giuffre tweeted out a reponse to the week's events: "Hey #GhislaineMaxwell just sitting outside, taking some time to destress after you & your lawyer's shenanigans. Like the view? If you didn't abuse 1000's of minors you would not be staring at your toilet as a piece of artwork. #TimesUp#SpeakOut#WhoIsNext#KidsToo."

# 39

## OUT OF THE WOODWORK

OF ALL THE MEN AND WOMEN IN JEFFREY EPSTEIN'S LIFE, THE individual with arguably the most to lose—and perhaps the most to want to hide—was the financier's onetime close friend Donald J. Trump. The lives of the dead child abuser and the president of the United States had intertwined in significant ways. It was at Mar-a-Lago, after all, that Epstein recruited the young Virginia Roberts, a staffer at the Trump resort. Trump and Epstein socialized together on numerous occasions, including the infamous 1992 party with NFL cheerleaders.[1] Trump is on record acknowledging Epstein's preference for very young girls.

With Epstein dead, will the public ever learn the extent of Epstein and Trump's relationship? The president seemed to stoke the fire when he spoke at a White House press briefing on July 21, 2020, when asked to comment on Ghislaine Maxwell's arrest. "I haven't really been following it too much. I just wish her well, frankly. I've met her numerous times over the years, especially since I lived in Palm Beach, and I guess they lived in Palm Beach. But I wish her well, whatever it is," Trump said. The remarks set off social media conspiracy theories, and the Lincoln Project, a conservative political action committee organized in 2019, posted an ad to Twitter with the caption "What does Ghislaine Maxwell have on @realDonaldTrump?"

In the wake of Epstein's death, several individuals came forward claiming to possess incriminating evidence about Epstein and other men connected to him. Shortly after Epstein's death, a man using the pseudonym Patrick Kessler met with lawyers David Boies and John Stanley Pottinger, and later with reporters for *The New York Times*. Kessler claimed he had thousands of hours of footage from Epstein's homes, as well as reams of data on his finances. Kessler promised to provide this information to reporters but disappeared without ever doing so.

With Ghislaine Maxwell's arrest, another possibility emerged of incriminating videotapes surfacing. On July 8, 2020, the UK tabloid the *Daily Mail* reported that Maxwell may have been sitting on "an alleged cache of sex tapes" as "an insurance policy to save herself from federal charges." The *Mail* attributed the claim to Christopher Mason, a journalist friend of Maxwell's since the 1980s.

There is one other figure who has claimed to possess incriminating video from Epstein's home. The man, who has received little attention in the mainstream press, is named John Mark Dougan, and his wild story is straight out of a spy novel.

JOHN MARK DOUGAN JOINED THE Palm Beach County Sheriff's Office in 2002 after a stint in the Marine Corps and starting a small web business of his own. He left the force in 2009.

The next year, Detective Joseph Recarey allegedly called Dougan and asked if he was at his house in Palm Beach Gardens. Dougan didn't know why Recarey was asking if he could come over, but he figured it might have something to do with Dougan's Internet side gig. Recarey was the lead detective involved in the 2005 Palm Beach investigation—the man who pieced together Epstein's criminal sex trafficking web luring young girls to his Florida mansion.

At the time of Recarey's call, Dougan was running PBSOTalk, a website with the stated goal of exposing corruption that Dougan alleged existed in the Palm Beach Sheriff's Office. "I had a lot of respect and a lot of whistleblowers," Dougan explained in an interview for this book. "A lot of people who gave me information."

When Detective Recarey showed up, Dougan said he came with "a bunch of file boxes." In Dougan's account, Recarey explained to Dougan that he was worried that either the state attorney's office or the sheriff's office might try to destroy the evidence in the boxes. Inside the boxes were CDs—about seven hundred, according to Dougan. Each CD was labeled with a date and room in which the video was taken.[2]

Recarey asked him to upload all the CDs onto a hard drive and to keep the information private. Dougan said the cache of materials also included documents that he scanned and uploaded to a private server. After uploading the videos ten at a time, Dougan said he had everything stored on a one-and-a-half-terabyte external hard drive. "It was just a file, a big encrypted file sitting on one of my hard drives," he claimed in an interview. Dougan said he later learned that the videos, purportedly shot between 1995 and 2005 at Epstein's Palm Beach mansion, allegedly depict men participating in sex acts with underage girls.[3] However, Dougan claimed Recarey did not discuss the content of the tapes at the time, and Dougan said he did not think about them for many years after he came to be in possession of them. He took the material only as a favor to Recarey.[4]

Copies of the digital dump were in Dougan's home when the FBI came calling in March 2016. Dougan had caught the attention of federal law enforcement in the wake of a bizarre episode involving a purported Russian hacker codenamed Badvolf, who had allegedly stolen countless names and addresses of local police officers and federal agents, which were then posted on the PBSOTalk website. (Dougan had resigned from the force in 2009 after submitting a tip to a superior that one of his colleagues was repeatedly alluding to beating up suspects on his Facebook page.)[5]

In March 2016, when the FBI raided Dougan's home, they

presented him with a search warrant seeking evidence of federal conspiracy and computer fraud crimes. The FBI seized Dougan's phone and computers; the Palm Beach County state attorney procured a warrant as well, and his home was searched by the sheriff's office.[6]

What happened next was nothing short of remarkable, a head-scratching twist. After the FBI raid, Dougan managed to slip away from police surveillance. He later emerged in Moscow, where, after seeking political asylum, he forged a new career as an IT and cyber-security consultant. After Epstein's July 2019 arrest, Dougan began posting about the existence of the alleged tapes on Facebook. In an interview, Dougan claimed that the hard drive had been taken in the 2016 FBI raid but that he had by this point realized what was on the tapes and made copies, which he said he took with him to Russia.

In September 2019, a month after Epstein's death, the *Times* of London reported that Dougan's alleged trove of digital and video data had sparked the interest of MI6, the British overseas intelligence gathering service. Among Dougan's data was purportedly compromising material on Prince Andrew.[7]

As Dougan sees it, "the logical conclusion is the FBI must have seen what was on the videos and they must have seen Prince Andrew and they must have contacted MI6," he explained. "The FBI isn't going to contact MI6 unless they have a reason to share information."[8]

Shortly after the story broke, Ron Chepesiuk, a prolific writer of true crime stories, visited Dougan in his Moscow home. Chepesiuk had reached out to Dougan a year earlier in the hope of writing a television show based on Dougan's life. For Chepesiuk, the fact that Dougan allegedly possessed these tapes added another level of intrigue to the strange saga.[9]

During the visit, Dougan floated the idea to Chepesiuk of sampling some of the tapes. "I was surprised that he trusted me that much to show me the tapes," Chepesiuk said in an interview for this book. "I can see from his point of view, he wanted to have somebody verify [it]."

One day, a week after his arrival in Moscow, Chepesiuk said he was sitting at a desk in Dougan's house when he heard what sounded like people having sex. "The first thing I saw when I looked at the screen on the computer, it looked like surveillance tape because it was looking down on this couple," he said.

Chepesiuk asked Dougan what was happening, and Dougan told the screenwriter he wanted to watch the tapes in the presence of someone else in case he was ever challenged about their existence. "I couldn't identify anybody in the tapes, but it [was a] young girl and an older guy," Chepesiuk said in an interview for this book.[10] In total, Chepesiuk claimed, he and Dougan watched just under three minutes of footage from about seven videos.

To Dougan, the existence of the alleged tapes poses a danger. If Prince Andrew was on those tapes, Dougan claimed, he could be targeted by MI6 or some other intelligence agency. These tapes "have signed my death ticket."[11]

The threat became real after Dougan dropped Chepesiuk off early the next morning at the airport. Dougan said he then noticed that he was being followed by a gray Mercedes. After being followed for thirty miles through the winding streets of Moscow, Dougan claimed that he ditched his Land Rover Defender in an alley and ran through an area of abandoned buildings and railroad tracks before hailing a cab home.[12]

Increasing the sense that he was in danger, Dougan said he later received a phone call from a British journalist who told him she had reason to believe Chepesiuk was going to be arrested at Heathrow by British intelligence during a layover before returning to South Carolina. Chepesiuk made it home without delay or incident.

Why not just release the alleged tapes to the lawyers representing Epstein's victims? Dougan claimed in an interview that that idea had not occurred to him. He said that Detective Recarey—who died in 2018 at the age of fifty—had asked him not to give the tapes to anyone. Yet Dougan claimed that he had in fact, as a security measure, sent the hard drive containing the tapes to a friend in the south of Russia. The tapes won't be released unless Dougan dies suspiciously or disappears, he said. As for the seven videos that he viewed with Chepesiuk, Dougan claimed to have held on to those as collateral. He said, "If people know that I have this and it's not going to be released unless something happens to me, they're not going to do something to me."[13]

Could the material Dougan showed Chepesiuk be legitimate? If it is, the criminal, political, and financial stakes would almost defy description. The fact that the material arrived in Russia in 2016, just as Donald Trump was in the thick of a presidential campaign, raises a litany of questions. Could Dougan's alleged material be connected to the *kompromat* that Vladimir Putin is often rumored to have on the man—Jeffrey Epstein's friend—who would become president of the United States?

Or is Dougan one more fraudster, in an era rife with them, a man with delusions of playing a pivotal role in a globe-spanning mystery?

As with most questions about Jeffrey Epstein's web, the answer is elusive.

# AFTERWORD

## "A WHOLE LOT OF GRAY"

During the reporting of this book, I visited the Florida cemetery where Jeffrey Epstein's remains are now interred in an unmarked tomb a thirty-minute drive from his former home on El Brillo Way.

Before I left there, I said a silent prayer for Jeffrey Epstein's many victims. I then drove south for twenty-two miles to the Treetops Motel in nearby Greenacres. There were no manicured lawns here. The low-budget motel was sometimes used by the Palm Beach County Sheriff's Office to carry out undercover prostitution stings.

I stood outside the dirt-smudged door to Room 212.

Inside this small room, a woman named Leigh Patrick took her last breath on May 30, 2017. A cleaning person found her body, partially covered with a sheet, on the bed.

Patrick died from an accidental heroin overdose. According to the police, her body was covered with bruises and sores. Leigh was exactly two months shy of her thirtieth birthday.

Two years earlier, Patrick had sat down with Palm Beach journalist Jose Lambiet. He told me he found Patrick's name after she was subpoenaed to testify in one of a series of lawsuits filed by victims against Epstein.[1] "At the time I interviewed her, she had just been in rehab and felt good about her future," Lambiet recalled to me. "She had applied for a job selling insurance and she was engaged."

Patrick's life had taken a dark turn when she was just sixteen, around 2003, when a friend took her to see Jeffrey Epstein. He gave her $300 to take her shirt off. Patrick told Lambiet that she was "creeped out," but, as Lambiet explained, "like so many girls before and after her, she went back." Lambiet took a long pause. "She regretted going back, she told me. And her life spiraled out of control for years to come. She was arrested numerous times. Leigh Patrick was never the same after meeting Jeffrey Epstein."

After her death, Lambiet tracked down Leigh's twin sister, who said Epstein had abused Leigh Patrick as a teen. "My sister suffered tremendously," said Selby Patrick. "And it started with Epstein. Something happened in her when she met him that got her out of control."[2]

Many victims of Jeffrey Epstein have waged personal battles of pain and anguish in the years and decades since being drawn into his web. Some ended up with drug addictions and stints in jail. Still others became sex workers.[3]

Some fought back against feelings of depression. Dainya Nida, who was molested by Epstein when she was sixteen, said she cut herself and attempted suicide.[4]

Another woman, identified in court only as Jane Doe 10, said she was assaulted by Epstein at age fifteen, and his abuse pushed her "to the point where I purchased a gun and drove myself to an isolated place to end my suffering."[5]

Courtney Wild, whose abuse by Epstein began at age fourteen when she was a junior high school student in braces, said she was robbed not only of her innocence but also of her "mental health."[6]

Jeffrey Epstein's death erased the possibility that he would stand trial on the new charges of sex trafficking brought against him by the U.S. Attorney's Office in Manhattan. Seventeen days following his death, federal prosecutors appeared at a court hearing to drop the charges, which required the approval of a judge. That judge, Richard

M. Berman, allowed Jeffrey Epstein's victims to finally have their day in court at the August 27, 2019, hearing.

Sixteen women turned out at Manhattan federal court. Judge Berman invited them to stand and form a line to the well of his courtroom. A half dozen other victims had their statements read into the record.[7]

For more than an hour, Jeffrey Epstein's accusers had the floor. One by one they spoke. Finally.

One victim named Anouska De Georgiou may have summed it up best: "I am every girl he did this to, and they're all me," she declared, "and today we stand together, those that are present and those that aren't."[8] She added: "He could not begin to fathom what he took from us."[9]

The chair at the defense table where Jeffrey Epstein should have been seated remained empty.


IT WOULD BE A CONSERVATIVE estimate to say that since the 1980s, Jeffrey Epstein spent more than $35 million related to his abuse of women and girls. The number, based on a review of court documents, police reports, interviews and other research conducted for this book, is a sum calculated from estimates of known payments Epstein made to victims and limited public details on what he's paid in financial settlements.[10] The amount is unfathomable, but it still constituted only a fraction of the financier's vast fortune.

In the original Palm Beach police files, one officer speculated that Epstein spent as much as $1,500 a day on his fixation. Alfredo Rodriguez, who worked for Epstein for six months, told police that Epstein considered him a "human ATM" and required him to keep a minimum of $2,000 on him at all times that he would use to pay the girls, even if Epstein wasn't home. Rodriguez was also instructed to buy iPods, jewelry, and "anything the girls would want," according to a court document.[11]

Within a year, Epstein would have spent an estimated $500,000. Epstein's legal settlements, meanwhile, have been bound in

confidentiality, and only a handful have been fully disclosed by victims. As of July 2020, thirty-nine settlements have been filed against
the financier or his estate, as identified either in legal records or by
the press.[12]

Epstein paid three victims a combined total of $5.5 million,
according to *The Palm Beach Post* in 2017. Two other victims were
paid $50,000 each, according to the *Daily Mail* in 2019.[13] Some
twenty victims were reportedly paid between $40,000 and $50,000
in their settlements, which adds up to just under $1 million.

The total amount paid is unknown, but it likely exceeds $20 mil-
lion in settlements and legal fees.


You can read the unsealed court documents, police reports, and
legal depositions in this case. They are factual. They are graphic. But
they seldom leave you with an accurate understanding of the complicated individuals whose lives were ruined by their association—no
matter how brief—with Jeffrey Epstein. One such person who I
wanted to see whole, who I wanted to understand in full color, was
Haley Robson. Robson became something of collateral damage as
Florida authorities built their case in 2005.

Robson was a sixteen-year-old student at Royal Palm Beach
Community High School when she was recruited at a local pool by a
friend to give Epstein a massage for some quick cash. While she shut
down his sexual advances during their only massage session together,
she returned to his house for over two years, bringing with her classmates and other girls. For her recruiting efforts, Haley was paid $200
each time one of them massaged Epstein. She provided six girls
between the ages of fourteen and sixteen; a seventh was rejected by
Epstein for being too old (she was twenty-three). Some of these girls
returned multiple times. Haley believes she accompanied her
"recruits" to Epstein's house a total of twenty-four times.

Police placed Haley under surveillance when they began probing
accusations about Epstein. When she was brought in for questioning,

Haley was "remarkably forthcoming" in her interviews with police, providing them with names and ages of all the girls. A report further said, "the affidavit suggests she willingly volunteered all information she had about Epstein and her role."

Despite her being a victim herself, police threatened to charge Haley under a statute of a lewd and lascivious act on a minor in the second degree, though she was never charged.

Nor did Robson receive immunity during Epstein's plea agreement like his four alleged potential coconspirators and assistants Nadia Marcinkova, Sarah Kellen, Lesley Groff, and Adriana Ross; all have denied wrongdoing.

Because Haley was named prominently with Kellen in the Palm Beach Police Department's probable cause affidavit against Epstein, she took on unwanted notoriety (*The New York Times* later referred to her as "a former stripper and Olive Garden worker").

And Robson's legal issues have not gone away. She was sued twice, and there was speculation in 2019 that New York investigators were interested in her as one of Epstein's "enablers," opening the door to possible federal prosecution. She has since cooperated with the FBI in their investigation.

Back in a 2009 deposition, Haley acknowledged debating whether to sue Epstein. "I decided this is my life and I have to take responsibility for my actions because I did volunteer," she said.

In an interview for this book, one of the original Florida lawyers who represented some of Epstein's victims said he recognized Haley's complicated situation. The attorney, Spencer Kuvin, said: "Haley Robson's a good example. Is she a victim, or a perpetrator? Is she a coconspirator, or a young girl who was turned into a victim [and] who was then brainwashed into becoming a perpetrator . . . ? It's an odd dynamic. Not all of it is black-and-white. There's a whole lot of gray."

I wanted to understand the gray in Haley Robson. Now a single working mom pulling her life together, she turned down all media requests at the time of the Florida case and for the next decade. I decided to appeal to her differently. I had learned that Haley was once a journalism student and liked writing. I invited her to write me a letter explaining the gray—in her own words. I greatly appreciate her courage in opening herself up to this self-inspection and allowing me to share it with this book's readers. Here are excerpts from her letter:

> I was a teenager when I met Jeffrey and became one of his victims. But that's not how the police and the media painted me. They viewed me as guilty—because I recruited other girls for Jeffrey.
>
> What the media doesn't know—and what I've never revealed until this writing—is how emotionally broken I was before I arrived at Jeffrey's mansion in Palm Beach.
>
> I'd been raped. I never pressed charges or told my friends. I buried myself in drugs and alcohol to cope with my pain. Then the man I fell in love with was murdered.
>
> The summer before I turned sixteen, my high school friends and I went clubbing every weekend. That's how I met "J." He and his friends were older—twenty-one or twenty-two.
>
> One night we were partying at someone's house. I was in the pool with "J." He tried to kiss me and after three shots of Bacardi we ended up in a bedroom. "J" was performing oral sex on me. I tried to stop him, but the next thing I knew he was pushing inside me. It was painful, and I started to cry.
>
> I'll never forget what he said—"Let me get my nut."
>
> I felt helpless. Before I could get up, his friend "D" came in. He was laughing. "D" pointed to a small blood spot on the bed and said, "I told you she was a bleeder."
>
> Then they both walked out. At that moment, I knew two things. I was a joke—and I'd never let anything like that happen to me again.
>
> I met Jeffrey through a classmate who approached me at a resort on Singer Island called The Canopy.
>
> My friend said there was an older, wealthier guy on Palm Beach island who paid girls $200 to massage him.

My first reaction was, "Yeah, sure, I'm definitely interested. Give me your number and we can set something up."

During the car ride, my friend said, "The more you do, the more you're going to make." I thought it would just be me in my underwear. I didn't think he would try to fondle me or touch me. I was wrong, of course.

I was first introduced to Jeffrey in the kitchen. My first reaction to seeing him? While he tried to act friendly, he seemed smug and strange. When I looked into his eyes, it was like the lights were on, but no one was home. Like he was empty inside.

The next time I saw him he was wrapped in a small towel, lying on a massage table in his bathroom/steam room. It was creepy. He removed the towel.

Then the topless massage turned into Jeffrey reaching out to touch my buttocks and my private parts while he masturbated himself. I pushed his hand away and told him, "No."

The disappointment on his face couldn't have been more obvious. I kept thinking, "Please don't let this get physical. I will not go through another sexual trauma."

It was just the two of us in the room. I know now that Jeffrey could have raped me as he did with so many others. Instead, he just finished himself.

Then he asked me to bring other girls, my friends—and he'd pay me.

I probably should have moved on with my life and put the whole thing behind as a bizarre experience. Instead, I made another mistake—and agreed to recruit other girls for him.

Jeffrey said, "I like the younger, the better." I thought he meant younger-looking—not younger girls.

The first girls I recruited were my friends. I knew he'd like them because they were built like me, athletic.

I drove the girls to Jeffrey's house, and I'd hang out in the kitchen or by the pool and wait for them to finish the massage. In all, I returned to Jeffrey's house some twenty-four times.

Sage was the youngest girl I brought to Jeffrey. She was fourteen, but at the time I thought she was a year or two older than me because she was dating my cousin and her body was more mature than mine.

But I had this intuition about her. One day she called me and asked me to go back to Jeffrey's house. That's when the cops recorded me—and suddenly I was caught up in their investigation.

The hardest part of the entire investigation for me was seeing my father's grief. He had been a police officer. When my lawyer said there was the possibility that I could be listed as a sex offender had I been charged and convicted, my dad—who's a very private man—broke down in tears. It was the only time I ever saw him cry.

After that, I followed my lawyer's advice and did exactly as I was told.

I have always—and I can't stress this enough—spoken my truth and have been willing to help law enforcement in this case.

I appeared in front of a grand jury. I was not charged or found guilty of any crimes.

After I turned eighteen, I made another bad decision. I walked into a strip club in West Palm Beach and was hired immediately.

I relocated to Orlando, moved in with a high school class-mate, and started working at a club called Dancer's Royale. I was known as Thalia.

An extremely handsome man who came in regularly caught my eye and we started hanging out. His name was Brian. He was a talented painter and a good cook.

He knew about my past and I knew about him—he'd just finished serving time in federal prison.

Brian was protective, caring, a gentleman. But he was also unfaithful.

While we were together, I kept having the same nightmare: two men took turns raping me while they forced Brian to watch. I screamed for him, but he couldn't do anything. They shot him and left me beaten and bloody on the floor. Then I'd wake up. It's just a nightmare, Brian told me.

I knew Brian made money by selling drugs. But I never wanted people to think they could use me to get to him or hurt him. So, I never told him that I loved him. I kept my feelings inside, where they were safe.

After two weeks of having that nightmare, I woke up on a Thursday in Brian's bed.

That morning, I left his house to pick up my car from the club. While I was driving back, I got a phone call saying Brian had been murdered.

When I pulled up to Brian's, there was crime scene tape, cops, and a huge crowd of people. He was murdered in broad daylight while his daughter was outside playing.

It was Thursday, June 22, 2006—a month after Epstein was charged in Florida.

As the investigation into Jeffrey continued, I was dragged into the media circus. But I wasn't put in the same category as the other victims.

People wrote about me when they didn't know a thing about me. A famous writer, James Patterson, referred to me as "Wendy Dobbs" in his book *Filthy Rich*. He never met me or spoke to me.

No one knew I'd been raped. No one knew my boyfriend had been murdered. I'm not making excuses or asking for forgiveness. I'd made mistakes as a teenager and I have to live with them for the rest of my life.

Looking back, I see very clearly that Jeffrey was a pedophile who manipulated me into sex trafficking.

When I heard Jeffrey had been arrested again and jailed

in New York last summer and that there were even more victims, I broke down.

I remember watching one victim being interviewed on television. I was with my parents, but I ran out of the room and sat on my bed, sobbing.

On a Saturday morning my phone buzzed with a text from my older sister. It was a heartfelt message about me finding inner peace and finally being able to move on with my life and heal.

Then it said Jeffrey had been found dead in his jail cell by suicide.

At that moment, I felt like I was going mad. Most of all, I felt torn and confused. How could one man cause so much pain? How could one man destroy so much beauty?

Looking back now, I realize Jeffrey Epstein was a calculating human being who groomed his victims to believe and feel things that were not real.

I know one day I'll have to explain all this to my daughter. Perhaps she will hate me. Maybe she'll be disgusted, feel sorry for me, or cry. But she will be very aware that there are monsters everywhere.

Today, I wish I could talk to Jeffrey's other victims. To the girls that I personally dealt with and recruited, I'd say I am truly sorry. There are no words for the amount of guilt I live with day in and day out.

My only goal is to keep moving forward, continue therapy, continue working, continue my education. Most of all, I want to continue being the best mother I can be for my daughter.

I've had to move and start new jobs what feels like a trillion times. But I'm not running anymore. I'm here. And I know that just because Jeffrey is dead doesn't mean things are over.

Still, sometimes I think to myself, who am I? All I have known is pain. If I heal, who will I become?

## ACKNOWLEDGMENTS

NO ATTEMPT TO TELL THE JEFFREY EPSTEIN STORY COULD BE UNDERTAKEN without recognition of the courageous women who have brought forward their personal accounts, all of them painful, whether it be to law enforcement, the courts, or the media.

I also extend gratitude to the lawyers who have valiantly stood by these survivors, some of them since the original Florida case, and continued to fight for justice.

Many months of research, reporting, and writing of this book took place during the coronavirus pandemic. I am extremely grateful to all of those who helped me through this time and persevered in the face of challenges none of us had ever experienced in the effort to complete this assignment.

At Crown, I thank David Drake for believing in this project, along with my editor, Paul Whitlatch, who was a calming voice and wise counselor during many arduous months and helped me stitch the seams of this work. And with Katie Berry's expert line editing, Paul deftly shaped and crafted the manuscript into something I am very proud of.

Others on the Crown team who deserve warm recognition are Gillian Blake, Annsley Rosner, Dyana Messina, Julie Cepler, Gwyneth Stansfield, and Christopher Brand. A special thanks to Loren Noveck and Emily DeHuff for their expert copyediting along with attorney Matthew Martin for his wise counsel.

I am also thankful to my literary agent, Lisa Leshne, for her steadfast support along with her continued friendship. And my appreciation goes out to Lisa's editorial associate, Samantha Morrice, for coming up with the book's title.

This book could not have been written without the tremendous contribution of Samuel M. Katz, a *New York Times* bestselling author and expert on international law enforcement, who helped crystallize my reporting from the very beginning into a cohesive narrative. Sam's steady resolve was a reassuring presence over the long haul—a virtual hand on my shoulder through the tiring months of quarantine. I will always remember the journey this book took us on together.

As I pointed out in the introduction, I am profoundly thankful for both Sharon Churcher's and Philip Messing's reporting contributions. I have known each of them for decades and have always admired their dedication and meticulous work. Phil additionally needs to be mentioned here for his Herculean efforts in bringing Part Six, "Secrets to the Grave," to life through his reporting and writing. I am indebted to him for the outstanding journalism he practiced and the wonderful spirit he brought to this project.

The surprise of reporting this book was working with a group of incredibly talented and whip-smart young researchers—all of them from the Craig Newmark Graduate School of Journalism at the City University of New York. They are Annie Todd, Sarah Gabrielli, Monroe Hammond, and Parker Quinlan. They all tackled their assignments like seasoned pros, and Annie and Sarah helped get me across the finish line in July 2020.

I EXTEND ADDITIONAL THANKS TO journalist Kate Ryan, a sexual violence survivor who passionately focused on the reporting of Epstein's accusers, along with Monroe Hammond.

I am profoundly thankful to my great photo editor, Meghan Benson, who tirelessly brought together many rare images for this book. Meghan was also the calm in my storm and became a supportive friend to me over many long months.

In addition to Meghan, who contributed to my first book, *All the*

*President's Women,* I had the privilege of working again with journalists Whitney Clegg and London-based Lucy Osborne. And a special shout-out to Whitney for hightailing it in her car from Maine to New Hampshire when Ghislaine Maxwell's surprise arrest came down on my deadline.

I am also grateful to Mike Mancuso, who helped again with crucial research, and to Palm Beach journalist Jose Lambiet for his superior reporting and his knowledge of this story dating back to Epstein's earliest days in Florida.

Others who richly deserve my thanks are author Michael Gross, photojournalist Maggie Andresen, journalist Emma Davis, and my longtime friend and Philadelphia writer Jon Caroulis for his support. I am grateful to Sea Gate resident Adam Davis for graciously allowing me, Sarah Gabrielli, and Phil Messing exclusive access to Epstein's childhood home.

On behalf of Phil, I also thank Dr. Michael Baden, Dr. Vernon Geberth, former NYPD chief of detectives Robert Boyce, former Bureau of Prisons warden Robert Hood, and William Mersey, as well as Michael "Miles" Tisdale, Laura Brevetti, Philip Rich, Sheryl Buchholtz, Alan Gasburg, Melody Stern, Bruce Reznick, and especially Bernard Laffer.

As THIS BOOK CAME TO life during the most challenging time of my life, I feel more grateful every day to my late mother and father, Naomi Millstein Levine and Matthew Levine, for always believing in me when I said I wanted to grow up to be a reporter.

# NOTES

## INTRODUCTION  THE SPIDER'S LAIR

1.  One of Epstein's many shell companies, Great St. Jim LLC, owns the larger of the two private islands, while Little St. James is held by a company called Nautilus Inc.; a limited liability company, LSJE LLC, was set up to pay employees on both islands. Tom Metcalf, Tom Maloney, Jonathan Levin, "The Shell Game: Untangling Jeffrey Epstein's Offshore Money Web," *Bloomberg*, July 19, 2019.
2.  Vanessa Grigoriadis, "'I Collect People, I Own People, I Can Damage People': The Curious Sociopathy of Jeffrey Epstein," *Vanity Fair*, August 26, 2019.
3.  Jonathan Levin, Greg Farrell, and Tom Metcalf, "Mystery Surrounds Jeffrey Epstein's Private Island in the Caribbean," *Los Angeles Times*, July 12, 2019.
4.  James Beal and Greg Woodfield, "Paedo's Paradise: Paedophile Jeffrey Epstein Installed a TEN-PERSON Shower for Orgies on his Caribbean Island, Witness Claims," *Sun* (UK), March 1, 2020.
5.  Ali Watkins, "Epstein Abused Girls on Island Until 2018, Suit Says," *New York Times*, January 16, 2020.
6.  Mola Lenghi, "Alleged Epstein Victim Recalls Harrowing Private Island Details: 'He Had Gun Strapped to His Bedpost,'" *CBS This Morning*, January 21, 2020.
7.  Caroline Graham, "Prince Andrew Brazenly 'Groped Girls' on a Balcony on Paedophile Jeffrey Epstein's Paradise Island, Claims Top U.S. Lawyer," *Mail on Sunday*, February 12, 2020. Denise George, attorney general of the U.S. Virgin Islands, said Andrew never sought to shield his activity from Epstein's staff, according to a former employee. Andrew, meanwhile, has vehemently denied Virginia Roberts's claims.
8.  Victoria Bekiempis, "'Depraved Human Being': Jeffrey Epstein Accusers Voice Their Anguish in Court," *Guardian*, August 27, 2019.
9.  Mola Lenghi, "Alleged Epstein Victim Recalls Harrowing Private Island Details: 'He Had Gun Strapped to His Bedpost,'" *CBS This Morning*, January 21, 2020.

10. Holly Aguirre, "'The Girls Were Just So Young': The Horrors of Jeffrey Epstein's Private Island," *Vanity Fair,* July 20, 2019.

11. Ibid.

12. Interview with St. Thomas cabdriver, January 1, 2020. The cabdriver requested anonymity.

13. Steve Eder, "Epstein's Isle, Where Cash Bought Clout," *New York Times,* August 29, 2019.

14. The public documents and reports cite the following victims and the years in which the rapes occurred: Amy McClure (1993), "Katie Johnson" (1994), Jennifer Araoz (2001), Jane Doe 15 (2004), Jane Doe 103 (2004–2005), Jane Doe 17, Teala Davies (2002–2004), "AH" (2003–2004), Mary Doe (2004), Juliette Bryan, Jane Doe (1997), Sarah Ransome (2006–2007), "Seloh" (2007), Anastasia Doe, Victim 8 (2005), Virginia Roberts, Teresa Helm, Jane Doe 3 (1990), Jane Doe 4 (1984), Jane Doe 5 (2003–2004), Jane Doe 1000 (1999), Jane Doe I (1990), Jane Doe II (1985), Jane Doe III (2003), Jane Doe IV, Jane Doe V, Jane Doe VI, Caroline Kauffman, Jane Doe X, Jane Doe XI, Anouska De Georgiou (late 1990s), Chauntae Davies (2002), Marijke Chartouni (2000), Nadia Marcinkova.

15. Interview with Adam Davis, at Epstein's boyhood home in Sea Gate, 3742 Maple Ave, Brooklyn, January 28, 2020.

16. Joshua Sokol, "The Thoughts of a Spiderweb," *Quanta* magazine, May 23, 2017.

## PART 1   THE BOY FROM BROOKLYN

1. Steve Eder, "Epstein's Isle, Where Cash Bought Clout," *New York Times,* August 29, 2019.

## 1   WONDER WHEEL

1. www.6sqft.com/from-nycs-first-gated-community-to-woody-guthrie-a -history-of-sea-gate/.

2. Ibid.

3. Ari Feldman, "What We Know About Jeffrey Epstein's Childhood," *Forward,* July 15, 2019.

4. James D. Walsh, "Jeffrey Epstein's Curious Ties to His Brother's Real-Estate Business," *New York* magazine ("Intelligencer"), August 14, 2019.

5. Philip Messing interview with neighbor Bruce Resnick, April 1, 2020.

6. Philip Messing reporting.

7. Kate Briquelet, "Epstein Had His Own Lodge at Interlochen's Prestigious Arts Camp for Kids," *Daily Beast,* August 19, 2019.

8. Philip Messing reporting.

9. Philip Messing interview with Bruce Resnick, April 1, 2020.

10. Philip Messing reporting.

11. Philip Messing reporting; interview with Melody Stern, February 8, 2020.

12. James Patterson, John Connolly, and Tim Malloy, *Filthy Rich: The Billionaire's Sex Scandal—The Shocking True Story of Jeffrey Epstein* (New York: Grand Central, 2016), 78.
13. www.legacy.com/obituaries/name/warren-eisenstein-obituary?pid= 169898022.
14. "Post Exclusive: Never-Before-Seen Jeffrey Epstein Biography Surfaces," *Palm Beach Post,* October 30, 2019.
15. Interview with Steven Hoffenberg, February 24, 2020.
16. "Post Exclusive: Never-Before-Seen Jeffrey Epstein Biography Surfaces," *Palm Beach Post,* October 30, 2019.
17. Philip Messing reporting.

## 2 TO SIR, WITH LOVE

1. Raquel Laneri, No. 13: "The Dalton," *Forbes,* April 29, 2010.
2. www.dalton.org/about/mission-statement/past.
3. www.dalton.org/admissions/welcome-to-admissions.
4. Mike Baker and Amy Julia Harris, "Jeffrey Epstein Taught at Dalton. His Behavior Was Noticed," *New York Times,* July 12, 2019.
5. Ibid.
6. Interview with Karin Williams, February 20, 2020.
7. Linda Robertson and Aaron Brezel, "'Poor, Smart and Desperate to Be Rich': How Epstein Went from Teaching to Wall Street," *Miami Herald,* July 16, 2019.
8. Tom Metcalf, "The Epstein Tapes: Unearthed Recordings from His Private Island," *Bloomberg,* August 14, 2019.
9. "Post Exclusive: Never-Before-Seen Jeffrey Epstein Biography Surfaces," *Palm Beach Post,* October 30, 2019.
10. Interview with Pam Brenner-Newton, February 18, 2020.
11. Interview with Dalton source, March 10, 2020.
12. Linda Robertson and Aaron Brezel, "'Poor, Smart, and Desperate to Be Rich': How Epstein Went from Teaching to Wall Street," *Miami Herald,* July 16, 2019.
13. Interview with second Dalton source, March 3, 2020.
14. Interview with Karin Williams, February 20, 2020.
15. Ibid.
16. Interview with second Dalton source, March 3, 2020.
17. Ibid.
18. Ibid.
19. Interview with Karin Williams, February 20, 2020.
20. Mike Baker and Amy Julia Harris, "Jeffrey Epstein Taught at Dalton. His Behavior Was Noticed," *New York Times,* July 12, 2019.
21. *Jeffrey Epstein v. Bradley J. Edwards et al.* Case No.: 50 2009 CA 040800XXXXMBAG.
22. Philip Messing reporting.
23. Linda Robertson and Aaron Brezel, "'Poor, Smart and Desperate to Be

Rich': How Epstein Went from Teaching to Wall Street," *Miami Herald,* July 16, 2019.

24.    Charlie Gasparino and Lydia Moynihan, "The Woes of Jeffrey Epstein: How He Maintained Wall Street Connections While Downplaying Child Sex Accusations," *Fox Business,* August 10, 2019.

25.    Linda Robertson and Aaron Brezel, "'Poor, Smart and Desperate to Be Rich': How Epstein Went from Teaching to Wall Street," *Miami Herald,* July 16, 2019.

## 3   MONEY NEVER SLEEPS

1.    Charlie Gasparino and Lydia Moynihan, "The Woes of Jeffrey Epstein: How He Maintained Wall Street Connections While Downplaying Child Sex Accusations," *Fox Business,* August 10, 2019.

2.    Interview with Steven Hoffenberg, February 24, 2020.

3.    Interview with Lynne Koeppel, February 27, 2020.

4.    Tom Metcalf, "The Epstein Tapes: Unearthed Recordings from His Private Island," *Bloomberg,* August 14, 2019.

5.    Interview with Steven Hoffenberg, February 24, 2020.

6.    Michael Wilson, "Moe Ginsburg, Inexpensive Fashion Specialist, Is Closing," *New York Times,* September 3, 2002.

7.    Tom Metcalf, "The Epstein Tapes: Unearthed Recordings from His Private Island," *Bloomberg,* August 14, 2019.

8.    Anna North, "Jeffrey Epstein Is Dead. His Story Isn't Over," Vox.com, August 10, 2019.

9.    Landon Thomas, Jr., "Jeffrey Epstein: International Moneyman of Mystery," *New York* magazine, October 28, 2002.

10.    Philip Messing phone interviews with Bernard Laffer, January 2020, February 2020, and March 2020.

11.    Ibid.

12.    Michael E. Tennenbaum and Donna Beech, *Risk: Living on the Edge* (New York: Rosetta Books, 2019), 87.

13.    Interview with Linda Eisenstein, March 16, 2020.

14.    Vicky Ward, "The Talented Mr. Epstein," *Vanity Fair,* March 2003.

15.    James Patterson, John Connolly, and Tim Malloy, *Filthy Rich: The Billionaire's Sex Scandal—The Shocking True Story of Jeffrey Epstein* (New York: Grand Central, 2016), 97.

## 4   THE "COSMO" GUY

1.    Janna Herron and Kevin McCoy, "From Private Island to Private Jet: What Is 'Billionaire' Jeffrey Epstein's Net Worth?" *USA Today,* July 14, 2019.

2.    Michael Quint, "Lessons in Drysdale's Default," *New York Times,* May 20, 1982.

3.    Jesse Kornbluth, "I Was a Friend of Jeffrey Epstein; Here's What I Know," *Salon,* July 9, 2019.

4.  medium.com/@jennyleelavertu/the-women-of-jeffrey-epstein
     -f76ae6801ffa.
5.  James Patterson, John Connolly, and Tim Malloy, *Filthy Rich: The Billionaire's Sex Scandal—The Shocking True Story of Jeffrey Epstein* (New York: Grand Central, 2016), 103–104.
6.  Jan Tuckwood, "Dubin Breast Center: Doctor Turns Her Experience into a Healing Center," *Palm Beach Report,* June 11, 2018.
7.  Interview with Steven Hoffenberg, February 24, 2020.
8.  Interview with Stuart Pivar, April 8, 2020.

## 5  DIRTY DEEDS, DIRTY MONEY

1.  SOUTHERN DISTRICT OF NEW YORK—JANE DOE 1; JANE DOE 2; JANE DOE 3; and JANE DOE 4, Plaintiffs v. DARREN K. IN-DYKE AND RICHARD D. KAHN, in their capacities as co-executors of THE ESTATE OF JEFFREY E. EPSTEIN; and ROES 2-10, Defendants. Case No.: 1:19-cv-07675-GBD.
2.  Ibid.
3.  Interview with Steven Hoffenberg, February 24, 2020.
4.  Ibid.
5.  Ibid.
6.  Jim Zarroli, "Jeffrey Epstein's Former Business Associate: I Want to Assist Victims," NPR, August 14, 2019.
7.  Ibid.
8.  Interview with Steven Hoffenberg, February 24, 2020.
9.  Marc Fisher, "Jeffrey Epstein: The Trail of Ruined Lives, Misery, and Bankruptcy Arch-Swindler and Pedophile Left in His Wake," *Independent,* August 11, 2019.
10. Interview with Steven Hoffenberg, February 24, 2020.
11. Ibid.
12. Marc Fisher, "Jeffrey Epstein: The Trail of Ruined Lives, Misery, and Bankruptcy Arch-Swindler and Pedophile Left in His Wake," *Independent,* August 11, 2019.
13. Interview with Steven Hoffenberg, February 24, 2020.
14. Darrel Hofheinz, "Palm Beach House in the Spotlight in Epstein Case," *Palm Beach Daily News,* July 8, 2019.

## 6  PATRON

1.  Carlye Adler, "Les Wexner Limited Brand," CNN, September 1, 2003.
2.  Stanley Green, "Leslie Wexner Makes a $100 Million Donation to Ohio State University," *Jewish Business News,* July 8, 2013.
3.  Carlye Adler, "Les Wexner Limited Brand," CNN, September 1, 2003.
4.  Stanley Green, "Leslie Wexner Makes a $100 Million Donation to Ohio State University," *Jewish Business News,* July 8, 2013.
5.  Associated Press, "Roy Raymond, 47; Began Victoria's Secret," *New York Times,* September 2, 1993.

6. James Patterson, John Connolly, and Tim Malloy, *Filthy Rich: The Billionaire's Sex Scandal—The Shocking True Story of Jeffrey Epstein* (New York: Grand Central, 2016), 118.

7. Stanley Green, "Leslie Wexner Makes a $100 Million Donation to Ohio State University," *Jewish Business News,* July 8, 2013.

8. Shoshy Ciment, "Inside the Relationship Between Victoria's Secret Head Les Wexner and Convicted Sex Offender Jeffrey Epstein, from 'Close Personal Friends' to Severed Ties," *Business Insider,* August 8, 2019.

9. Interview with Thomas Volscho, March 6, 2020.

10. William D. Cohan, "'He Picks the Wrong Friend, Then There's All Hell to Pay': How Jeffrey Epstein Got His Hooks into Les Wexner," *Vanity Fair,* August 8, 2019.

11. Khadeeja Safdar, Rebecca Davis O'Brien, Gregory Zuckerman, Jenny Strasburg, "Jeffrey Epstein Burrowed Into the Lives of the Rich and Made a Fortune," *Wall Street Journal,* July 25, 2019.

## PART 2  HIGH SOCIETY

1. Jeffrey Mervis, "What Kind of Researcher Did Sex Offender Jeffrey Epstein Like to Fund? He Told *Science* Before He Died," Sciencemag .org, September 19, 2019.

## 7  DADDY'S LITTLE GIRL

1. Caroline Davies, "The Murky Life and Death of Robert Maxwell—and How It Shaped His Daughter Ghislaine," *Guardian,* August 22, 2019.

2. espionagehistoryarchive.com/2019/12/20/robert-maxwell-the-kgb/.

3. www.youtube.com/watch?v=1FVocA9ggT4.

4. Craig R. Whitney, "Robert Maxwell, 68: From Refugee to the Ruthless Builder of a Publishing Empire," *New York Times,* November 6, 1991.

5. www.youtube.com/watch?v=1FVocA9ggT4.

6. Robert Rockaway, "Gangsters for Zion," *Tablet* magazine, April 19, 2018.

7. espionagehistoryarchive.com/2019/12/20/robert-maxwell-the-kgb/.

8. Dennis Barker and Christopher Sylvester, "Robert Maxwell Obituary," *Guardian,* November 6, 1991.

9. Interview with Sharon Churcher, March 18, 2020.

10. www.youtube.com/watch?v=1FVocA9ggT4.

11. Ibid.

12. Peter Fearon, "How Ghislaine Rose from the Ashes—Maxwell's Heirs Building a New Business Empire," *New York Post,* March 23, 2000.

13. Sarah Cartledge, Ghislaine Maxwell exclusive interview, *Hello!* magazine, February 23, 1997.

14. Elisabeth Maxwell, *A Mind of My Own: My Life With Robert Maxwell* (New York: Harper Collins, 1994).

15. Interview with source, April 12, 2020.

16. Eric Lutz, "Just How Much Does Ghislaine Maxwell Know?," *Evening Standard*, August 28, 2019.
17. Ibid.
18. Peter Fearon, "How Ghislaine Rose from the Ashes—Maxwell's Heirs Building a New Business Empire," *New York Post*, March 23, 2000.
19. Emma Parry and Grant Hodgson, "Men Love Her: 'Sex Obsessed' Alleged Jeffrey Epstein Madam Ghislaine Maxwell 'Has Found Herself New Boyfriend,' Former Pal Reveals," *Sun* (UK), December 3, 2019.
20. Interview with source, March 11, 2020, regarding Maxwell wanting to sell branded condoms; Maxwell quote: Sarah Cartledge, Ghislaine Maxwell exclusive interview, *Hello!* magazine, February 23, 1997.
21. EIR News Service, September 17, 2004.
22. Michael Robotham, "Revealed: The Unlikely Romance Between a Business Spy and the Crooked Financier's Favourite Daughter," *Mail on Sunday*, November 5, 1992.
23. Noah Kirsch, "Long Before Ghislaine Maxwell Disappeared, Her Mogul Father Died Mysteriously," *Forbes*, February 28, 2020.
24. Mick Brown and Harriet Alexander, "How Ghislaine Maxwell Went from Daddy's Girl to Epstein's Right-Hand Woman," *The Telegraph* (UK), December 13, 2019. John F. Kennedy, Jr., died in a plane crash in 1999. Ghislaine Maxwell's first love, Count Gianfranco Cicogna, also lost his life in a plane crash, in 2012.
25. Interview with confidential source, April 15, 2020.
26. Craig R. Whitney, "Robert Maxwell, 68: From Refugee to the Ruthless Builder of a Publishing Empire," *New York Times*, November 6, 1991.
27. Robert Verkaik, "The Mystery of Maxwell's Death," *Independent*, March 10, 2006.
28. Sarah Cartledge, Ghislaine Maxwell exclusive interview, *Hello!* magazine, February 23, 1997.
29. Peter Fearon, "How Ghislaine Rose from the Ashes—Maxwell's Heirs Building a New Business Empire," *New York Post*, March 23, 2000.
30. Tom Bower, "Ghislaine Maxwell, Daughter of Robert Maxwell, Fell Under the Spell of Rich and Domineering Men," *Times* (UK), August 12, 2019.
31. Jackson Diehl and Glenn Frankel, "Israel Gives Maxwell Farewell Fit for Hero," *Washington Post*, November 11, 1991.
32. Glenn Frankel, "Media Baron Sues Seymour Hersh," *Washington Post*, October 25, 1991.
33. Eric Lutz, "Just How Much Does Ghislaine Maxwell Know?," *Evening Standard*, August 28, 2019.
34. Ian Mohr, "Royal Cousin Christina Oxenberg: Ghislaine Maxwell Threw Semi-Nude Tea Party, Abused Dog," *New York Post*, January 16, 2020.
35. Peter Fearon, "How Ghislaine Rose from the Ashes—Maxwell's Heirs Building a New Business Empire," *New York Post*, March 23, 2000.

## 8 POWER COUPLE

1. Emma Parry and Grant Hodgson, "'Madam' Guilt: Jeffrey Epstein's 'Pimp' Ghislaine Maxwell Says 'Biggest Mistake of Her Life' Was Recruiting Prince Andrew: Sex Accuser," *Sun* (UK), November 29, 2019.
2. Interview with Stuart Pivar, April 8, 2020.
3. Leland Nally, "Jeffrey Epstein, My Very, Very Sick Pal," *Mother Jones*, August 2019.
4. Interview with source, February 27, 2020.
5. Interview with Laura Goldman, January 23, 2020.
6. Interview with source, January 24, 2020.
7. Interview with Nikki Haskell, March 21, 2020.
8. Ben Widdicome, "The Secret History of Jeffrey Epstein's New York Townhouse," *Town & Country*, July 10, 2019.
9. Matthew Haag, "$56 Million Upper East Side Mansion Where Epstein Allegedly Abused Girls," *New York Times*, July 8, 2019.
10. Interview with former NYPD officer, Washington State, April 10, 2020.
11. Vicky Ward, "The Talented Mr. Epstein," *Vanity Fair*, March 2003.
12. Interview with source, March 8, 2020.
13. Interview with source, January 23, 2020.
14. Interview with New York source, January 24, 2020.
15. Interview with source, March 23, 2020.
16. Interview with source, January 23, 2020.
17. Interview with Christina Oxenberg, May 3, 2020.
18. Interview with New York City source, April 12, 2020.

## 9 NO ANGEL

1. www.businessinsider.com/victorias-secret-rise-and-fall-history-2019-5.
2. Sarah Ellison and Jonathan O'Connell, "Epstein Accuser Holds Victoria's Secret Billionaire Responsible, as He Keeps His Distance," *Washington Post*, October 5, 2019.
3. Emma Parry, "'I Was Helpless': Epstein's 'First Victim' Tells of Harrowing Rape and Urges Prince Andrew and Ghislaine Maxwell 'to Give Answers,'" *Sun* (UK), November 26, 2019.
4. Ibid.
5. Lee Brown, "Ex-Model Amy McClure Accuses Jeffrey Epstein of 1993 Rape," *New York Post*, November 27, 2019.
6. Ibid.
7. Kate Briquelet, "Epstein Had His Own Lodge at Interlochen's Prestigious Arts Camp for Kids," *Daily Beast*, August 19, 2019.
8. Ibid.
9. U.S. District Court, Southern District of New York, Case No. 1:20-cv-00484.
10. Ibid.

## 10 THE PALM BEACH NEIGHBOR

1. Philip Bump, "Donald Trump's Father Was Arrested at Ku Klux Klan Riot in New York in 1927, Records Reveal," *Independent*, August 14, 2017.
2. Vivian Wang, "Why the Trump White House Is Caught Up in the Jeffrey Epstein Scandal," *New York Times*, July 7, 2019.
3. Maggie Haberman and Annie Karni, "Trump and Epstein Partied and Commented on Women in 1992 Video," *New York Times*, July 17, 2019.
4. Barry Levine and Monique El-Faizy, *All the President's Women: Donald Trump and the Making of a Predator* (New York: Hachette Books, 2019), 261.
5. Annie Karni and Maggie Haberman, "Jeffrey Epstein Was a 'Terrific Guy,' Donald Trump Once Said. Now He's 'Not a Fan,'" *New York Times*, July 9, 2019.
6. Barry Levine and Monique El-Faizy, *All the President's Women: Donald Trump and the Making of a Predator* (New York: Hachette Books, 2019), 63–65.
7. Jon Swain, "Rape Lawsuits against Donald Trump Linked to Former TV Producer," *Guardian*, July 7, 2016.
8. Interview with Heather Braden, March 15, 2019.
9. David A. Fahrenthold, Beth Reinhard, and Kimberly Kindy, "Trump Called Epstein a 'Terrific Guy' Who Enjoyed 'Younger' Women Before Denying Relationship with Him," *Washington Post*, July 8, 2019.
10. Nicole Einbinder, "Jeffrey Epstein Had 14 Phone Numbers Connected to Trump in His Contacts," *MSN Insider*, July 10, 2019.
11. Kate Briquelet, "The Craziest Bits from New Epstein Book: Jacko, Trump, Prince Andrew, and the CIA," *Daily Beast*, March 31, 2020.

## 11 ALARM BELLS

1. "The First Women to Report Jeffrey Epstein," *New York Times*, August 26, 2019.
2. Ben Widdicome, "The Secret History of Jeffrey Epstein's New York Townhouse," *Town & Country*, July 10, 2019.
3. Mike Baker, "The Sisters Who First Tried to Take Down Jeffrey Epstein," *New York Times*, August 26, 2019.
4. www.scribd.com/podcast/447750589/The-First-Women-to-Report-Jeffrey-Epstein#.
5. Mike Baker, "The Sisters Who First Tried to Take Down Jeffrey Epstein," *New York Times*, August 26, 2019.
6. Mola Lenghi, "What's Next for Epstein's Zorro Ranch, Where Accusers Say They Were Raped and Trafficked," CBS News, August 31, 2019.
7. Milan Simonich, "Tax Records Show Jeffrey Epstein's Power, Influence," *Santa Fe New Mexican*, April 25, 2020.
8. Steve Terrell, "Epstein's Tracks in NM Remain Murky," *Santa Fe New Mexican*, July 14, 2019.

9.  Mike Baker, "The Sisters Who First Tried to Take Down Jeffrey Epstein," *New York Times,* August 26, 2019.

10. Sarah Ellison and Jonathan O'Connell, "Epstein Accuser Holds Victoria's Secret Billionaire Responsible, as He Keeps His Distance," *Washington Post,* October 5, 2019.

11. "Jeffrey Epstein Accuser Maria Farmer Says Ghislaine Maxwell Threatened Her Life, FBI 'Failed' Her," CBS News, November 19, 2019.

12. Sarah Ellison and Jonathan O'Connell, "Epstein Accuser Holds Victoria's Secret Billionaire Responsible, as He Keeps His Distance," *Washington Post,* October 5, 2019.

13. Ibid.

14. Ibid.

15. Sharon Churcher, "No Angel—Is Jeffrey Epstein's Unholy Alliance with the Victoria's Secret Boss the REAL Reason the Show Was Scrapped?," *Sun* (UK), November 28, 2019.

16. Mike Baker, "The Sisters Who First Tried to Take Down Jeffrey Epstein," *New York Times,* August 26, 2019.

17. Sarah Ellison and Jonathan O'Connell, "Epstein Accuser Holds Victoria's Secret Billionaire Responsible, as He Keeps His Distance," *Washington Post,* October 5, 2019.

18. Claire Selvin, "Jeffrey Epstein's Art World Connections: A Guide," *ARTnews,* August 27, 2019.

19. Leland Nally, "Jeffrey Epstein, My Very, Very Sick Pal," *Mother Jones,* August 2019.

20. Ibid.

21. www.youtube.com/watch?v=6CFFfwruCQE.

22. Whitney Clegg interview with Alicia Arden, March 26, 2020.

23. Ibid.

24. Section 46—Type of Weapon, instrument or force; Santa Monica Police Department Crime Report, dated as (Date & Time Crime Occurred) 05-12-97, 1530–1700.

25. Whitney Clegg interview with Alicia Arden, March 26, 2020.

26. Katie Campione and Jennifer Peltz, "Early Epstein Accuser: Police Could Have Stopped Him in 1997," AP News, August 19, 2019.

27. Whitney Clegg interview with Alicia Arden, March 26, 2020.

28. Ibid.

29. Katie Campione and Jennifer Peltz, "Early Epstein Accuser: Police Could Have Stopped Him in 1997," AP News, August 19, 2019.

30. Sarah Ellison and Jonathan O'Connell, "Epstein Accuser Holds Victoria's Secret Billionaire Responsible, as He Keeps His Distance," *Washington Post,* October 5, 2019.

31. Emily Steel, Steve Eder, Sapna Maheshwari, and Matthew Goldstein, "How Jeffrey Epstein Used the Billionaire Behind Victoria's Secret for Wealth and Women," *New York Times,* July 25, 2019.

32. Interview with Christina Oxenberg, May 3, 2020.

33. Libertina Brandt, "Jeffrey Epstein's Estate Was Just Sued in the U.S. Virgin Islands by His Former Girlfriend, Ghislaine Maxwell. Here's an Inside Look at His 2 Private Islands There," *Business Insider*, March 19, 2020.

## 12   THE RUNAWAY

1. Manuel Roig-Franzia, "Trump Made Florida His Official Residence. He May Have Also Made a Legal Mess," *Washington Post*, May 7, 2020.
2. Sarah Fitzpatrick, Anna Schecter, Chelsea Damberg, and Rich Schapiro, "How a British Teen Model Was Lured into Jeffrey Epstein's Web," NBC News, September 20, 2019.
3. Staff Report, "Man Admits Smuggling Women for Prostitution," *South Florida Sun-Sentinel*, August 23, 2001.
4. United States District Court Southern District of Florida—Case No. 08-80736-CIV-MARRA.
5. Case 18-2868, Document 278, 08/09/2019, 2628230, cited in Virginia Roberts, "The Billionaire's Playboy Club," unpublished memoir, p. 564 of 648.
6. Interview with Sharon Churcher, April 30, 2020.
7. United States District Court Southern District of Florida—Case No. 08-80736-CIV-MARRA.
8. Lia Eustachewich, "Virginia Roberts Giuffre's Dad Sky Roberts: 'I Know She's Telling the Truth,'" *New York Post*, December 3, 2019.
9. Interview with Sharon Churcher, April 30, 2020.
10. United States District Court Southern District of Florida—Case No. 08-80736-CIV-MARRA.
11. Ibid.
12. Ibid.
13. Sharon Churcher interview with Virginia Giuffre, 2011.
14. Ibid.
15. United States District Court Southern District of Florida—Case No. 08-80736-CIV-MARRA.
16. Emily Michot and Julie K. Brown, "How a Teen Runaway Became One of Jeffrey Epstein's Victims," *Miami Herald*, November 26, 2018.
17. Interview with Sharon Churcher, April 30, 2020.
18. Ibid.
19. Ibid.
20. United States District Court Southern District of Florida—Case No. 08-80736-CIV-MARRA.

## 13   24-KARAT PRISON

1. Interview with Sharon Churcher, April 30, 2020.
2. Connie Bruck, "Alan Dershowitz, Devil's Advocate," *New Yorker*, August 5 and 12, 2019.

3.　United States District Court Southern District of Florida—Case No. 08-80736-CIV-MARRA.

4.　Case 18-2868, Document 278, 08/09/2019, 2628230, cited in Virginia Roberts, "The Billionaire's Playboy Club," unpublished memoir, p. 564 of 648.

5.　United States District Court Southern District of Florida—Case No. 08-80736-CIV-MARRA.

6.　*Giuffre v. Dershowitz* (1:19-cv-03377) District Court, S.D. New York, July 29, 2020.

7.　Ben Ashford, "Celebrity Attorney Alan Dershowitz Loses Legal Bid to Gain Access to Bombshell Confidential Papers Naming Late Pedophile Jeffrey Epstein's Closest Associates," *Daily Mail,* July 2, 2020.

8.　Stephen Rex Brown, "Jeffrey Epstein Accuser Sues Alan Dershowitz as New Sex Trafficking Victim Reveals Herself," New York *Daily News,* April 16, 2019.

9.　Andrew Rice, "Alan Dershowitz Cannot Stop Talking," *New York* magazine, July 19, 2019.

10.　Vivian Wang, "They Were Sexually Abused Long Ago as Children. Now They Can Sue in N.Y.," *New York Times,* January 28, 2019.

11.　Connie Bruck, "Alan Dershowitz, Devil's Advocate," *New Yorker,* August 5 and 12, 2019.

12.　Interview with Sharon Churcher, April 30, 2020.

13.　Ibid.

14.　Ellen Cranely, "Ex-Model Says Jean-Luc Brunel, Model Agent and Jeffrey Epstein's Friend, Spiked Her Drink and Raped Her," *Business Insider,* October 20, 2019.

15.　Julie Brown, "Even from Jail, Sex Abuser Manipulated the System," *Miami Herald,* December 4, 2018.

16.　Jean-Luc Brunel interview with Michael Gross, copyright 1995 by Michael Gross for Idee Fixe Ltd. All rights reserved. Gross published *Model: The Ugly Business of Beautiful Women* (New York: William Morrow, 1995). He was interviewed by Barry Levine in New York City, March 5, 2020. Gross said Epstein at one point was interested in acquiring the Elite modeling agency. "I had a source who told me Epstein was one of the underbidders for Elite and this was one year before MC2. I didn't know who Epstein was at the time. Just some dude with money."

17.　Interview with Sharon Churcher, April 30, 2020.

18.　Jean-Luc Brunel interview with Michael Gross, copyright 1995 by Michael Gross for Idee Fixe Ltd. All rights reserved.

19.　Amanda Arnold, "What We Know About Jean-Luc Brunel, One of the Men Closest to Epstein," *New York* magazine ("The Cut"), September 26, 2019.

20.　J. K. Trotter, "Flight Data from Jeffrey Epstein's Private Jets Show a Lavish Travel Schedule as the Walls Closed In," *Insider,* July 12, 2019.

21.　Amanda Arnold, "What We Know About Jean-Luc Brunel, One of the

Men Closest to Epstein," *New York* magazine ("The Cut"), September 26, 2019.

22. Linda Robertson, Julie K. Brown, and Nicholas Nehemas, "Did a Miami-Based Modeling Agency Fuel Jeffrey Epstein's 'Machine of Abuse'?," *Miami Herald,* December 26, 2019.

23. United States District Court Southern District of Florida—Case No. 08-80736-CIV-MARRA.

24. Ibid.

25. Andrew Whalen, "What Is the Lolita Express? Epstein's Infamous Sex Plane Included VIPs like Bill Clinton," *Newsweek,* July 9, 2019.

26. Marie Lodi, "What We Know About Jeffrey Epstein's Private Jet, the 'Lolita Express,'" *New York* magazine ("The Cut"), July 9, 2019.

27. Sharon Churcher, "Andrew and the 17-Year-Old at Centre of Under-Age Sex Case That Has Scandalized America," *Mail on Sunday*, February 27, 2011.

28. United States District Court Southern District of Florida—Case No. 08-80736-CIV-MARRA.

## 14   THE "NEGATIVE CHARISMA" PRINCE

1. Jason Rodrigues, "1979: Lord Mountbatten Killed by IRA Bomb," *Guardian,* May 19, 2015; John Bingham, "Margaret Thatcher: Seconds from Death at the Hands of an IRA Bomber," *Telegraph,* April 8, 2013.

2. Interview with London source, March 3, 2020.

3. Ibid.

4. Zoe Williams, "The Party Prince: How Andrew Got His Bad Reputation," *Guardian,* November 18, 2019.

5. Interview with Sharon Churcher, April 30, 2020.

6. Sharon Churcher, "Prince Andrew and the 17-Year-Old Girl His Sex Offender Friend Flew to Britain to Meet Him," *Daily Mail,* March 2, 2011.

7. Interview with Sharon Churcher, April 30, 2020.

8. https://cd6d9e9a-fe32-4a06-a5b3-75550ffdabc1.filesusr.com/ugd/7a1419_45212967a73d441cac313fdf6f4251eb.pdf.

9. Interview with Sharon Churcher, April 30, 2020.

10. United States District Court Southern District of Florida—Case No. 08-80736-CIV-MARRA.

11. Interview with Sharon Churcher, April 30, 2020.

12. Ibid.

13. Lee Brown, "Former Royal Cop Challenges Prince Andrew's Alibi in Virginia Roberts Giuffre Sex Scandal," *New York Post,* February 23, 2020.

14. United States District Court Southern District of Florida—Case No. 08-80736-CIV-MARRA.

15. Interview with Sharon Churcher, April 30, 2020.

16. Sebastian Murphy-Bates, "Woman, 39, Who Claims Prince Andrew Groped Her Breast When She Was 21 Is Pictured for the First Time in Ten Years," *Daily Mail,* November 24, 2019.

17. Interview with Sharon Churcher, April 30, 2020.
18. Sharon Churcher, "Andrew and the 17-Year-Old at Centre of Under-Age Sex Case That Has Scandalized America," *Mail on Sunday,* February 27, 2011.
19. Flora Drury, "Pictured: Prince Andrew Surrounded by Topless Women on Thai Holiday with Paedophile Billionaire Epstein as Friend Says Duke 'Has Always Been a T**s and Bums Man,'" *Daily Mail,* January 7, 2015.
20. Interview with Sharon Churcher, April 30, 2020.
21. A former friend of Maxwell and Epstein, who attended parties with the couple and Andrew, agreed to speak for the book on the condition of anonymity.
22. Interview with Sharon Churcher, April 30, 2020.
23. Ibid.
24. Ibid.

## 15　FRIENDS IN HIGH PLACES

1. Jaquelyn M. Scharnick, "Mogul Donor Gives Harvard More than Money," *Harvard Crimson,* May 1, 2003.
2. Vanessa Grigoriadis, "'I Collect People, I Own People, I Can Damage People': The Curious Sociopathy of Jeffrey Epstein," *Vanity Fair,* August 26, 2019.
3. Privileged Pursuant to FS 766.2054(4) and/or Work Product—*Edwards v. Epstein.*
4. Emily Shugerman and Suzi Parker, "Jeffrey Epstein Visited Clinton White House Multiple Times in Early '90s," *Daily Beast,* August 19, 2019.
5. Gabriel Sherman, "Clinton and Ghislaine Became Super Close: As the Epstein Scandal Spirals, a New Focus on Old Names," *Vanity Fair,* July 23, 2019.
6. Privileged Pursuant to FS 766.2054(4) and/or Work Product—*Edwards v. Epstein.*
7. Michael Gold, "Bill Clinton and Jeffrey Epstein: How Are They Connected?," *New York Times,* July 9, 2019.
8. Vanessa Grigoriadis, "'I Collect People, I Own People, I Can Damage People': The Curious Sociopathy of Jeffrey Epstein," *Vanity Fair,* August 26, 2019.
9. Lisa Miller, "Titans of Industry Join Forces to Work for Jewish Philanthropy," *Wall Street Journal,* May 4, 1998.
10. TOI Staff, "Barak Vows to Sue Daily Mail for 'Sordid Insinuations' over His Ties to Epstein," *Times of Israel,* July 17, 2019.

## 16  THE SPIDER

1.  Rosie Perper, "The Mysterious Foreign Passport Found in Jeffrey Epstein's Mansion Was Used to Enter at Least 4 Countries in the 1980s, Prosecutors Say," *Business Insider,* July 18, 2019.
2.  Vanessa Grigoriadis, "'I Collect People, I Own People, I Can Damage People': The Curious Sociopathy of Jeffrey Epstein," *Vanity Fair,* August 26, 2019.
3.  Hannah Skellern, "Price Andrew Accuser Virginia Roberts Says Every Single Room of Jeffrey Epstein's $77 Million Mansion Had Cameras and Questions Why the FBI Still Hasn't Made Any Arrests," *Daily Mail,* February 22, 2020.
4.  Ibid.
5.  Ibid.
6.  "Jeffrey Epstein Accuser Maria Farmer Says Ghislaine Maxwell Threatened Her Life, FBI 'Failed' Her," CBS News, November 19, 2019.
7.  Phone interview with Spencer Kuvin, April 16, 2020.
8.  Kate Sheehy, "Jeffrey Epstein Accuser: I Was 14 Years Old and Still in Braces When Abuse Began," *New York Post,* July 8, 2019.
9.  Luke Kenton, "'We Weren't Prostitutes or Whores—We Were Children': Three Jeffrey Epstein Victims Open Up About Coming to Terms with the Horrific Abuse They Endured at His Palm Beach Mansion After 'Blaming Themselves for Years,'" *Daily Mail,* January 8, 2020.
10. Julie K. Brown, "How a Future Trump Cabinet Member Gave a Serial Sex Abuser the Deal of a Lifetime," *Miami Herald,* November 28, 2018.
11. Sharon Churcher and Privileged Pursuant to FS 766.2054(4) and/or Work Product—*Edwards v. Epstein.*
12. Ibid.
13. Kate Sheehy, "Jeffrey Epstein Accuser: I Was 14 Years Old and Still in Braces When Abuse Began," *New York Post,* July 8, 2019.

## 17  BURN EVERYTHING

1.  Vanessa Grigoriadis, "'I Collect People, I Own People, I Can Damage People': The Curious Sociopathy of Jeffrey Epstein," *Vanity Fair,* August 26, 2019.
2.  Vicky Ward, "The Talented Mr. Epstein," *Vanity Fair,* March 2003.
3.  Ibid.
4.  David Folkenflik, "A Dead Cat, A Lawyer's Call and 5-Figure Donation: How Media Fell Short on Epstein," NPR, August 22, 2019.
5.  Marc Tracy, "Ex-Vanity Fair Writer Says Editor Stopped Her from Exposing Epstein in '03," *New York Times,* July 9, 2019.
6.  *Jane Doe 15 v. Indyke and Kahn,* 11-19-19.

## 18  WEIRD SCIENCE

1.  Phone interview with Charles Denson, February 19, 2020.
2.  James B. Stewart, Matthew Goldstein, and Jessica Silver-Greenberg,

"Jeffrey Epstein Hoped to Seed Human Race with His DNA," *New York Times,* July 31, 2019.

3.  Chris White, "Exclusive: Inside Jeffrey Epstein's New Mexico Ranch: Jaw-Dropping Pictures Show Pedophile's Eight-Person Party Shower, Life-Sized Installation of a Crucified Jesus, and Underground Strip Club Where Teens Would Entertain VIP Guests," *Daily Mail,* November 20, 2019.
4.  TOI Staff, "Report: Epstein Wanted to Spread His DNA by Impregnating 20 Women at His Ranch," *Times of Israel,* August 1, 2019.
5.  James B. Stewart, Matthew Goldstein, and Jessica Silver-Greenberg, "Jeffrey Epstein Hoped to Seed Human Race with His DNA," *New York Times,* July 31, 2019.
6.  ped.fas.harvard.edu/.
7.  James B. Stewart, Matthew Goldstein, and Jessica Silver-Greenberg, "Jeffrey Epstein Hoped to Seed Human Race with His DNA," *New York Times,* July 31, 2019.
8.  Ibid.
9.  E. J. Dickson, "Why Some Men Are Obsessed with Inseminating as Many Women as Possible," *Rolling Stone,* August 23, 2019.
10.  Roddy Boyd, "Epstein's Subprime Exposure," *New York Post,* July 17, 2007.
11.  Interview with Stephen Davis, February 20, 2020.

## 19   ROYAL PALM HIGH

1.  Philip Weiss, "The Fantasist," *New York* magazine, December 7, 2007.
2.  Darrell Hoffheinz, "Palm Beach House in the Spotlight in Epstein Case," *Palm Beach Daily News,* July 18, 2019.
3.  Ibid.
4.  Holly Baltz, "VIDEO: Inside Jeffrey Epstein's Palm Beach Mansion: Take the Full Tour," *Palm Beach Post,* December 7, 2019.
5.  Yaron Steinbuch, "Video From 2005 Raid on Jeffrey Epstein's Estate Shows Images of Underage Girls," *New York Post,* August 28, 2019.
6.  Madison Feller, "How Exactly Is Alleged Sex Trafficker Jeffrey Epstein Connected to President Trump?," *Elle,* May 27, 2020.
7.  www.usnews.com/education/best-high-schools/florida/districts/palm -beach/royal-palm-beach-high-school-5400.
8.  Interview with Chief Michael Reiter in *Jeffrey Epstein: Filthy Rich* (Netflix original documentary TV series, May 2020), directed by Lisa Bryant, based on the James Patterson book *Filthy Rich* (q.v.).
9.  James Patterson, "The Paedophile Next Door: Author JAMES PATTERSON Was Fascinated and Appalled by Jeffrey Epstein. His True-Life Probe into the Behaviour of His Billionaire Florida Neighbour May Be His Most Chilling Thriller," *Daily Mail,* August 16, 2019.
10.  "Jeffrey Epstein: How the Case Unfolded in Palm Beach County," *Palm Beach Post,* November 13, 2019.

11. Paul Lewis and Jon Swaine, "Jeffrey Epstein: Inside the Decade of Scandal Entangling Prince Andrew," *Guardian*, January 10, 2015.
12. James Patterson, "The Paedophile Next Door: Author JAMES PATTERSON Was Fascinated and Appalled by Jeffrey Epstein. His True-Life Probe into the Behaviour of His Billionaire Florida Neighbour May Be His Most Chilling Thriller," *Daily Mail*, August 16, 2019.
13. Ian Cohen, "Decorated Former Palm Beach Detective Who Led Epstein Investigation Dies at 50," *Palm Beach Daily News*, June 1, 2018.
14. Probable Cause Affidavit: Palm Beach Police Department, Case #05-368(1)—May 1, 2006.
15. Ibid.
16. Ibid.
17. medium.com/@the_war_economy/investigation-jeffrey-epstein -d2ad68e2e845.
18. Philip Weiss, "The Fantasist," *New York* magazine, December 7, 2007.
19. Madeleine Aggeler, "What We Know About Sarah Kellen, Who Allegedly 'Recruited' Girls for Jeffrey Epstein," *New York* magazine ("The Cut"), August 29, 2019.
20. Ibid.
21. Philip Weiss, "The Fantasist," *New York* magazine, December 7, 2007.
22. Larry Keller, "After Long Probe, Palm Beach Billionaire Faces Solicitation Charges," *Palm Beach Post*, July 27, 2006.
23. Probable Cause Affidavit: Palm Beach Police Department, Case #05-368(1)—May 1, 2006.
24. Ibid.
25. Paul Lewis and John Swaine, "Jeffrey Epstein: Inside the Decade of Scandal Entangling Prince Andrew," *Guardian*, January 10, 2015.
26. Witness Juan P. Alessi Examination by Detective Recarey, J. Consor and Associates Reporting and Transcription 561.835.9738.
27. Probable Cause Affidavit: Palm Beach Police Department, Case #05-368(1)—May 1, 2006.
28. Chris Spargo, "'He Bragged She Was His Sex Slave': Jeffrey Epstein 'Purchased Nadia Marcinkova as a Girl from Her Family, Shot Child Porn of Her with Underage Teen and Forced Her into Threesomes,'" *Daily Mail*, July 28, 2019.
29. www.planeandpilotmag.com/article/learning-to-fly-all-about-priorities/ ?start=6.
30. Palm Beach Police Department Incident Report, 07/19/2016.
31. medium.com/@the_war_economy/investigation-jeffrey-epstein -d2ad68e2e845.
32. Ken Bensinger, "Plenty of Innuendo, But No Hard Evidence of New Clinton Sex Scandal," *BuzzFeed News*, January 28, 2015.
33. Jane Musgrave, John Pacenti, and Lulu Ramadan, "Jeffrey Epstein: To the First Prosecutors, Teen Victims Were Prostitutes," *Palm Beach Post*, November 15, 2019.

## 20   FLORIDA JUSTICE

1. Susan Spencer-Wendel, "A Decade After Lake Worth Middle School Shooting: Nathaniel Brazill Regretful, Ambitious," *Palm Beach Post,* May 23, 2010.
2. www.wpbf.com/download/2009/0716/20080264.pdf.
3. Philip Weiss, "The Fantasist," *New York* magazine, December 7, 2007.
4. Interview in *Jeffrey Epstein: Filthy Rich* (Netflix documentary), 2020.
5. keepitsimplenews.com/why-did-jeffrey-epstein-get-such-a-lenient-sentence/#cmf_footnote_25.
6. Philip Weiss, "The Fantasist," *New York* magazine, December 7, 2007.
7. Connie Bruck, "Alan Dershowitz, Devil's Advocate," *New Yorker,* August 5 and 12, 2019.
8. Ibid.
9. Larry Keller, "Palm Beach Chief Focus of Fire in Epstein Case," *Palm Beach Post,* August 14, 2006.
10. Philip Weiss, "The Fantasist," *New York* magazine, December 7, 2007.
11. Michele Dargan, "Ex-Chief Details Hurdles in Epstein Probe," *Palm Beach Daily News,* December 13, 2009.
12. Interview with Jose Lambiet, April 19, 2020.
13. Ibid.
14. Jane Musgrave, John Pacenti, and Lulu Ramadan, "Jeffrey Epstein: To the First Prosecutors, Teen Victims Were Prostitutes," *Palm Beach Post,* November 15, 2019.
15. Ibid.
16. *Jeffrey Epstein: Filthy Rich* (Netflix documentary), 2020.
17. Connie Bruck, "Alan Dershowitz, Devil's Advocate," *New Yorker,* August 5 and 12, 2019.
18. Larry Keller, "Palm Beach Chief Focus of Fire in Epstein Case," *Palm Beach Post,* August 14, 2006.
19. Interview with Chief Michael Reiter in *Jeffrey Epstein: Filthy Rich* (Netflix documentary), 2020.
20. Interview with Sarah Ransome in *Jeffrey Epstein: Filthy Rich* (Netflix documentary), 2020.
21. Chris Dyer, "Jeffrey Epstein Victim Sarah Ransome Describes Her Desperate Bid to Escape His Notorious 'Pedophile Island' by Swimming Through Shark-Infested Waters After Being 'Raped Three Times' the Same Day," *Daily Mail Online,* September 16, 2019.
22. Interview with Sarah Ransome in *Jeffrey Epstein: Filthy Rich* (Netflix documentary), 2020.
23. Chris Dyer, "Jeffrey Epstein Victim Sarah Ransome Describes Her Desperate Bid to Escape His Notorious 'Pedophile Island' by Swimming Through Shark-Infested Waters After Being 'Raped Three Times' the Same Day," *Daily Mail Online,* September 16, 2019.

### 21 OPERATION LEAP YEAR

1. Interview with New York City source, June 9, 2020.
2. Frank Cerabino, "Cerabino: Epstein Case First Went Wrong Right Here," *Palm Beach Post,* December 8, 2018.
3. Interview with Spencer Kuvin, April 20, 2020.
4. Jose Lambiet, "Lewinsky Prosecutor Joins Defense of Clinton Crony," *Palm Beach Post,* September 12, 2007.
5. Interview with Spencer Kuvin, April 16, 2020.
6. Ibid.
7. Ibid.
8. Jane Musgrave, "Jeffrey Epstein Victim Goes Public: I Want to Know Why," *Palm Beach Post,* January 31, 2020.
9. Ibid.
10. Philip Weiss, "The Fantasist," *New York* magazine, December 7, 2007.
11. Larry Keller, "Palm Beach Chief Focus of Fire in Epstein Case," *Palm Beach Post,* August 14, 2006.
12. Stephen Wright, "Did Legal Deal Protect the Duke? Paedophile Billionaire's Plea Bargain Halted Police Investigation," *Daily Mail,* January 4, 2015.

### 22 ACOSTA: THE INSIDE MAN

1. Case of *Jeffrey Epstein v. Scott Rothstein, Bradley J. Edwards, and L.M.* in the Circuit Court of the Fifteenth Judicial Circuit in and for Palm Beach County, Florida, Case No. 502009CA040800XXXXMBAG.
2. Connie Bruck, "Alan Dershowitz, Devil's Advocate," *New Yorker,* August 5 and 12, 2019.
3. John Cassidy, "Alex Acosta Had to Go, but the Jeffrey Epstein Scandal Is Really About Money and Privilege," *New Yorker,* July 12, 2019.
4. Interview with Ann Marie Villafaña in *Jeffrey Epstein: Filthy Rich* (Netflix documentary), 2020.
5. Composite Exhibit A: Non-Prosecution Agreement and Addendum, Case 1:10-cv-21588-ASG.
6. Interview with attorney Jack Scarola in *Jeffrey Epstein: Filthy Rich* (Netflix documentary), 2020.
7. The document provided earlier was obtained by the Palm Beach newspaper.
8. Landon Thomas, Jr., "Financier Starts Sentence in Prostitution Case," *New York Times,* July 1, 2008.
9. Helaine Olen, "What Jeffrey Epstein's Crimes Say About Our Era," *Washington Post,* July 11, 2019.
10. Landon Thomas, Jr., "Financier Starts Sentence in Prostitution Case," *New York Times,* July 1, 2008.
11. "Palm Beacher Pleads in Sex Case," *Palm Beach Post,* July 1, 2008.
12. *Jeffrey Epstein: Filthy Rich* (Netflix documentary), 2020.
13. Charles Doyle, "Crime Victims' Rights Act: A Summary and Legal

Analysis of 18 U.S.C. §3771," Congressional Research Service, December 9, 2015.

14.    Matt Zopotosky, Devlin Barrett, Kimberly Kindy, and Renae Merle, "Acosta Said Prosecutors Wanted to Guarantee Jeffrey Epstein Would Go to Jail. The Reality Is More Complicated," *Washington Post*, July 11, 2019.

15.    Nicole Goodkind, "'No Regrets Is a Very Hard Question': Alex Acosta Defends Jeffrey Epstein Plea Deal," *Newsweek*, July 10, 2019.

16.    Interview with Alan Dershowitz in *Jeffrey Epstein: Filthy Rich* (Netflix documentary), 2020.

17.    keepitsimplenews.com/why-did-jeffrey-epstein-get-such-a-lenient -sentence/#cmf_footnote_20 and vault.fbi.gov/jeffrey-epstein.

## 23   ROCK STAR

1.    Interview with Michael Gauger in *Jeffrey Epstein: Filthy Rich* (Netflix documentary), 2020.

2.    Christine Stapleton, "Jeffrey Epstein: Jail Records Show Sex Offender Got Special Treatment," *Palm Beach Post*, July 21, 2019.

3.    Interview with Jane Musgrave in *Jeffrey Epstein: Filthy Rich* (Netflix documentary), 2020.

4.    Christine Stapleton, "Jeffrey Epstein: Jail Records Show Sex Offender Got Special Treatment," *Palm Beach Post*, July 21, 2019.

5.    Ali Watkins, "Jeffrey Epstein's New York Hunting Ground: Dance Studios," *New York Times*, September 3, 2019.

6.    Ibid.

7.    Terri Parker, "Lawsuit: Epstein Also Had Work-Release Sex While in Palm Beach Mansion," WPBF 25 News, August 21, 2019.

8.    Joe Capozzi, "Jeffrey Epstein: PBSO Open Probe of Deputies Who Watched Sex Offender," *Palm Beach Post*, July 19, 2019.

9.    *Jeffrey Epstein: Filthy Rich* (Netflix documentary), 2020.

## PART 5   JUSTICE DELAYED

1.    Connie Bruck, "Alan Dershowitz, Devil's Advocate," *New Yorker*, August 5 and 12, 2019.

## 24   SYMPATHY FOR THE DEVIL

1.    Jacob Bernstein, "Whatever Happened to Ghislaine Maxwell's Plan to Save the Oceans?" *New York Times*, August 14, 2019.

2.    Michele Dargan, "Jeffrey Epstein House Arrest Missteps Not Deemed Uncompliant," *Palm Beach Daily News*, April 1, 2012.

3.    Jane Musgrave, "Billionaire Sex Offender Jeffrey Epstein's Year-Long Probation to End Next Week," *Palm Beach Post*, July 11, 2010.

4.    Ibid.

5.    Michele Dargan, "Jeffrey Epstein House Arrest Missteps Not Deemed Uncompliant," *Palm Beach Daily News*, April 1, 2012.

6. Mike Baker, "Sheriff to Investigate Jeffrey Epstein 'Work Release' After Allegation of Nude Meeting," *New York Times,* July 19, 2019.
7. *Jeffrey Epstein: Filthy Rich* (Netflix documentary), 2020.
8. Lousie Boyle, "Exclusive: How Jeffrey Epstein Pulled Strings for His 20-Something 'Lady Friend' to Intern for Hollywood's Queen of Publicity—Ultimately Leading to Her Downfall from Grace because of Ties to the Dead Pedophile," *Daily Mail,* February 7, 2020.
9. Emily Flitter and James B. Stewart, "Gates Met with Epstein Many Times, Despite His Criminal Past," *New York Times,* October 13, 2019.
10. Amie Tsang, "Barclays Chief Faces Inquiry in the U.K. over His Ties to Epstein," *New York Times Business,* February 14, 2020.
11. Alana Goodman and Daniel Harper, "New Book Claims Bill Clinton Had an Affair with Ghislaine Maxwell," *New York Post,* May 27, 2020; Conchita Sarnoff, *TrafficKing: The Jeffrey Epstein Story* (New York: Simon and Schuster, 2015).
12. George Rush, "Billionaire Jeffrey Epstein Shells Out More Money in Latest Sex Abuse Lawsuit," New York *Daily News,* December 19, 2009.
13. Joe Pompeo, "'He Was Living in Peace, Like Dr. Mengele in Paraguay': Manhattan Media Remembers Jeffrey Epstein, the Monster Hiding in Plain Sight," *Vanity Fair,* July 10, 2019.
14. Interview with George Rush, April 12, 2020.
15. Ibid.
16. Alex Williams, "Peggy Siegal, Best Hostess in a Supporting Role," *New York Times,* February 13, 2016.
17. Philip Weiss, "The Fantasist," *New York* magazine, December 7, 2007.
18. Lousie Boyle, "Exclusive: How Jeffrey Epstein Pulled Strings for His 20-Something 'Lady Friend' to Intern for Hollywood's Queen of Publicity—Ultimately Leading to Her Downfall from Grace because of Ties to the Dead Pedophile," *Daily Mail,* February 7, 2020.
19. Ben Widdicombe, "Tarnished by Epstein Scandal, Power Publicist Peggy Siegal Attempts a Hollywood Comeback," *Town & Country,* November 6, 2019.
20. Russell Brandom, "AI Pioneer Accused of Having Sex with Trafficking Victim on Jeffrey Epstein's Island," *Verge,* August 9, 2019.
21. Sara Dorn, "MIT Scientist Says Epstein Victim Virginia Giuffre Was 'Entirely Willing': Report," *New York Post,* September 14, 2019.
22. Marc Tracey and Tiffany Hsu, "Director of M.I.T.'s Media Lab Resigns After Taking Money from Jeffrey Epstein," *New York Times,* September 7, 2019.
23. Ibid.
24. www.edge.org/the-billionaires-dinner.
25. Ibid.
26. Evgeny Morozov, "Jeffrey Epstein's Intellectual Enabler," *New Republic,* August 22, 2019.

27. Peter Aldhous, "How Jeffrey Epstein Bought His Way into an Exclusive Intellectual Boys Club," *BuzzFeed,* September 26, 2019.
28. Evgeny Morozov, "The Epstein Scandal at MIT Shows the Moral Bankruptcy of Techno-Elites," *Guardian,* September 7, 2019.
29. Evgeny Morozov, "Jeffrey Epstein's Intellectual Enabler," *New Republic,* August 22, 2019.
30. Peter Aldhous, "How Jeffrey Epstein Bought His Way into an Exclusive Intellectual Boys Club," *BuzzFeed,* September 26, 2019.

## 25 NOTORIOUS

Note: This chapter is based on multiple interviews the author had with journalist Sharon Churcher from February 2020 to May 2020.
1. Rich Schapiro and Oren Yaniv, "Jeffrey Epstein Accuser Was Not a Sex Slave, But a Money Hungry Sex Kitten, Her Former Friends Say," New York *Daily News,* March 1, 2015.
2. Julie K. Brown, "Cops Worked to Put Serial Sex Abuser in Prison. Prosecutors Worked to Cut Him a Break," *Miami Herald,* November 28, 2018.

## 26 CIVIL ACTIONS

1. Josh Saul, "Ex-Teen Prostitute Files Suit in Billionaire Sex-Slave Case," *Page Six,* September 1, 2015.
2. Lee Brown, "Jeffrey Epstein Wanted to Marry Ex-Girlfriend's Teenage Daughter Who Called Him 'Uncle Jeff,'" *New York Post,* December 18, 2019.
3. Meghan Morris and Casey Sullivan, "Hedge-Fund Giant Glenn Dubin and His Wife, Eva, Told Jeffrey Epstein's Probation Officer They Were '100% Comfortable' with the Sex Offender Around Their Kids. New Documents Show the Extent of the Billionaire Couple's Relationship with Epstein," *Business Insider,* August 10, 2019.
4. Lee Brown, "Jeffrey Epstein Wanted to Marry Ex-Girlfriend's Teenage Daughter Who Called Him 'Uncle Jeff,'" *New York Post,* December 18, 2019.
5. Interview with Nadia Vostrikov, April 2, 2020.
6. Ibid.
7. Amy Brandt, "'I Was in Disbelief': Jeffrey Epstein Targeted Dancers at NYC Studios, with Others Acting as Recruiters," *Pointe,* September 3, 2019.

## 27 UNDERGROUND NEWS

1. Interview with Michael Tennenbaum in *Jeffrey Epstein: Filthy Rich* (Netflix documentary), 2020.
2. Jacob Silverman, "Letting Jeffrey Epstein's Pals Off the Hook," *New Republic,* June 17, 2020.
3. Richard Johnson, "Jeffrey Epstein's East Side Mansion Houses Russian Playmates," *New York Post,* March 8, 2016.

4. Ibid.
5. Ibid.
6. Anna Nemtsova, "The Russian Sleazeball Peddling Girls to Billionaires," *Daily Beast,* July 29, 2019.
7. Rosie Perper and Bill Bostock, "Israel's Former Prime Minister Says He Visited Convicted Sex Offender Jeffrey Epstein's Private Caribbean Island, but Never Partied with Him or Met Younger Girls," *Business Insider,* July 16, 2019.
8. Interview with confidential source, July 2020.
9. Neil Murphy and Tiffany Lo, "Jeffrey Epstein and Harvey Weinstein Pictured at Princess Beatrice's 18th Birthday," *Daily Mirror,* December 9, 2019.
10. Tatiana Siegel, "Julie K. Brown and the Female Collaborator Who Helped Bring Down Jeffrey Epstein," *Hollywood Reporter,* December 14, 2019.
11. Tiffany Hsu, "The Jeffrey Epstein Case Was Cold, Until a Miami Herald Reporter Got Accusers to Talk," *New York Times,* July 9, 2019.

## 28  MIDNIGHT IN PARIS

1. Julie K. Brown, "Federal Prosecutors Broke Law in Jeffrey Epstein Case, Judge Rules," *Miami Herald,* February 21, 2019.
2. Jonathan Swan and Marisa Fernandez, "Ben Sasse Asks Justice Department to Investigate Itself on Jeffrey Epstein," *Axios,* December 5, 2018.
3. Théo Hetsch, Olivier Liffran, and Pauline Pennanec'h for Radio France, "Jeffrey Epstein 'A Polite and Generous Man' Who 'Loved the Company of Women' According to His French Handyman," *France Info,* August 30, 2019.
4. Leena Kim, "Everything We Know About Jeffrey Epstein's Vast Real Estate Portfolio," *Town & Country,* May 28, 2020.
5. Norimitsu Onishi, "A Victim's Account Fuels a Reckoning over Abuse of Children in France," *New York Times,* January 7, 2020.
6. "France to Set Legal Age of Sexual Consent at 15," BBC News, March 6, 2018.
7. Théo Hetsch, Olivier Liffran, and Pauline Pennanec'h for Radio France, "Jeffrey Epstein 'A Polite and Generous Man' Who 'Loved the Company of Women' According to His French Handyman," *France Info,* August 30, 2019.
8. Ibid.
9. Ibid.
10. Ibid.
11. Ben Widdicome, "The Secret Plan to Rehabilitate Jeffrey Epstein's Image," *Town & Country,* July 16, 2019.
12. Ibid.
13. Alexander Robertson, "Prince Andrew Met with Ghislaine Maxwell AFTER Jeffrey Epstein Probe Was Reopened: Duke Saw Paedophile's

'Madam' in London as She Took Part in Supercar Rally to Monaco with Paris Hilton and Chloe Green," *Daily Mail*, November 21, 2019.

## PART 6   SECRETS TO THE GRAVE

1. Ben Widdicombe, "The Secret Plan to Rehabilitate Jeffrey Epstein's Image," *Town & Country*, July 16, 2019.

## 29   THE STING

1. Interview with confidential law enforcement source, March 6, 2020.
2. FAA spokeswoman Arlene Salac, emailed reply, March 26, 2020. FAA link: www.faa.gov/licenses_certificates/aircraft_certification/aircraft _registry/special_nnumbers/.
3. *United States v. Jeffrey Epstein*, criminal indictment brought by the government in relation to the July 2020 charges.
4. J. K. Trotter, "Flight Data from Jeffrey Epstein's Private Jets Show a Lavish Travel Schedule as the Walls Closed In," *Insider*, July 12, 2019.
5. According to flight logs contained in documents unsealed in August 2019 as part of a civil lawsuit filed by one of Epstein's alleged victims against an Epstein associate.
6. Christopher Magan, "New Jersey's Teterboro Airport Was Travel Hub of Jeffrey Epstein's Sex Traffic Ring, Pilots Are Subpoenaed in Sex Trafficking Case," *USA Today*, August 16, 2019.
7. Virginia Heffernan, "The Twisted Flight Paths of 'Global Girl' and the Lolita Express," *Wired*, July 23, 2019.
8. Tyler Durden, "Epstein Sold 'Lolita Express' Weeks Before Arrest: Court Document," Zerohedge.com, July 11, 2019, www.zerohedge.com/news/ 2019-07-11/epstein-sold-lolita-express-weeks-arrest-court-document.
9. Samantha Lock, "Vile High Club: Inside Jeffrey Epstein's 'Lolita Express' Private Jet That He Partied On with Prince Andrew with Padded Floors for 'Sex with Young Women,'" *Sun* (UK), July 19, 2019.
10. William D. Cohan, "'He Had, Like, This Big Round Bed with Mirrors on the Wall': How the Private Jet Became the Singular Fetish Object of the Modern Billionaire," *Vanity Fair*, November 6, 2019.
11. Philip Messing interview with Lt. Eugene Whyte, NYPD, January 30, 2020.
12. Ibid.
13. Chris Spargo, "Jeffrey Epstein DID Use His Fake Passport for Travel to Spain, UK and More Reveals U.S. Attorney's Office After Pedophile's Defense Team Said There Was No Proof of Use," *Daily Mail*, July 19, 2019.
14. Annie Karni, Eileen Sullivan, and Noam Scheiber, "Acosta to Resign as Labor Secretary over Jeffrey Epstein Plea Deal," *New York Times*, July 12, 2019.

## 30  FAVOR BANK

1. Lauren Aratani, "Rats and Raw Sewage: Jeffrey Epstein Jail Blighted by 'Horrible' Conditions," *Guardian*, August 17, 2019; Jeanne Theoharis, "I Tried to Tell the World About Epstein's Jail. No One Wanted to Listen," *Atlantic*, August 16, 2019.

2. Joseph Goldstein, "Manhattan Jail That Holds El Chapo Is Called Tougher than Guantanamo Bay," *New York Times*, January 23, 2017.

3. This description of him was based upon an internal memorandum from a United States Marshal Service processing form that was obtained through a Freedom of Information Act request.

4. Ali Winston and Darwin Bond Graham, "Private Donors Supply Spy Gear to Cops," *ProPublica*, October 13, 2014.

5. Len Levitt, "'Using' the NYC Police Foundation," *AM New York*, June 8, 2015.

6. Philip Messing interview with Robert Boyce, January 30, 2020, and a follow-up phone interview February 1, 2020.

7. Ibid.

8. Ibid.

9. www.youtube.com/watch?v=a_d0QdRSQ0M.

10. www.justice.gov/usao-sdny/press-release/file/1180481/download.

11. Ali Watkins, "Jeffrey Epstein Is Indicted on Sex Charges as Discovery of Nude Photos Is Disclosed," *New York Times*, July 8, 2019.

12. Devlin Barrett, "Second Sex-Crimes Case Against Jeffrey Epstein Shows Reach of Federal Law," *Washington Post*, July 9, 2019.

13. Brendan Pierson, "Financier Epstein Pleads Not Guilty to Sex Trafficking Charges Involving Girls," Reuters, July 8, 2019.

14. www.courtlistener.com/recap/gov.uscourts.flsd.357669/gov.uscourts.flsd .357669.1.3.pdf.

15. Brendan Pierson, "Financier Epstein Pleads Not Guilty to Sex Trafficking Charges Involving Girls," Reuters, July 8, 2019.

16. Tom Hays and Larry Neumeister, "Jeffrey Epstein Denied Bail in Sex Trafficking Case," Associated Press, July 18, 2019.

17. Ibid.

18. www.scribd.com/document/418536949/Judge-BermanJeffrey-Epstein -bail-decision; Benjamin Weiser and Ali Watkins, "Jeffrey Epstein Is Denied Bail in Sex Crimes Case," *New York Times*, July 18, 2019.

## 31  JAILHOUSE CONFESSIONS

1. Barry Levine and Philip Messing interviews with William Mersey, February 10, 2020. Additional phone interviews were also conducted by Messing on February 13, 2010; March 14, 2020; March 31, 2020; and May 4, 2020.

2. Philip Messing interviews with Michael Tisdale, April 27, 2019, and May 8, 2020.

3. Barry Levine and Philip Messing interviews with William Mersey,

February 10, 2020. Additional phone interviews were also conducted by Messing on February 13, 2010; March 14, 2020; March 31, 2020; and May 4, 2020.

4.  Ibid.

5.  Ali Watkins, Danielle Ivory, and Christine Goldbaum, "Inmate 76318-054: The Last Days of Jeffrey Epstein," *New York Times,* August 17, 2019.

6.  Interviews with Michael Tisdale and William Mersey.

7.  www.justice.gov/usao-sdny/press-release/file/1218466/downloadTo.

8.  Ali Watkins, Danielle Ivory, and Christine Goldbaum, "Inmate 76318-054: The Last Days of Jeffrey Epstein," *New York Times,* August 17, 2019.

9.  Tom Hays, "Financier Jeffrey Epstein Found Injured in Jail Cell," Associated Press, July 25, 2020.

10. Reuven Fenton and Bruce Golding, "Ex-Cop Accused of 'Roughing Up' Epstein Thrown Back into Solitary Confinement," *New York Post,* September 17, 2019.

11. Reis Thebault, "Video from Epstein's First Apparent Suicide Attempt Lost Due to 'Technical Errors,' Prosecutors Say," *Washington Post,* January 9, 2020.

12. Ibid.

13. Philip Messing phone interview with David Schoen, January 23, 2020.

14. Matt Spillane, "Lawyer for Nicholas Tartaglione Denies Client Involved in Jeffrey Epstein's Jail Injuries," *Rockland/Westchester Journal News,* July 25, 2019.

15. Phone interview with Bruce Barket, February 7, 2020.

16. Associated Press, "Video in Apparent Jeffrey Epstein Suicide Attempt 'No Longer Exists,'" *Los Angeles Times,* January 9, 2020.

17. Reis Thebault, "Video from Epstein's First Apparent Suicide Attempt Lost Due to 'Technical Errors,' Prosecutors Say," *Washington Post,* January 9, 2020.

18. Ali Watkins, Danielle Ivory, and Christine Goldbaum, "Inmate 76318-054: The Last Days of Jeffrey Epstein," *New York Times,* August 17, 2019.

19. Jane Musgrave, "Billionaire Sex Offender Jeffrey Epstein's Year-Long Probation to End Next Week," *Palm Beach Post,* June 11, 2010.

## 32  LAST RITES

1.  Larry Neumeister and Jim Mustian, "Judge Sets Tentative Date for Jeffrey Epstein's Trial," Associated Press, in *U.S. News and World Report,* July 31, 2020.

2.  Curt Anderson, "1 Justice Department, 2 Views on Sex Charges Against Epstein," Associated Press, July 9, 2019.

3.  John Gramlich, "Only 2% of Federal Criminal Defendants Go to Trial, and Most Who Do Are Found Guilty," Pew Research Center, June 11, 2019.

4. "United States Attorneys' Annual Statistical Report: Fiscal Year 2018," table 3C, p. 15.

5. Karen Freifeld and Jonathan Allen, "Movie Producer Weinstein to Surrender on Sex Assault Charges," Reuters, May 24, 2018.

6. James C. McKinley, Jr., "Harvey Weinstein Faces New Sex Assault Charges in Manhattan," *New York Times,* July 2, 2018.

7. James Beal, "Beast Bust-Up: Paedo Jeffrey Epstein 'Kicked Harvey Weinstein Out of His Home After He Assaulted One of His Sex Slaves,'" *Sun* (UK), March 30, 2020.

8. Dave Schechter, "Jeffrey Epstein Consulted Atlanta Attorney Days Before Death," *Atlanta Jewish Times,* August 12, 2019.

9. Philip Messing phone interview with David Schoen, January 23, 2020.

10. Ibid.

11. Priscilla DeGregory and Kate Sheehy, "Jeffrey Epstein Signed Will Just Two Days Before Suicide," *New York Post,* August 19, 2019.

12. www.yourtango.com/2019327736/who-mariel-colon-miro-new-details -lawyer-who-represents-jeffrey-epstein-el-chapo.

13. www.scribd.com/document/422423833/Jeffrey-Epstein-will?ad_group =93051X1547088Xb30d7add56eab94329dafe81588aefff&campaign =SkimbitLtd&keyword=660149026&medium=affiliate&source=hp _affiliate.

14. Erik Larson "Jeffrey Epstein Pal Maxwell Loses Last-Ditch Attempt to Seal Papers," *Bloomberg,* August 9, 2019.

15. Dan Mangan and Kevin Breuninger, "Court Releases Documents About Jeffrey Epstein, Accused in Sex Traffic Case, and His Alleged Procurer Ghislaine Maxwell," CNBC, August 9, 2019.

16. Ibid.

17. Stephen Rex Brown, "Even Jeffrey Epstein's Girlfriend, the Last Person to Speak on Phone with Him Before Suicide, Shocked He Killed Himself: Source," New York *Daily News,* March 3, 2020.

18. Philip Messing interview with confidential source.

19. Daniel Bates, "EXCLUSIVE: This Is the Dentist Girlfriend of Jeffrey Epstein Who He Phoned from Prison Just Before He Hanged Himself—But Gave No Hint He Was So Despondent He Was About to Commit Suicide," *Daily Mail,* March 3, 2020.

20. Karyna Shuliak's dental license for Florida: appsmqa.doh.state.fl.us/ MQASearchServices/HealthcareProviders/LicenseVerification?LicInd =21168&Procde=701&org=%20. Karyna Shuliak's dental license for California: search.dca.ca.gov/results.

21. Philip Messing interview with confidential source.

22. Philip Messing phone interviews with Shuliak attorney Maurice Sercarz, April 15, 2020, and April 16, 2020.

## 33  NIGHT MOVES

1.   Eric Levenson, "A Timeline of What Jeffrey Epstein and His Prison Guards Did in His Final Hours," CNN, November 19, 2019.
2.   www.bop.gov/foia/docs/fy_2019_national_menus.pdf.
3.   www.justice.gov/usao-sdny/pr/correctional-officers-charged-falsifying -records-august-9th-and-10th-metropolitan.
4.   Michael R. Sisak, "Feds Fight Back as Epstein Death Conspiracy Theories Swirl," Associated Press, November 23, 2019.
5.   Philip Messing phone interviews with Robert Hood on April 4, 2020; April 19, 2020; and April 26, 2020.
6.   This and other details from the FOIA request were obtained via a FOIA request made to the FDNY on January 28, 2020. Subsequent references to specific times cited in this chapter come from this transcript released as part of the FOIA request to the FDNY.
7.   Dwyer cited "the nature of this incident, the coverage that followed and the ongoing litigation and investigations" as rationales for not providing a real time guide with regards to the 911 call as reflected in the released FOIA transcript.
8.   Philip Messing phone interviews with Peter Gleason on March 30, 2020; April 17, 2020; April 19, 2020; and April 27, 2020.

## 34  SIDESHOW

1.   Mark Epstein is quoted from a phone conversation with journalist Philip Messing on April 15, 2020. Epstein had told Messing: "I'm calling you back because you're a Coney Island guy, out of respect." During the call, Epstein mentioned the media interest following his brother's death. He said: "Look, do you know how many people have called me? I've been called by media outlets from all over the world! I just got a call from Australian *60 Minutes* and they told me they wanted to do an entire show on my brother. I had one guy who called me from Texas and the guy said he wanted to film me using like five cameras. He said he'd put me up in a Texas hotel, like that's supposed to give me a hard-on or something! What can he sell something like that for?" Before hanging up, Mark Epstein added: "My only job is to find out the circumstances of my brother's death. I'm not participating in anything. This is not about me at all—I don't want notoriety."
2.   Chas Danner, Margaret Hartmann, and Matt Stieb, "Everything We Know About Jeffrey Epstein's Death," *New York* magazine, August 19, 2019.
3.   Matt Zapotosky, Devlin Barrett, Renae Merle, and Carol D. Leonnig, "Jeffrey Epstein Dead After 'Apparent Suicide' in New York," *Washington Post,* August 10, 2019.
4.   "Jeffrey Epstein: Financier Found Dead in New York Prison Cell," BBC News, August 10, 2019.

5.  Morgan Chalfant, "Barr Criticizes Prison's 'Serious Irregularities' After Epstein Death," *Hill,* August 12, 2019.
6.  William K. Rashbaum, Benjamin Weiser, and Michael Gold, "Jeffrey Epstein Dead in Suicide at Jail, Spurring Inquiries," *New York Times,* August 10, 2019.
7.  Natnicha Churwiruch, "Plan to Move Epstein Warden to Prison Leadership Job," Associated Press in *Bloomberg,* January 24, 2020; Kevin Johnson, "New York Warden Reassigned After Jeffrey Epstein's Death; Two Staffers Placed on Leave," *USA Today,* August 13, 2020.
8.  David Shortell, "Bureau of Prisons Chief Removed in Wake of Jeffrey Epstein Suicide," CNN, August 19, 2019.
9.  Robert D. McFadden, "Whitey Bulger Is Dead in Prison at 89; Long-Hunted Boston Mob Boss," *New York Times,* October 30, 2018.
10. www.justice.gov/usao-sdny/press-release/file/1218466/download.
11. Barry Levine and Philip Messing interviews with William Mersey and Michael Tisdale, February 10, 2020. Additional phone interviews were also conducted by Messing on February 13, 2010; March 14, 2020; March 31, 2020; and May 4, 2020.
12. www.justice.gov/usao-sdny/press-release/file/1218466/download.
13. Philip Messing phone interviews with Robert Hood on April 4, 2020, April 19, 2020, and April 26, 2020.

### 35  POSTMORTEM

1.  Mabel Kabani, "The Handwritten Note Found in Jeffrey Epstein's Jail Cell," *60 Minutes Overtime,* January 5, 2020.
2.  Sarah Weinman, "Why You Might Not Want to Believe Michael Baden, Celebrity Pathologist, on Epstein's Death," *New York* magazine ("Intelligencer"), October 31, 2019.
3.  Michael R. Sisak, Michael Balsamo, and Larry Neumeister, "Medical Examiner Rules Epstein Death a Suicide by Hanging," Associated Press in *U.S. News and World Report,* August 16, 2019.
4.  theconsciousresistance.com/wp-content/uploads/2019/08/Epstein-vicctims-transcripts.pdf.
5.  Ibid.
6.  Azi Paybarah, "Epstein's Autopsy 'Points to Homicide,' Pathologist Hired by Brother Claims," *New York Times,* October 30, 2019.
7.  Phone interview with Asa Worthy-Davis, May 18, 2020.
8.  Philip Messing phone interviews with journalist who spoke to two sources in medical examiner's office, January 30, 2020, and May 24, 2020.
9.  Phone interview with Dr. Baden, March 3, 2020.
10. Philip Messing interview with Vernon Geberth, June 4, 2020.
11. Michael Balsamo and Michael R. Sisak, "Jeffrey Epstein's Jail Guards Had Been Offered Plea Deal," Associated Press in *Bloomberg,* November 15, 2019.

12. Tareq Haddad, "Prison Guards on Duty at Time of Jeffrey Epstein Death Reject Plea Deal: What Are They Accused Of?," *Newsweek,* November 17, 2019.

13. Katie Benner, Danielle Ivory, Christina Goldbaum, and Ashley Southall, "Before Jail Suicide, Jeffrey Epstein Was Left Alone and Not Closely Monitored," *New York Times,* August 11, 2020.

14. Michael Balsamo, "AG Barr: Epstein's Death Was a 'Perfect Storm of Screw-ups,'"Associated Press, November 22, 2019.

15. Michael Crowley, "Trump Shares Unfounded Fringe Theory About Epstein and Clintons," *New York Times,* August 10, 2019.

16. Michael Gold and Jonah Engel Bromwich, "Epstein Conspiracy Theories: De Blasio and Others Join Speculation," *New York Times,* August 12, 2019.

17. www.rasmussenreports.com/public_content/lifestyle/people/january _2020/most_now_think_jeffrey_epstein_was_murdered.

## 36 CHEATING JUSTICE

1. Ben Ashford, "EXCLUSIVE: Jeffrey Epstein Has Been Laid to Rest in Unmarked Tomb Beside His Parents at a Jewish Mausoleum in Florida That Was Arranged by His Brother, Who Raged It's 'Nobody's F**king Business' to Know Where the Pedophile Had Been Buried," *Daily Mail,* August 21, 2019.

2. Ibid.

3. Jerusalem Post Staff, "Jeffrey Epstein Buried in Unmarked Grave with Family Names Removed," *Jerusalem Post,* September 5, 2019.

4. Emily Steel, Steve Eder, Sapna Maheshwari, and Matthew Goldstein, "How Jeffrey Epstein Used the Billionaire Behind Victoria's Secret for Wealth and Women," *New York Times,* July 25, 2019.

5. Adam K. Raymond, "Leslie Wexner: Jeffrey Epstein 'Misappropriated' Millions from Me," *New York* magazine ("Intelligencer"), August 8, 2019.

6. Sharon Churcher, "No Angel—Is Jeffrey Epstein's 'Unholy Alliance' with the Victoria's Secret Boss the REAL Reason the Show Was Scrapped?" *Sun* (UK), November 28, 2019.

7. Shira Hanau, "Wexner Report Claims Epstein Played 'No Meaningful Role' in Foundation," *New York Jewish Week,* February 25, 2020.

8. Mark Williams, "Leslie Wexner Steps Down as Chairman and CEO of L Brands," *USA Today,* May 14, 2020.

9. Kate Briquelet, "Epstein's Pal Jean-Luc Brunel Quietly Sells Off His Infamous Modeling Biz," *Daily Beast,* October 1, 2019.

10. AP, "French Group Says It Has 10 Witnesses of Epstein-Linked Abuse," *Times of Israel,* August 22, 2019.

11. Interview with Homayra Sellier, April 17, 2020.

12. Mark Landler, "A Prince's Accuser Speaks Out: 'It Was Disgusting,'" *New York Times,* December 3, 2019.

13. Sara Nathan and Laura Italiano, "Andrew's Sweaty Defense," *New York Post,* November 17, 2019.

14. Aaron Katersky, "NY Prosecutors Request Testimony from Prince Andrew for Jeffrey Epstein Investigation," ABC News, June 8, 2020.

15. Ibid.

16. Kenneth P. Vogel, "Prince Andrew Sought Washington Lobbyist to Help with Epstein Case," *New York Times,* July 5, 2020.

17. Megan Sheets, "Prince Andrew's Lawyers 'Consulted Washington Lobbyist with Ties to the Trump Administration About Helping Him Handle Jeffrey Epstein Fallout,'" *Daily Mail,* July 5, 2020.

18. Brad Hunter, "Prince Andrew Pulverized! Ex–Sex Slave Says, 'Sweat Raining Everywhere,'" *Toronto Sun,* December 2, 2019.

## 37  "TUCKEDAWAY"

1. Sara Nathan and Mara Siegler, "Jeffrey Epstein's Gal Pal Ghislaine Maxwell Spotted at In-N-Out Burger in First Photos Since His Death," *New York Post,* August 15, 2019.

2. Louise Boyle, "EXCLUSIVE: Ghislaine Maxwell STAGED In-N-Out Photo in Los Angeles with Her Close Friend and Attorney, Using Confidante's Dog Dexter in the Snapshot," *Daily Mail,* August 19, 2019.

3. Nicole Hong, Benjamin Weiser, and Mihir Zaveri, "Associate Accused of Recruiting Teen Girls for Epstein Is Arrested," *New York Times,* July 3, 2020.

4. Interview, *New York Times* correspondent Megan Toohey, Twohey, *All In* with Chris Hayes, MSNBC, July 2, 2020.

5. Gabrielle Bruney, "Ghislaine Maxwell Knows More About Jeffrey Epstein than Anyone. But No One Knows Where She Is," *Esquire,* May 29, 2020.

6. Sara Nathan and Mara Siegler, "Jeffrey Epstein's Gal Pal Ghislaine Maxwell Spotted at In-N-Out Burger in First Photos Since His Death," *New York Post,* August 15, 2019.

7. Adam Gabbatt, "Jeffrey Epstein Associate Ghislaine Maxwell Sues His Estate," *Guardian,* March 19, 2020.

8. Erica Orden and Kara Scannell, "In Pursuit of Ghislaine Maxwell, Authorities Allege Mysterious Financial Dealings with Jeffrey Epstein," CNN, July 3, 2020.

9. Nicole Hong, Benjamin Weiser, and Mihir Zaveri, "Associate Accused of Recruiting Teen Girls for Epstein Is Arrested," *New York Times,* July 3, 2020.

10. Victoria Bekiempis, "How Ghislaine Maxwell Lived a 'Life of Privilege' on the Run," *Guardian,* July 2, 2020.

11. Emily Shugeman, William Bredderman, Susan Zalkind, and Bill Donahue, "Inside the Secret Sale of Ghislaine Maxwell's Swanky New Hampshire Hideout," *Daily Beast,* July 3, 2020.

12. Emma Parry and Sharon Churcher, "Mystery Links—Ghislaine Max-

well's Luxury 'Hideout' Bought by Mysterious Company Linked to Alleged Lover Scott Borgerson," *Sun* (UK), July 4, 2020.

13. Emily Shugeman, William Bredderman, Susan Zalkind, and Bill Donahue, "Inside the Secret Sale of Ghislaine Maxwell's Swanky New Hampshire Hideout," *Daily Beast,* July 3, 2020.

14. Bruce Golding, "Ghislaine Maxwell Wrapped Cellphone in Foil to 'Evade Detection,' Feds Say," *New York Post,* July 13, 2020.

15. Mark Seal, "'Ghislaine, Is That You?': Inside Ghislaine Maxwell's Life on the Lam," *Vanity Fair,* July 3, 2020.

16. Whitney Clegg interview with Richard Morris, July 2, 2020.

17. Benjamin Weiser and Nicole Hong, "Ghislaine Maxwell Tried to Hide When F.B.I. Knocked, Prosecutors Say," *New York Times*. July 13, 2020.

18. Mark Seal, "'Ghislaine, Is That You?': Inside Ghislaine Maxwell's Life on the Lam," *Vanity Fair,* July 3, 2020.

19. Interview with source, July 3, 2020.

20. Gabrielle Fonrouge, Lia Eustachewich, Larry Celona, and Bruce Golding, "Accused 'Perv'eyor of Epstein's Girls Arrested," *New York Post,* July 3, 2020.

21. Interview with source, July 3, 2020.

22. Mark Seal, "'Ghislaine, Is That You?': Inside Ghislaine Maxwell's Life on the Lam," *Vanity Fair,* July 3, 2020.

## 38  A MOST WANTED WOMAN

1. Whitney Clegg interview with Richard Morris in Bradford, New Hampshire, July 2, 2020.

2. Gabrielle Fonrouge, Lia Eustachewich, Larry Celona, and Bruce Golding, "Accused 'Perv'eyor of Epstein's Girls Arrested," *New York Post,* July 3, 2020.

3. Ibid.

4. Caroline Graham and Greg Woodfield, "'Let's Say We Didn't Knock Politely': Officers Describe How FBI Agents Smashed Down Ghislaine Maxwell's Door and Hauled Her Off in Handcuffs After She Gave Them the Slip in Year-Long $5m Game of 'Cat and Mouse,'" *Mail on Sunday,* July 4, 2020.

5. Nicole Hong, Benjamin Weiser, and Mihir Zaveri, "Associate Accused of Recruiting Teen Girls for Epstein Is Arrested," *New York Times,* July 3, 2020.

6. Ibid.

7. Interview with source, July 12, 2020.

8. Benjamin Weiser and Nicole Hong, "Ghislaine Maxwell Tried to Hide When F.B.I. Knocked, Prosecutors Say," *New York Times,* July 13, 2020.

9. Larry Neumeister and Tom Hays, "Judge Orders Ghislaine Maxwell to Remain Behind Bars Until Her 2021 Trial on Charges Tied to Jeffrey Epstein," *Time,* July 14, 2020.

10. Katy Forrester, "Living a Nightmare: Ghislaine Maxwell's 'In-Laws' Are

'Traumatized' and Don't Believe She Is Married to Millionaire Scott Borgerson," *Sun* (UK), July 20, 2020.

11. Colin Kalmbacher, "Ghislaine Maxwell's Case Being Handled by SDNY Public Corruption Unit Could Spell Trouble for U.S. Elites," *Law & Crime,* July 2, 2020.

12. Maureen Callahan, "Protect Her—for the Sake of the Victims," *New York Post,* July 3, 2020.

13. Tamar Lapin, "'Rapist' Maxwell as 'Evil as Jeff' Gal," *New York Post,* July 4, 2020.

14. Alan Dershowitz, "The Ghislaine Maxwell I Know," *Spectator,* July 3, 2020.

15. Tamara Tabo, "Dersh Deposed: Alan Dershowitz Accuses Former Federal Judge of Billion-Dollar Scheme," *Above the Law,* October 19, 2015.

16. Jeffrey Martin, "Judge Rules Virginia Giuffre's Lawyers Must 'Destroy' Jeffrey Epstein Files," *Newsweek,* July 2, 2020.

17. "Dershowitz Says He's Suing Netflix over Sexual Allegations in Epstein Series," *Times of Israel,* June 25, 2020.

18. James Hill, "Ghislaine Maxwell to Appeal Judge's Order Unsealing Records in Civil Case," ABC News, July 23, 2020.

### 39   OUT OF THE WOODWORK

1. Eric Lutz, "Video: Trump Caught Partying with Epstein, Touching Women at 1992 Party," *Vanity Fair,* July 17, 2019.

2. Annie Todd interview with John Mark Dougan, April 4, 2020.

3. Annie Todd interview with John Mark Dougan, April 4, 2020.

4. Ibid.

5. Andy Cush, "Why a Russian Hacker Declared War on the Palm Beach County Sheriff's Office," *Gawker,* March 16, 2016.

6. Ibid.

7. Laura Italiano, "Damning Evidence on Prince Andrew Could Be in Russian Hands: MI6," *New York Post,* September 21, 2019.

8. Annie Todd interview with John Mark Dougan, April 4, 2020.

9. Phone interview with Ron Chepesiuk, April 17, 2020.

10. Ibid.

11. Annie Todd interview with John Mark Dougan, April 4, 2020.

12. Ibid.

13. Ibid.

### AFTERWORD   "A WHOLE LOT OF GRAY"

1. Interview with Jose Lambiet, April 28, 2020.

2. Jose Lambiet, "Exclusive: 'She Suffered Tremendously—and It Started with Jeffrey Epstein.' Twin Sister of Woman Who Overdosed on Heroin Years Later After 'Being Abused by Financier as a Teen' Blames Her Downward Spiral and Death on Billionaire Pedophile," *Daily Mail,* July 15, 2019.

3.   Cassady Potts, "Journalist Julie K. Brown Recounts Jeffrey Epstein Investigation, Discusses Representation of Vulnerable Communities," onwardstate.com, October 2019.

4.   Jane Musgrave, "Epstein Victim Sheds Anonymity to Seek Answers: 'Why Can't I See the Documents Now?,'" *Palm Beach Post,* January 31, 2020.

5.   Dylan Howard with Melissa Cronin and James Robertson, *Epstein: Dead Men Tell No Tales; Spies, Lies & Blackmail* (New York: Skyhorse, 2019), 96.

6.   Madeleine Carlisle, "23 of Jeffrey Epstein's Accusers Finally Got Their Day in Court. Here's What They Said," *Time,* August 27, 2019.

7.   Ali Watkins, Benjamin Weiser, and Amy Julia Harris, "Denied Justice, Accusers Share Fury at Epstein," *New York Times,* August 28, 2019.

8.   Ibid.

9.   Madeleine Carlisle, "23 of Jeffrey Epstein's Accusers Finally Got Their Day in Court. Here's What They Said," *Time,* August 27, 2019.

10.  Interview with Jose Lambiet, March 26, 2020.

11.  2006 Palm Beach Police report entered in evidence in *Giuffre v. Maxwell* via PACER.

12.  This number is figured from a source who told Jose Lambiet in an interview that twenty victims took settlements. The other nineteen came from PACER filings.

13.  Jose Lambiet, "Exclusive: 'She Suffered Tremendously—and It Started with Jeffrey Epstein.' Twin Sister of Woman Who Overdosed on Heroin Years After 'Being Abused by Financier as a Teen' Blames Her Downward Spiral and Death on Billionaire Pedophile," *Daily Mail,* July 15, 2019.

# INDEX

## ABOUT THE AUTHOR

BARRY LEVINE is a veteran investigative reporter and editor in print and television. He received *The Huffington Post*'s Game Changer award in 2010 and led a reporting team to a Pulitzer Prize nomination for investigative reporting and national news reporting. He is the coauthor of *All the President's Women* and lives in New York.